RUSSIAN IN ARIZONA

A History of its Teaching

by:

Lee B. Croft
Barry Boosman
Katherine Lutz
James C. Nielsen
Aimee M. Raymer

**Institute for Issues in the History of Science
IIHS
Tempe/Arizona (U.S.)
Perm'/Russian Federation
MMVII**

Copyright © 2007 by Lee B. Croft

This work is published under the auspices of the Institute for Issues in the History of Science (IIHS), a scholarly organization having locations in Tempe, Arizona, USA, and in Perm, Russian Federation. The members of this institute are affiliates of Arizona State University's Melikian Center for Russian, Eurasian, and East European Studies (Prof. Stephen K. Batalden, Director) and its Center for Biology and Society (Regents' Professor Jane Maienschein, Director) or of the Russian Academy of Natural Sciences (RANS), Perm Division (Prof. Valentin F. Olontsev, Academician). Correspondence concerning this publication should be directed to author Lee B. Croft, Professor of Slavic Languages and Literatures, School of International Letters and Cultures, Arizona State University, Tempe, AZ 85287-0202, USA, or at Lee.Croft@ASU.EDU.

IIHS Institutional History Series

Editorial Board:

Prof. Stephen K. Batalden Arizona State University	Prof. Lee B. Croft Arizona State University
Prof. Albert Feldman Mesa Community College, Emeritus	Prof. Ann Hibner Koblitz Arizona State University
Regents' Professor Jane Maienschein Arizona State University	Prof. Valentin F. Olontsev RANS-Perm Division, RF

Prof. Danko Šipka
Arizona State University

Croft, Lee B. (1946--); Boosman, Barry; Lutz, Katherine; Nielsen, James C.; and Raymer, Aimee M. *Russian in Arizona: A History of its Teaching.* Institute for Issues in the History of Science. Tempe, AZ, USA and Perm, Russian Federation. 2007. 260 pages with 57 illustrations and index. This book (www.lulu.com/content/881610) has ISBN: 978-1-4303-2355-6. The color-photo version of this B/W book (www.lulu.com/content/868256) is also available at www.lulu.com.

This book is dedicated to the memory of Joe Malik, Jr…
"a good man to have in your corner."

TABLE OF CONTENTS

Dedication..pp. 3
Table of Contents...pp. 4
List of Illustrations and Photos..pp. 5
Introduction by Lee B. Croft (LBC)...pp. 6
Acknowledgments...pp. 9
A Personal History of ASU's Russian Section by LBC..............pp. 10
"Who Has Taught Russian in the State of Arizona?"..................pp. 70
Some Statistical Ruminations..pp. 80
Russian Teacher Profiles..pp. 82
   (**ASU**: Burton, 82; Couch, 84; Croft, 88; Dhaliwal, 97; Ekmanis, 99; Livingston, 101; Mashuri, 103; Šipka, 104; **Glendale CC**: Story, 106; **Mesa CC**: Willeford, 111; High School Programs: **Mesa Westwood**: Barrett, 114**; Phoenix Central**: Vontsolos, 117**; Northern Arizona U.**: Slobodchikoff, 120; **U. of A**.: 122; Program History, 125; Reminiscences of Joe Malik, Jr., 126; Remarks at Malik's funeral by LBC, 134; Malik obituary, 135; LBC AzAATSEEL presentations, 136; UA Faculty profiles continue: Barker, 139; Dunkel, 142; Fielder, 143; Garrard, 145; Gutsche, 150; Leafgren, 153; Phillips, 154; Polowy, 165; Simkhovich, 167)
Executive Summary from ASU's 2004 Program Review...............pp. 169
Essay on Prof. Croft's Office Chair...pp. 178
Students of Russian at ASU by LBC ....pp. 181
"Why do the Students take Russian?"...pp. 184
Letters from Former UA Russian Students..................................pp. 188
"How do we Teach Them?" by LBC..pp. 195
Student Profile (ASU)...pp. 199
Letter to Student Editor Jeanne Palumbo: "Where are they now?"....pp. 205
ASU Russian BA Graduates, 1996-2003.....................................pp. 214
List of Fellowship/Scholarship Winners......................................pp. 221
Recent Emails from Former ASU Russian Students....................pp. 222
ASU and U of A DOBRO SLOVO members..............................pp. 240
WHAT HAVE WE LEARNED?..pp. 246
INDEX...pp. 247.

List of Illustrations and Photographs

Joe Malik, Jr., dedication, 3; Table One: ASU DFL Heads and Chairs, 11-12; S. Couch/Lee and Hayden Croft, 16; Steve and Sandra Batalden with Eleni Buzarovska and Lesley Hoyt Croft, 18; Col. Bruce Powers and Rolfs Ekmanis with dog Alf in Colorado, 20; Peter Horwath and LBC in Sedona, 29; Dora Burton, LBC, and Deborah Losse at Losses', 40; ASU Molnija Satellite Schematic, 46; Nick Vontsolos, Don Livingston, Dirk Willeford, Tatiana Kazanina and 1936 Ford Phaeton at Crofts', 49; ASU Russian Enrollment/Graduates, 1970-2000 by LBC and Adam Orford, 54; Tatyana Dhaliwal and Jeanette Owen at Crofts', 68; Danko Šipka and Mario Filipovic at spitted lamb, 69; 1989 group on mini-tour of Leningrad UARA facilities, 74; UA grad students and 2007 TA's, 80; **Profiled Russian Teachers:** Dora Burton, 82; Vladimir Mochalov sketch of Mark Preslar and Sandy Couch, 85; Lesley Hoyt Croft/LBC/Cathy Croft, 88; Fred Giffin/Valentin Olontsev, 90; LBC CLAS Award brochure, 91; 1979 ASU RESEARCH NEWS article on LBC award, 92; 1985 AZ REPUBLIC article on LBC award, 93; 1985 TEMPE SUNDAY NEWS article on LBC award, 94; V. Olontsev/LBC/Steve Batalden at 2005 medal ceremony, 95; Hayden Croft/LBC/Kathryn Hoyt/Lesley Hoyt Croft at ceremony, 95; Tatyana Dhaliwal, 97; ASU INSIGHT article on R. Ekmanis, 100; Don Livingston, 101; David Mashuri, 103; Danko Šipka, 104; Joyce Story with Chagall print, 106; Joyce Story at Crofts', 108; Dirk Willeford Advises Mikhail Gorbachev, 112; Pat Barrett, 114; Nick Vontsolos, 118; Anne Slobodchikoff, 121; 2006 UA Faculty Retreat, 123; Sandy Couch/Joe Malik, Jr.-Big Figures, 128; LBC/Joe Malik/Steve Batalden at Maliks', 132; Malik Obituary, 135; LBC/Joe Malik/Del Phillips awardee, 137; Adele Barker, 140; Alex Dunkel, 142, Grace Fielder, 144; John Garrard, 146; George Gutsche, 150; The Pushkinists' Dinner (Sconce, Croft, Falen, and Gutsche, 2005), 152; John Leafgren and daughters, 153; Del Phillips/LBC/Nick Vontsolos, 155; Terry Polowy, 166, Roza Simkhovich, 168; Young Rolfs Ekmanis, 169; ASU INSIGHT article about ASU program, 172; Outstanding UA student Ken Cargill and mentors, 211; ASU (241-2) and UA (243-4) DOBRO SLOVO membership lists, 240; 2007 ASU DS initiates, 245; and DS students with LBC in 1936 Ford, 245.

Introduction
by:
Lee B. Croft

This book is published by the "Institute for Issues in the History of Science." But it concerns the teaching of the Russian language (and the Russian culture) in the State of Arizona. Such teaching is both a science…linguistics, second-language acquisition, psychologically sophisticated techniques of "surrogate exposure" and etc…and it is an art…communicating attitudes as it builds communicative skills, expressing the individual self as it deals with mass expression, enriching, hopefully, the common understanding of humanity and one's role in it. The history of the teaching of Russian in the State of Arizona, then, does deal with an "issue in the History of Science." The issue is human potentiation. Have the teachers of Russian in the State of Arizona so potentiated its residents over the years that their efforts have been "worth it" to the paying citizenry or not? That is the issue.

It seems strange to many people in other parts of the United States that Russian is taught in Arizona. The stereotype of Arizona that these people have in their minds is that of a sunny state in the great southwest desert to which northerners flee from their inclement winter weather. They see in their minds' eye dessicated cattle skulls, skittering lizards and giant saguaro cacti. They know of the pervasive cultural influence from proximate Mexico and its Spanish-speaking population. No cultural connection to distant and very foreign Russia is apparent to them, and therefore they think it strange when they hear that someone is teaching Russian there, in Arizona. "How did you end up doing that?" they often ask. "Why is it taught there?" "Has it been taught there long?"

To the citizens of Arizona too, the teaching of Russian also seems strange. "Why would an Arizonan want to learn Russian?" they ask. And even their educational administrators, unfortunately, often think it strange…something on the fringe, something less than essential in the prioritization for the always scarce resources. This book is an attempt to detail how Arizona's teachers of Russian have, despite the at-large perception of its strangeness and its constantly inadequate administrative support, greatly potentiated the students who comprise the State's and the Country's next generation. These students have played important roles in our nation's relations with other important peoples in the global arena, and their impact in this arena has benefitted, and continues to benefit, us all.

So "how long has Russian been taught in Arizona?" The concise answer is that Russian has been taught in the State of Arizona constantly since it was begun in 1946 by Dr. George Portnoff, Head of the Department of Foreign Languages at what is now Arizona State University in Tempe, Arizona. Dr. Portnoff taught the language because he was ethnically Russian and he spoke it well. But he was responding to an increased general interest in Russia, a country which had been our ally in World War II, but was rapidly becoming, under Soviet Dictator Josef Stalin, our new primary adversary in the global conflict of ideologies. The fact that Arizona already had appreciable populations of Slavic immigrants in its labor force, and even Russian Orthodox, Molokan, and Jewish religious groups represented in the fabric of Phoenix society by this time (cf. **Phoenix—Where Worlds Meet**, a March 27-28, 1982 publication of PACT ("Phoenix Arts Coming Together") with its article on the Czechs and Slovaks by Emil Volek, the Croatians by C.I. Zovko, the Poles by Joan Rattay, and the "Three Communities" of Russians by Carl Goldberg) had no reflection of these populations' languages in Arizona's educational institutions until this time. Current numbers of Russian speakers in Arizona can be found at Andrew John Conovaloff's website, www.russianaz.org. Here we find that the 2000 census listed 40,616 people of Russian ancestry in Arizona, 4,073 of whom who, over the age of five, speak Russian in the home. Extrapolating from the 1990 census data showing only 1153 such speakers (showing an increase of 25.3%/year), we can figure that in 2007 there are close to 20,000 people here who speak Russian in their homes.

The study of Russian in Arizona begun by Dr. Portnoff, as elsewhere in the U.S., gained tremendous momentum with the Soviet Union's launch of the Sputnik satellite in October of 1957. This launch was a real "wake-up call" to Americans, signifying the presence of a real threat to our technological superiority and, indeed, to our collective security. Within five years of this launch, Russian programs were springing up in all the most prominent U.S. universities, colleges, and even high schools. In Arizona, Dr. Joe Malik, Jr. was hired away from the University of Texas by the University of Arizona in Tucson and given a mandate to "start a Russian program" based on the small enrollment built after 1957 by part-timer Martha Breger, the Russian-speaking wife of prominent local Rabbi Marcus Breger. This was in 1960. In 1962, Dr. Sanford C. Couch was hired at Arizona State University in Tempe with a mandate to "design and begin a Bachelor's Degree program in Russian." These two "major figures" in <u>RUSSIAN IN ARIZONA</u> built nationally prominent academic programs in this state: BA and MA programs in Russian under Prof. Malik in Tucson, and BA and BA in Ed. programs in Russian under Prof. Couch in Tempe. Three of these programs (U. of A.'s BA and MA, and ASU's BA...the Russian BA in Ed. was terminated in 1997-8) have turned out hundreds of graduates since their inception, and these graduates have had a large impact on the global ideological struggle that provided the impetus for the development of their *alma maters'* programs.

When people ask me how I, a non-Russian from the Montana wheat-and-oil-patch town of Cut Bank, began the study of Russian, I tell them that I had been, in my undergraduate studies, a Mathematics major. Because I was in a Bachelor of Science program at ASU, a foreign language was not required of me. But, I was considering graduate studies in Mathematics and my advisor told me that an MA in Math would require that I demonstrate research-access proficiency in one foreign language...and that if I pursued a Ph.D. I would need to demonstrate proficiency in two. Even though a Math MA would only take three semesters of course work to complete, the required foreign language proficiency would take four or more. Obviously, a person considering graduate study of Math should begin to take the anticipated foreign languages in advance. But which language was I to take? My advisor, a retired navy admiral whose name I have forgotten (he told me I was a "strong student" in Math...certainly not true) told me that if I were interested in the "history of Math" I should take German, but that if I were interested in what is happening at the cutting edge of Mathematical science right then I should take Russian, because Russian is already, he said, "our second language of science." So I chose Russian and that was how I started to study it. And study it I have...now more than forty years.

Thirty-four years ago this year I began to teach Russian as a professor at ASU, being an alumnus of both ASU in Tempe (BS in Math, 1968) and the U. of A. in Tucson (MA in Russian, 1970) as well as Cornell University in Ithaca, New York (Ph.D. in Slavic and General Linguistics, 1973). Since 1975 I have been the "Coordinator of Russian" at ASU, and, in this capacity, have had something to do with ALL the other teachers of Russian in the entire state of Arizona. I think I am, in fact, in a rare circumstance wherein I can say that I know, or at least know of, EVERYONE who has ever taught Russian anywhere in the state of Arizona. Such a circumstance entails a certain responsibility...the responsibility that I write this knowledge down, that I record as best I can all these people's contribution to the effort in its current totality.

As of just this year, ASU requires that its graduates, in their last year of attendance, take a course called the "capstone experience." This course pairs these students, just prior to their graduation, with a senior professor in their subject area (in this case, me) to complete a project which makes use of their accumulated knowledge and skills to produce something of value to them. The first four of these Russian "capstone" students are Barry Boosman, Katherine Lutz, James C. Nielsen, and Aimee M. Raymer. Our picture will be on the back cover. Together, as part of our "capstone experience" under an ASU RUS-498 credit listing, we are authoring this book, <u>RUSSIAN IN ARIZONA</u>. I admit that this capstone experience was my idea—indeed it may be the textual "capstone" of my own career, but the students embraced it with enthusiasm, contributing their interviews of key teachers of Russian in different locales around the state, their photography, their writing, typing, and editing skills. And I hope that having their names on the resultant history will be of benefit to them in their subsequent careers.

Acknowledgements

We would like to acknowledge the aid of several people in the production of this book. First, several of the faculty members treated in it saw the worth of the project, thinking it a story that should be told, and they sent additional suggestions and valuable information: current UA Head Teresa Polowy, former UA Head George Gutsche, UARA Director Delbert Phillips, ASU Profs. Emeritus Sandy Couch and Rolfs Ekmanis, and current Prof. Danko Šipka. Paula Malik, the widow of Joe Malik, Jr., was very helpful in remembering key details of the history of RUSSIAN IN ARIZONA. The ASU freshman son of author Lee Croft, Hayden L. Croft, worked all semester typing and editing on the computer to "digitize" old letters, reports, and files. Lesley Hoyt Croft helped with the processing of the photographs. Hayden Library Copy Center employee and Engineering graduate student Akhila Inumpudi did sterling work in graphic design to realize our conception of the book's cover. We thank all these people sincerely, but we, the authors, are responsible for any errors or oversights.

A PERSONAL HISTORY OF ASU'S RUSSIAN SECTION
by:
Lee B. Croft

Не приведи Бог служить по учебной части,
всего боишься. Всякий мешается, вякому
хочется показать, что он тоже умный человек.

Lord, don't lead us to serve in the academic ranks,
you're afraid of everything. Everyone is meddling,
everyone wants to show that they are the
intelligent ones.
--Nikolai V. Gogol

I'll start my history of this section with an excerpt from the more general "Historical Perspective" of the Department of Foreign Languages that I co-wrote with Prof. Wayne M. Senner of the German Section as part of the Department of Foreign Languages' 1981 Decennial Review Process. The idea here is to show the historical roots of the adversarial climate in which the Department, and our Russian Language Section, struggled to grow.

I'm now quoting from the 1981 document, "The Department of Foreign Languages: A Historical Perspective," by Lee B. Croft and Wayne Senner.

"Foreign Language instruction has been a struggling part of this institution almost since its founding in 1885. Latin was a part of the general instruction of early Assistant Principal Augusta Hildebrandt from 1892, later augmenting as well the language instruction of Laura W. Sharpe. On March 13, 1893, Charles Trumball Hayden, the 'First President of the board of education of the Territorial Normal School,' wrote a letter to the legislative assembly of the territory of Arizona in which he included these statements:

'I earnestly suggest that a professor be provided for the Territorial Normal School to teach the Spanish Language. To attempt to teach or govern a people whose language you do not understand, is certainly a condition to be avoided.

For practical purposes in the school room, and all the purposes of our government and social and commercial relations that intimately effects the government from our location and surroundings the Spanish Language is of the first importance to us

Your individual experience probably corresponds with my own that would cultivate the living and cremate the dead languages with all other dead matter, preserving the translations (the ashes), proven by science to be the source of the greatest fertilizing power.'

Nevertheless, Spanish Language instruction was not offered soon thereafter. In the catalogues after 1885, however, Latin (taught by Amina J. McNaughton, wife of early President-Principal Dr. James McNaughton, 1895-9), as well as German and French (taught by Frances B. Abell) were listed as 'auxiliary classes.' The 1910-11 catalogue, which is the first to use the term 'Department,' even though individual faculty members were not designated as department heads or chairpersons, includes both a 'Department of Latin' and an apparently instructorless 'Department of Spanish.' At this time there was no evidence of continuing instruction in German and French.

Only after 1925 when the Arizona State Legislature approved the school as an institution of higher education under the name of Tempe State Teachers' College was Spanish Language instruction regularly offered in addition to Latin. The push for National accreditation then re-introduced German and French in 1929.

Accreditation in 1931 brought about the formal organization of the Department of Foreign Languages under the headship of Dr. Fernand Cattlain (see table 1 for a listing of department heads and chairs).

TABLE 1: DEPARTMENT OF FOREIGN LANGUAGES: HEADS AND CHAIRS

Dr. Fernand Cattlain (French)		Head	1931-45
Dr. George Portnoff (Russian)		Head	1945-48
Dr. Irma Wilson (French)	Acting Head 1948-52	Head	1952-56

Dr. Russell K. Bowman (French)	Head	1956-64
Dr. Herbert A. Van Scoy (Spanish)	Head	1964-71
Dr. Albert Buffington (German)	Acting Head	1971
Dr. Douglas C. Sheppard (Spanish)	Head	1971-75
Dr. Michael J. Flys (Spanish) by By-laws	Chair	1975-81
Dr. Peter Horwath (German) Acting Chair 1981-2	Chair	1982-91
Dr. Pier R. Baldini (Italian)	Chair	1991-1997

(During Chair Baldini's tenure the department was renamed the "Department of Languages and Literatures" abbreviated DLL)

Dr. David W. Foster (Spanish)	Chair	1997-2001
Dr. Deborah Losse (French)	Chair	2001-2004
Dr. Pier R. Baldini (Italian)	Chair	2004-2006

(During Interim Chair Baldini's 2004-6 tenure the decision was made to change the Department of Languages and Literature into the "School of International Letters and Cultures" abbreviated SILC)

Dr. Robert 'Joe' Cutter (Chinese)	Chair	2006-

(Beginning in July 2007, Chair Cutter's formal title will be "Director of the School of International Letters and Cultures")

As Head, Dr. Cattlain waged a protracted battle for institutional recognition even as the institution itself struggled with opposition from the University of Arizona in Tucson to the idea of this institution's being empowered to grant degrees other than in Education. During this period only degrees in Education were awarded, the first B.A. in Ed. being given in 1929 and reissued in 1931 (the first B.A.'s in Ed. in Spanish (5) coming with three in 'Foreign Languages' and one in French in 1934, followed in 1936 by one German; and the 1938 M.A.'s in Ed. included one in French, with Spanish following soon after, at least by 1946 (record deficit during the war years here)).

Dr. Cattlain's own struggle shows in his report of 1938-9 in which he expresses his disenchantment with the members of the administration when members of the Alpha Mu Gamma National Foreign Languages Honorary, which has long played a supportive role in departmental affairs, were prohibited from selling cool drinks at registration, thus limiting financial resources for endowing an award for the best graduating student in the field of foreign languages. And in his May 1945 report, written in long-hand on a grade report sheet, he decried the general lack of respect for foreign language learning, especially in such a Spanish–speaking area, and complained of the lack of institutional support in the area of providing 'maps, charts, and other realia.' At the end of this report, Dr. Cattlain mentions his resignation for reasons of health and states: 'This is the only paper I have left.'

An interesting side-light to this institution's battle to grant liberal arts degrees is found in President Grady Gammage's report to the Arizona State Board of Regents dated June 13, 1945. In this report, entitled 'Problems of Arizona State College at Tempe' (the institution's name at that time), President Gammage compared the Arizona State College faculty with the faculties of thirty accredited colleges of arts and sciences. He found the Arizona State College faculty in foreign languages to be 5.6 faculty positions short of parity in instructional adequacy. His recommendational comment on this was that due to '...a lessening of emphasis on foreign languages as a requirement of college education...It would therefore seem inadvisable to build Tempe's foreign language department up to the indicated average, although some addition is apparently needed, or will be when the war is over.' The subsequent May 26th 1946 'Report of the Special Survey Committee of the Board of Regents' then recommended that 'Tempe be given the right to award the Bachelors' degrees in Liberal Arts and Sciences, i.e. without any requirements in education, within the following limitations:...(b) Tempe should give not more than two years of French and not more than two years of German, limited to the first two years of college work, and should give a modern foreign language major only in Spanish.' *It is under this attitude of restriction that Dr. George Portnoff, the second head of the Department of Foreign Languages, labored. To his credit goes the addition of Russian to Departmental offerings in 1946 (he taught the first Russian classes personally).*

When, in 1949, the first non-education B.A. degree was awarded in Spanish, the Department of Foreign Languages' faculty consisted of Dr. Irma Wilson (Acting Head), Dr. Mary Escudero (Mary, who taught at ASU until 1980 or so, was also a Cornell alumna who had studied Russian there with Avgusta L'vovna Jaric in 1946...and Avgusta was still there in 1973 teaching my Ph.D. cohort), Dr. Suzanne D'Orssaud, Dr. Aldis Hatch, and part-time instructors Homan, Dembo, and *Mrs. Anna Wall*, who had taken over the Russian the previous year. Despite the dramatic increase in general enrollment which characterized the post-war years, the foreign languages faculty actually decreased in size to 1953, when the faculty listed Drs. Von der Heydt, Wilson, D'Orssaud, Escudero, and Mrs. Wall.

Only in the late 1950's did the Department of Foreign Languages begin to show the first signs of the qualitative and numerical growth that characterized its development in the sixties and the seventies. In 1956, Head Russell Bowman saw the first language laboratory installed, and in 1959 the M.A. programs in French, German, and Spanish were initiated. In the same year the first non-education B.A. degree in French was awarded, and the following year another was awarded in German. The first M.A. degrees in all three languages were awarded in 1961.

In 1965 the department, over thirty faculty strong, awarded its first B.A. in Russian to Col. D. Bruce Powers and added Portuguese (taught by Dr. Quino Martinez) and classical Greek (taught by Dr. George Carver) to its curriculum. Instruction in Italian (Dr. Carmello Virgillo), Chinese (Dr. Tom Nielson), and Japanese (Ms. Tamayi Cyoni) was started in 1966, 1967, and 1968 respectively, with first B.A.'s coming in Chinese in 1972 and in Japanese in 1978. After a detailed proposal, the department initiated its Ph.D. program in Spanish in 1968 and Granted the first Ph.D. degree in Spanish to Carmen Corricides in 1972."

Here I end the quotation from the 1981 (Table 1 is updated) departmental history. In general I think it is fair to write that ASU's Department of Foreign Languages has long struggled in an adversarial climate to develop and that it has only relatively recently grown to considerable size. The contention made in 1981 that ASU's Department of Foreign Languages is the WORLD'S LARGEST such academic department (judged by the number of full-time ranked faculty—50—or by involved students—close to 5,000 per session, but distinctly NOT by financial resource) is still undisputed. (In 2006 the successor Department of Languages and Literatures had 80 full-time faculty (and another 80 FA's and TA's as part-time people) teaching over 7000 students per semester). The size has been a problem in that the many diverse interests occasionally clash (linguists vs. literati, natives vs. non-natives, graduate-offering programs vs. undergraduate or service programs, and language section vs.

language section). The factionalization has had political significance within the institutional framework. We ousted one Head (Dr. Douglas Sheppard in 1975) by faculty petition, then hired another (Dr. Michael Flys) who transformed the departmental structure (essentially transcending seniority for merit, and institutionalizing the quasi-administrative sectional "Coordinators" and determining a host of operational processes through a set of departmental by-laws) only to serve his last two years (1979-81) in violation of the by-laws he himself wrote. The years under Chairman Peter Horwath were reconciliative due to his personal charm, but diminishing resources and diminishing institutional prioritization slowed the department's rapid rate of program growth and added an additional element of stress to our professional lives—concern with maintaining the status quo—programmatic survival. Subsequent Chairs (Pier Baldini, Deborah Losse, and David Foster) were often confronted with financial cutbacks and increased intra-institutional competition for the more limited available resources. The need to remain institutionally "large" in this competition prevented our splitting into smaller units ("Where would the new smaller sections be physically housed?" "How could they afford to pay new separate secretarial staffs, buy new office equipment, etc., etc.?).

In this problematical framework swam the "Russian Section" (more recently the "Slavic Section" and now the SILC "Faculty of German, Romanian and Slavic"). The Section's particular history, as mentioned above, began after World War II (1946) with the instruction of Dr. George Portnoff, the department Head and a native-speaker of Russian. Dr. Portnoff retired in 1948. His wife, Collice Portnoff, was a professor of English and continued to teach at ASU into my time as faculty in it. After Dr. George Portnoff's retirement, Russian language instruction continued from 1948 to 1962 on a part-time basis under the instruction of Mrs. Anna Wall, a woman of Ukrainian heritage who had, by 1962, an intermittent two-year program involving about twenty students. Then DFL Head, Dr. Russell Bowman of French, hired *Dr. Sanford C. Couch* (University of Wisconsin-Madison Ph.D., 1961) to begin building a Bachelor's Degree program in Russian. Dr. Couch designed a four-year curriculum, wrote the course descriptions and got the courses approved by all the requisite committees. He set about writing and publishing his own textual materials (Практический курс русского языка (A Practical Course of the Russian Language), parts I, II, III, and IV) and supporting laboratory tapes for the first two years of this instruction, completing the first-year's version of his basic text set by 1964 and the second-year's version by 1966 (these texts were used through multiply revised versions until Dr. Couch's retirement in 2002). Enrollment grew quickly, responding to the public interest in the cold-war politics (USA vs. USSR) of the time, and, in 1963, Dr. Couch was able to replace Mrs. Wall with *Rolfs Ekmanis*, a fellow graduate student at the University of Wisconsin who was then past his comprehensive doctoral examinations for the Ph.D. at the University of Indiana and was teaching in Florida while working on his dissertation. In 1964 Dr. Couch's protests of Head Russell Bowman's "non-democratic" modes of departmental administration led Bowman to fire Dr. Couch. But instead of effecting Dr. Couch's departure, Head Bowman only brought about departmental mutiny and his own removal as Head.

(L-R): Sandy Couch, Lee and Hayden Croft. Photo by Lesley Hoyt Croft, ca. 1989.

The increasing enrollment in Russian language classes in those days was driven by our country's cold war rivalry with the Soviet Union under the "know thy enemy" rationale. The U.S. higher-education professoriate in the Russian Lang/Lit/Soviet Studies subject area was unanimously anti-

Soviet in character. At every university and college in the land were professors in this subject area who differed personally, and by most of their social and political views, in every way under the sun, BUT they were virtually unanimous in their opposition to the Soviet government, its "enslavement" in their terms, of the highly cultured Russian people. Our goal under these professors tutelage was: 1) to confront the Soviet ideology, to thwart its aims and goals, especially its aims and goals of world domination; and 2) to bring about a great "change of mind," to effectuate the Russian people's rejection and change of their authoritarian form of government, so abrogating of an individual's human needs in subordination to collective or "mass" welfare. Many members of this U.S. Russian/Soviet-area professoriate were themselves emigres from the cultures impacted by the Leninist/Stalinist governments and their actions. Their goal was to equip their students with the means to confront and to change this adversarial government. Dr. Couch often stated that every Russian-competent university student we trained and put on the streets of Moscow among the Russian people, every student we enabled to argue with Russians in their own language about everything that matters, was worth "ten missiles" in the determination of who would prevail in our cold war with the Soviets. The irony is that, through the late 1980's years of Mikhail Gorbachev's "perestroika" and "glasnost," through the Polish "Solidarity" freedom movement and the destruction of the Berlin Wall, and even to the final 1991 world-unprecedented self-dissolution of the Soviet Union, we did not really believe that our powers of ideological confrontation and persuasion by word and example, incremental to the individual students we placed into the fray, could actually bring about such a sea change in world politics as we then witnessed. Prof. Ronald Grigor Suny of the University of Michigan put it well in his recent essay, "Fifteen Years Apres Le Deluge: What's Left of Marx?" in the Newsnet of the American Association for the Advancement of Slavic Studies (AAASS, Vol. 47, NO.1 (January 2007)). He wrote: "For those of us who started this profession four decades ago, at the end of the 1960's, the present seems to be another planet! It is not the world we anticipated. Then the objects of our study, the Soviet Union and Communist regimes in East Europe, were alive if not well, and *few could have imagined that the AAASS would outlive the very regimes it had been constituted to investigate* (italics mine)." This is so true. Each of us in the profession from those years had their individual epiphanies in the realization. I remember getting a note from Rolfs Ekmanis, who had been engaged in setting up a news bureau of Radio Free Europe in his homeland of Latvia, that "the job is done." I wrote this myself on a posting of a stunning article, published in both Известия and Soviet Life by an author called Alexei Kiva entitled "Do We Need to Repent?" When I read that article in those organs I knew that indeed the job was done.

Sandra Batalden, Eleni Buzarovska, Stephen Batalden and Lesley Hoyt Croft in Flagstaff at the Bataldens', summer 2006. Photo by Lee B. Croft.

In 1965, Dr. Couch added his "Scientific Russian" courses (RUS-303, 304) to the curriculum, filling them with students despite their early morning time. He wrote textbooks for these courses too, the successive editions of which were used into the 21st century. Rolfs Ekmanis, who had begun to publish steadily in the field of Baltic Literature, contributed the three literature survey courses (RUS-321, 322, 323) to the curriculum, winning a political struggle in the academic context of the time to teach them in English, thus to add significant numbers of non-majors to our sectional enrollment. And, significantly, Ekmanis began the bureaucratic labor of building our ASU Library's collection of Baltic and Slavic books and serials. By the time of my arrival in 1973, Ekmanis was working with a $300.00/year total acquisitions allowance, and, in 1974, he and I went together with ridiculous lack of success to Head Librarian Donald Koepp to protest the outright cancellation of the Balto-Slavic book budget. Only was our library effort revived after the arrival here of Dr. Stephen K. Batalden of Russian History and his wife, Slavic Librarian Sandra Batalden in 1976. The Bataldens managed strategic acquisitions of retired scholars' book collections in exchange for tax deductions and eventually achieved a "blanket order" policy for library acquisitions in the area, arranging the orders through a series of Soviet and East European-permitted vendors (e.g. Four Continent Books of NYC and then Les Livres Etrangers of Paris).

1965 was also the year that *Mrs. Irina Borisovna Krylova* was brought from Michigan to instruct the Basic Conversation courses (RUS-211, 212), the Intermediate Composition and Conversation courses (RUS-311, 312), and the Advanced Composition and Conversation courses (RUS-411, 412). Mrs. Krylova was a native Russian from Moscow who had emigrated to the U.S. after World War II. Her husband, a Moscow Lawyer, had been arrested by the NKVD just before the war and she never saw him again (even though he was "rehabilitated" during the thaw during the Khrushchev years and allowed to return from the GULAG system to Moscow where Dr. Couch became aware of his existence. By this time, approximately 1968, Mrs. Krylova decided not to reestablish contact with him). Mrs. Krylova's instruction was highly personal in nature, requiring memorization of poetry as well as grammatical rules from the Pulkina-Zastava-Nekrasova text (Русский язык для студентов иностранцев). She lived near campus and did not drive, so that students helped her travel around and shop. She retired at advanced age in 1973 and when she died (ca. 1985), only three people (her daughter, Sandy Couch and I) attended her funeral.

In 1965 also, our first Bachelor's Degree in Russian was awarded to a faculty husband (his wife was Dr. Doris Powers of English) and retired military engineer (he had an engineering degree from M.I.T.), Col. D. Bruce Powers. Col. Powers subsequently wrote a "Dictionary of Irregular Russian Verb Forms" which was published by John Wiley and Sons' Textbook Publishers (New York, London, Sydney, Toronto, 1968). This dictionary was thoroughly damned in a Slavic and East European Journal review (Vol. XVI, No. 1 (Spring 1970), pp. 107-9) by no less a scholar than Harvard's Prof. Horace Lunt, who especially ridiculed the irregular use of the term "irregular" in the title. According to the bitter Powers, Wiley Publishers decided on the basis of this scathing review not to issue a second edition of the dictionary despite the first run's sellout. Later on, in the early 1980's, after publishing a literary translation with Ardis Publishers, then at the University of Michigan, Powers told this tale to editors Carl and Ellendea Proffer, who then agreed to republish the dictionary under the amended title "Dictionary of Russian Verb Forms" (Ardis Publishers, Ann Arbor, MI, gives only the original 1968 copyright date though it was issued in 1985 or 1986). Powers, then in his nineties and living in retirement in Colorado, reported that the dictionary sold well. I can recall with humor how one particularly mischievous band of Teaching Assistants from the University of Arizona's Russian MA program (thinking here of TA's Rick Ruth, Dan Winters, Al Cannon, and

Col. Bruce Powers, Dr. Rolfs Ekmanis and the Powers' dog, "Alf," at their Colorado estate, ca. 1990.

Others) used to bait Col. Powers at our semesterly Arizona chapter of AATSEEL. They would speak with him and deliberately insert into the conversation words that rhymed with "Lunt," like "runt," "hunt," "bunt," "shunt," and others. By doing this they would elicit a rant from Col.

Powers about "that pompous Lunt, the #$%+#:^*," much to their amusement.

In 1966 our "person courses" (RUS-421 Pushkin, RUS-423 Dostoevsky, RUS-424 Tolstoy, and RUS-425 Chekhov) were fixed into the curriculum. And RUS-426 Soviet Literature (later retitled "Soviet Dissident Literature" and still later "Non-Russian Literatures of the USSR"...all taught by Dr. Ekmanis) was subsequently added to the catalogue. Soon after this, Dr. Ekmanis became a member of the Modern Language Association Bibliography Committee for "Baltic and Slavic Literatures," using this professional connection to boost our library acquisitions in this area and to advocate ASU's hiring of professional library staff in our area. At this time too he began to provide audiotaped commentary on Baltic literature, culture, and news to the U.S. government's surrogate broadcast radio organs, Radio Free Europe/Radio Liberty (RFE/RL) under the pseudonym "Maris Rauda." His anti-Soviet perspective infused also his work on his influential book, <u>Latvian Literature Under the Soviets, 1940-1975</u>, published by Nordlands Publishing Co. of Belmont, MA in 1978.

I (*Lee Croft*) transferred to ASU as a student of Mathematics in early 1966 after visiting here in the Fall of 1965. To me, ASU was a "huge" place, its student population at the time (ca. 16,000...a fraction of its current 60,000) was five times the population of the town in which I grew up and three times the size of the university from which I transferred. I had begun a quarter of Russian earlier at Montana State University in Bozeman under instructor Dmitri Berkoff (the text was by Von Gronicka and Bates as I remember it), but I enrolled in Dr. Couch's RUS-101 in the Fall semester of 1966. For the next three years (past my 1968 B.S. in Math.) I took every Russian course I could from Couch, Ekmanis, and Krylova. As a Mathematics major I never made the acquaintance of any other Mathematics major I could call a friend, never sat in more than one class with the same cohort. But I had many Russian-class comrades who are still well remembered. Murlin Croucher, later Slavic Librarian at the University of Indiana at Bloomington who was an evaluator of our library's Slavic collection as part of our 1996-7 program review, was a student in the ASU Russian program with me. Barbara Rasnick, who later became an esteemed instructor of English here at ASU, was a fellow student. Neil Merrill, later an employee of the CIA and a high-school teacher in Mesa, was a fellow student. I remember fondly also an older student, a Glendale maker of jewelry named Dan Klein, whose daughter Susan was also a student of Russian at that time. In 1967-8, when student anti-Vietnam-war protestors went "on strike" and tried to take over the Language and Literature Building (they were burning a uniformed US Marine effigy on the front mall and had hung a severed and fly-swarmed rotting horse's head from a large light-blue star-spangled pendant made to resemble the Congressional Medal of Honor) and prevent class attendance there, Dan and I led our Russian class into a second floor classroom, telling the protestors that we would not be intimidated out of learning what we had paid to learn. Dr. Couch conducted the class as if there were no outside disturbance at all…his students knew that they could not afford to take any "day off."

As a student I was unaware of the published research of any of the faculty members, though I was positively impressed by the language texts of Prof. Couch. But now I know that, after completing his doctorate in 1967, Dr. Ekmanis was able to emerge into prominence as a literary and cultural researcher, especially in the area of Latvian (his native) Literature. And, with the department's gradual adoption of published research as a measure of professional achievement, Dr. Ekmanis advanced rapidly in professional status. By 1972, both he and Dr. Couch were at Full Professor's rank and approximately equal pay.

In the summer of 1968, after having received the B.S. degree in Mathematics, I was hired as a quality control inspector at Talley Industries in Mesa. My job was to inspect the internal canisters of parachute-suspended illuminating flares and of fragmentation grenades. This job, involving the handling of high explosives, was judged critical to the nation's military effort in Vietnam and so I was draft exempt. But, not liking the job, I requested and received a renewal of my "2-S" student draft exemption to return to ASU in the 1968-9 academic year in an effort to requalify myself as a high-school teacher. I took 21 semester hours in the Fall and tried to take 23 in the Spring, including the required student teaching experience. The most useful of the "education" courses I took that year was the "Methods of Foreign Language Teaching" course (FLA-400, I think, was the listing) I took from Spanish Instructor Lola Mackey…she was wonderful. But, of course, I was trying to take too many semester hours without having filed the required "overload petition." The College of Liberal Arts administration informed me that this would not be allowed UNLESS I got letters of support from all the Heads of the departments in which I was taking these courses. This was how I first met Dr. Herbert Van Scoy, Head of the Department of Foreign Languages at that time. Dr.

Van Scoy signed the form allowing me the overload. And he still remembered this when, only four years later, I sent him an application from Cornell University to be considered as an Assistant Professor of Russian in his department.

The "retooling" of my career from Mathematics to Russian happened during my student teaching experience at Saguaro High School in Scottsdale. At Saguaro in the Spring of 1969 I was, even while enrolled in a full load of courses in Math and Russian and Education, commuting in my 1962 Pontiac to teach honors Calculus and observe the classes of Russian taught by Glendon Bergfalk. Bergfalk, a retired gas-station owner, had taken classes in Russian with me at ASU and I considered him a senior friend. But, during that semester he became ill, was hospitalized, and died. A Saguaro High School Assistant Principal named Walter S. Hoffman (later a prominent high-school sports photographer) who was also a Mathematics teacher proposed that I give up the Calculus course (where I was, he had observed, struggling) and take over the three Russian classes entirely. They could replace a Math teacher easily, but not a Russian teacher. Hoffman told me that I could commence to "just teach out the semester in Russian." No other tasks (dance and sports event chaperoning, for example) would be expected of me, and he (Hoffman) would sign my certification papers in both Math and Russian. I loved the teaching of Russian at Saguaro High School and Mr. Hoffman's word was good. I was, in fact, certified as a high school teacher of both Math. and Russian in the State of Arizona in summer of 1969. But although I have supervised the training of many high school teachers of Russian, I have never really taught high-school Russian myself. During that same summer of 1969, I applied for and received a graduate teaching assistantship to support Master's Degree work in Russian at the University of Arizona in Tucson. There I had coursework from Dr. Joe Malik, Jr., Dr. Boriss Roberts, and from Lecturer Nick Vontsolos. Delbert Phillips was the supervisor of teaching assistants (me, Louis Prazma and Paul Weadon, in 1969-70) and he was inspirational. I finished the M.A. in Russian there in one year and a summer session (during which I was actually working on the drilling rigs in Montana, having already done the work). I completed also a course in "Junior College Education" (Prof. Waldo Anderson) that enabled my Arizona State certification as a community college teacher of Russian (1970). And, most significantly, I applied for and received—thanks to the recommendations of the UA faculty-- admittance to Cornell University's Ph.D. program, funded by the Ford Foundation's Humanities and Social

Sciences Fellowship that gave me a tuition waiver, a stipend, and an allowance for my four dependents (my third child, son Bill, was born on the very day I got this life-changing news…March 23, 1970).

In 1968-9 Dr. Couch had completed a self-study document preparatory to initiating a Master's Degree Program in Russian at ASU. This document, very brief and cursory by today's bureaucratic standards, concluded that another doctoral-level faculty member was needed in order to bring the M.A. Program into viability. And so Brian Dulley, "just finishing" his Ph.D. at Brown University in Linguistics (he did not finish while here) and "fresh from program triumphs" at U-Colorado, was hired. He promptly announced that he would refuse to use Dr. Couch's text and that he wouldn't allow his students to be exposed to Dr. Couch's "non-native speech" on the lab tapes. Dr. Couch suspended the use of his own textual materials in the students' interest and permitted the substitution of Ben T. Clark's Russian for Americans, and its associated tapes were purchased by the lab. Nevertheless, there were soon two student contingents, the "Couchians" and the "Dullards." Of course, in this uncooperative climate the Master's Degree literally "went south," to Dr. Joe Malik at the U. of A. in Tucson, where it still resides. Dr. Couch made Dr. Malik "a deal" not to oppose the M.A. going to the U. of A. (the Arizona Board of Regents' educational advisors traditionally ask U. of A. to evaluate ASU program proposals and ASU to evaluate U. of A. program proposals), where Dr. Malik was just separating his "Russian Department" (now the Department of Russian and Slavic Languages and Literatures) from the earlier "Department of German and Russian," to which he had come from the University of Texas in 1960 with a University of Arizona mandate to "begin Russian in Arizona." In return for this lack of opposition from ASU's Dr. Couch, Malik promised to admit our graduates on a preferential basis…a policy which benefitted me only the next year (I was, as described above, at this time at ASU as a Math graduate student, but taking almost all Russian courses and student teaching at Saguaro High School in an effort to get high-school certified as a teacher).

It turned out, of course, that Brian Dulley was unwise to so blatantly oppose the senior professor here, and he was not offered a 1969-70 contract. Professor Couch reinstalled his own textual materials. A sidenote to this is Dulley's remaining in the Arizona community of Slavists. In 1970, Dr. Peter Horwath, then in a Dean's position at the soon-to-be-defunct Prescott College in Prescott, Arizona, came to the U. of A.'s Russian Department, where I was then a teaching assistant working on my

M.A., to see Dr. Malik (and me) about Dulley. Despite my relation of the above, Dr. Horwath hired Dulley, and Dulley continued to teach Russian at Prescott College until, at age 39, dying suddenly in front of his class of a brain hemorrhage in 1974. This was Prescott College's last year of operation under that administrative incarnation, and Dr. Horwath had already bailed out by that time to join our Department of Foreign Languages as an Associate Professor of German (subsequently to gain Full Professor's rank and become our chair from 1981 to 1991).

Cornell University and its faculty (especially Dr. Richard L. Leed, my doctoral supervisor) were very good to me. I was able to study there intensively, inspired by founder Ezra Cornell's coeducational dictum "I would found an institution where any person can find instruction in any study," together with an impressive cadre of later subject-area scholars, analysts and professors in the field: Thomas G. Marullo of Notre Dame; Sister Mary Colleen Dillon of Thomas More College; Andrew Zigelis of Drew University and the University of Georgia; John Mohan of Grinnell College, Adrian Gan of Mt. Holyoke College, Kathleen Parthe of the University of Rochester, Alice Stone Nakhimovsky of Colgate University, R. David Zorc of McNeil Language Technologies, Charles M. Winkler of the Institute for the Analysis of Military Threat, linguist Mark Orton, and a number of others. I had coursework there from a number of prominent professors in Linguistics and in Slavic Languages and Literatures: Professors Richard L. Leed, Gerald Kelley, Leonard H. Babby, Walter Pintner, George Gibian, Antonia Glasse, William Tjalsma, Patricia Carden, Robert A. Hall, Anthony Lozano, Frederick Foos (an ousted devotee of Eckankar now living in Maui); and I made the acquaintance or worked with very able instructors Avgusta L'vovnoa Jaric (Russian), Predrag Cvitanovic (then we called it Serbo-Croatian, but now at ASU we call it Bosnian/Croatian/Serbian), K. Paulius Zygas (Lithuanian...he is now, coincidentally, a professorial colleague of mine in Architecture here at ASU), Alexander Kraft (Russian), Boris Glasse (Russian), and Alla Novosiltsev (Russian). Also a visiting professor there at Cornell from Harvard was Dr. Richard Brecht, now Director of the National Foreign Languages Center (my dissertation heavily cites parts of his and he came to my dissertation defense). By the summer of 1973 I had defended my doctoral dissertation, <u>The Semantics of Modality in Russian Syntax</u> (Leonard H. Babby, now at Princeton University, was my dissertation supervisor, though Richard L. Leed was my doctoral program director) at Cornell University and had returned for a Summer Assistant Professorship there from the previous semester's employment as an instructor of "Serbo-Croatian" at Colgate University in Hamilton, New York (I was myself taking Serbo-Croation 102 at Cornell from a fellow graduate student, now an endowed professor of theoretical physics at Georgia Tech, Predrag Cvitanovic, while teaching Serbo-Croation 101 at Colgate…an arrangement of great financial aid to me made by my Professors Leed and Babby). After ninety-some inquiries, ten interviews (including Kansas State University, University of Virginia, Loyola of New Orleans, the CIA's Language School, and others), and two go-and-lectures (at Clark University and the University of Wyoming), I had no job for Fall 1973. But one day in mid July, while contemplating Cayuga Lake from my office in historic Morrill Hall, I got a telephone call and heard a familiar voice. It was "Sandy Couch, calling from Tempe." He had heard from "Joe Malik at the last AATSEEL convention" that I was finishing up and looking for a job. Mrs. Krylova, he told me, "was retiring," and I should send my vita to the Department of Foreign Languages Head's office immediately. In one week I had a job offer and was to report to ASU by August 20. Of course, I had a wife and three children, a high-mileage 1965 Chrysler car, and no money for gas. So…would I get any travel money, it being a long road from Ithaca, New York back to Tempe, Arizona? Inquiries with the Head (Dr. Herbert Van Scoy, acting in the summer for Dr. Douglas Sheppard), Dean (George Peek), and the Academic Vice-President (Dr. Karl Dannenfeldt) came to naught…no travel money… "it was against a state law," they said. And no advance on the $12,000 salary either…couldn't be done. So I sold our furniture, even the beds and mattresses, all my tools, all winter clothes, all the kids' toys, and almost everything else in a series of moved-around garage sales. The trip took place in 100-mile increments of car overheating. And when we got to Tempe we rented an unfurnished apartment within a long walking distance from the university and slept for months on the floor. In order to buy a refrigerator and other necessities we went so far into debt that I didn't get clear until 1985. But I had a job doing what I wanted, and I loved it.

I relate the above travail so as to give a picture of what it was like to work at ASU in the early 1970's, before the realities of modern big-university academia struck us hard. First, it was four and five-course loads of daily grading-intensive classes. The Department was run by a group of senior cronies of the Head. My early efforts to build interest and enrollment by posting fact sheets, stationing students at the registration tables, selling T-shirts, and the like were not welcomed by these people. I recall former DFL Head Russell Bowman coming over to me as I plastered another bulletin board with my "take Russian" propaganda, saying: "Young man, I think you're treading rather heavily upon the bounds of academic propriety with these activities." Of course, I only intensified my efforts to boost enrollment...river floats, volleyball and softball challenges, translation contests, etc., etc...and it worked.

In my first year I got unpleasantly involved in the Department's development of an affirmative action policy. I thought the first version, written by a Head-selected group of minority faculty, was clearly a specified-quota reverse-discrimination document...unjust, and I said so loudly (forever cementing my perception in the Department as a "brash" young man—I might mention here that in 1973 at 26 I was the youngest professor of 43, and now, almost twenty years later (I wrote this in 1993) and a grandfather of 45 years, I'm still "young" by our Department's graying standard...I believe only four of our present 50 are younger than I). I even wrote an alternative, find-the-best-person-regardless-of-natal-circumstance version of my own and circulated it. In a departmental election my version and yet another got as many votes as the original Head-commissioned version. Dr. Sheppard said he'd pass the decision on to the Dean and University Counsel. He then reported that all our versions had been declared "illegal" by the university counsel and that we'd just have to abide by a college-level policy to be drafted later. But later we found out that only his original Head-commissioned version had been shown to anyone at all. This and other scandals resulted in a petition to oust Head Sheppard (which, as an untenured faculty member, I was asked not to sign...though I wanted to). As a person I always got along with this fellow Montanan well, but as Head he left much to be desired. I recall asking him for a "merit raise" after my first year. He thought about it for a few days, "consulting with others," and then called me into his office to say that he would grant me a merit raise of $50.00, but he cautioned me: "Don't tell anyone else about it."

DFL Head Sheppard also rejected our sectional request to change our formal titles from "Professors of Russian" to "Professors of Slavic and East European Languages," saying that such a change was "illegal" (he was fixated on legality after undergoing some previous course of litigation while at SUNY-Buffalo) without an act of the state legislature. Then he rebuffed our timely proposal to be the first university in the world to offer an academic position to Alexander Solzhenitsyn, just then in process of exiting the Soviet Union pursuant to his stigmatization there after winning the 1970 Nobel Prize for Literature for his revelations concerning the Soviet system of incarceration in the "Gulag Archipelago." Drs. Couch, Ekmanis and I had all signed this proposal, reasoning that, if for God knows what reason the hermitic Solzhenitsyn might decide to settle here in the desert Southwest, the university could surely find the money to hire its first Nobel Prize laureate, and that, if he refused and went elsewhere (or even ignored our offer and did not respond), then at least our university and our Russian Section would get the publicity of being the first to offer Solzhenitsyn an academic position. It was our feeling that we had a win-win proposition for our administrators to consider. When Dr. Sheppard wrote us a memo refusing to advance the idea to ASU President John W. Schwada as we had written it (the proposal was dated February 13, 1974), both Dr. Couch and Dr. Ekmanis urged me to "go ahead and take it directly to the Board of Regents," which I did personally at their next meeting, held in ASU's Administration Building, second floor. I now chuckle to recall their response. ASU Vice President for Academic Affairs Karl Dannenfeldt came out of the meeting to the hallway where I was told to wait for a response, handed the proposal back to me, and said: "Good idea. Keep on thinking." Then he walked away and we never heard anything more about it (though we soon read in the newspapers about other universities in Europe and the United States making their offers to Solzhenitsyn). This was not to be the last administrative frustration of our "good ideas" by any means.

In 1974 I became involved in our university's effort to forge an academic exchange with Universitet Kiril i Metodij (UKIM) in Skopje, Macedonia (then Josip Broz Tito's Yugoslavia). Skopje, Macedonia, was Tempe, Arizona's first (and the nation's first) "sister city." My function was to aid in hosting the exchangees from UKIM here at ASU. Some of these scholars had interesting aims and goals, like the limnologist (lake bottom sediment expert) attached to the Biology Department on a full professor's replacement salary (a fortune to an East European professor at the time) who confided to me that he most wanted to "purchase a Corvette car" with his money while here, but who then took sick and spent much of his time here in the hospital. But one of these early exchangees, a scholar of Herman Melville attached to the ASU Department of English named Violeta Milenkovska, expressed a desire to Dr. Peter Horwath, who administered the ASU/UKIM exchange from its infancy and deserves much of the credit for its current success, to teach the Macedonian Language here. Peter Horwath asked me to arrange for a credited course

(RUS-494 Special Topics) for this and to proselytize my students into taking it. This successful effort was the nascence of our long championship of the Macedonian language and, indeed, the Macedonian culture in the world outside Macedonia. One day I received a telephone

Peter Horwath and Lee Croft at Cedic Family's Serbian-American Academy on the Oak Creek in Sedona, Arizona. Photo by Lesley Hoyt Croft, ca. 1991.

call from a local Macedonian émigré librarian and bookseller, Mary Choncoff. She had heard that I, the Coordinator of Russian at ASU (my title at the time did not mention "Slavic Languages," but only "Russian"), planned to teach (or, more acccurately, to have taught) the Macedonian Language. What did I think I was doing? What kind of language did I think Macedonian was? Who, in my opinion, were the Macedonians? I answered that the Macedonian Language I was having taught was a SLAVIC language, linguistically independent by the criteria of mutual spoken intelligibility and grammatical structure from the other proximate

Slavic languages (i.e. Serbo-Croatian or Bulgarian) and that the Macedonians whose language I planned to have taught were also predominately SLAVS who had inhabited their territory since the sixth century AD. As I explained this to Mary, who, of course, knew it better than I did, she began to cry on the telephone. She had been afraid that I would be, in ignorance or from some deliberate sociopolitical agenda, indulging the "opposition views" of the Bulgarians and especially the Greeks, who felt that their claim on the illustrious historical characters of Phillip of Macedon and his son, Alexander the Great, was somehow threatened by these Slavic "parvenues." In the years to come, I continued to be involved in the teaching of Macedonian as we hosted UKIM faculty and students here and sent our graduate students, the first of ASU's Fulbright recipients (Paulette Lowe, Robb Berry, Michael Zavada, Linda Susan Snipes, Linda Abernathy, Suzanne Galvin, Bonifacio Contreras, Edward Brennan, Susan Moore, Jamie Struckmeyer, Julie Nachtigal and several more) to Skopje. This ASU/UKIM exchange is now ASU's oldest academic exchange, but it had to survive several threats from ASU administrators attempting to trim the financial "bottom line." Fortuitously, Peter Horwath had initially had the actual exchange agreement signed not by an ASU Vice President for Academic Affairs, but by Alonzo Metcalf, a Vice President for Business Affairs. When later minions of the Academic Vice Presidents asked to see the exchange agreement...this, we knew, so that they could cancel or cut it...Peter Horwath and I maintained that we could not find it in our files and that Vice President Metcalf's files, he having retired, were inaccessible. Later UKIM exchangee Evica Konecni significantly advanced the Macedonian instruction by her excellence. In later years she was the first instructor of Macedonian when I founded the Critical Languages Institute (CLI) at ASU under a grant from the American Council of Learned Societies (ACLS). Subsequent teachers, both in the CLI and in the academic year, have included Eleni Buzarovska, Liljana Mitkovska and Marija Kusevska (authors of the Macedonian to English speakers' text developed here) and Lupco Spasovski. In 1999, after the death of Mary Choncoff, who had been like a real "grandmother" to our UKIM exchangees here all those years—giving them sheets and pillowcases, kitchen implements and utensils, a bicycle, and inviting them often to her home—Dr Stephen Batalden, Dr. Don Traicoff (a Mesa physician of Macedonian heritage, who, together with his wife Gloria, is a superb program supporter in many ways) and I founded and endowed a subaccount in the ASU Foundation entitled "The Mary Choncoff Memorial Fund for Macedonian-American Understanding." The Fund pays for a yearly "Mary Choncoff Lecture" and the speakers have included many luminaries from Macedonian society. This year's (March 29, 2007) speaker is Dr. George Mitrevski of Auburn University, a Macedonian-born scholar and teacher of Slavic Studies and Computer pedagogical applications.

The Critical Languages Institute under my administration of it from 1991 to 1997 included also the intensive summer offerings of Serbo-Croatian (taught by Maria Budisavljevic-Oparnica, a former student of Russian here) and Kazan Tatar (taught initially by Agnes Kefeli-Clay, an ASU History Ph.D. and wife of Religious Studies Professor Eugene Clay). Since 1997 the Critical Languages Institute has flourished under the Administration of Dr. Stephen Batalden, aided by Dr. Danko Šipka (2002-5) and now by Dr. Ariann Stern-Gottschalk.

In 1974-5 I was appointed to the committee to select a new Head. I worked hard on this committee in advocacy of Dr. Couch's candidacy, but Dr. Michael Flys, a Professor of Spanish from Bowling Green University was selected instead. I remember the committee conference with Dean Charles Woolf about what his pay level would be. I couldn't help pointing out the irony of the situation in which we could pay a candidate's way here to interview for a position, but were prohibited by "State law" from paying Flys' way here once he had won the position. Dean Woolf's comment was, "Oh, we can get around that." Of course such consideration could be extended to an incoming Head, but not to a financially struggling Assistant Professor as I had been two years before. Fortunately for him, Dr. Woolf was not the same Dean who had refused my earlier request. Gogol said it well: "Lord, lead us not to serve in the academic ranks."

By the time Dr. Flys took his position in Fall 1975, Dr. Couch was on leave as the resident director of the CIEE (Council on International Educational Exchange) programs in the USSR. After a rigorous search we selected *Dr. Martha Awdziewicz* of Brown University as a temporary replacement for Dr. Couch. Dr. Flys, politically perceiving that I was the known advocate of his primary search opponent (the "inside candidate," Couch), asked me to serve as his "Assistant Chair," (he preferred the title "Chair," implying administration by a set of by-laws) which I consented to do (and did until 1979). I soon became his confidant and ally in the construction of a set of defining by-laws. These by-laws had the virtue of mandating fair and democratic procedure, specifying things like the method of assigning summer teaching contracts (which my own appointment letter said I'd never get), and providing for elected instead of crony-appointed advisory and personnel committees and setting terms for offices including the "Chair," and etc. In those days the only thing Flys and I disagreed on was the merit of Dr. Awdziewicz. I thought she was a superb teacher, a splendid colleague. He gave her a negative primary evaluation and we had harsh words about it. She gave his case against her armament by not publishing anything in that single year (as if one could). And so, after I had, by great effort, managed to weather a very threatening Board-of-Regents-initiated budgetary "red-flagging" of our "low production" Bachelor's Degree program (Dr. Senner, then acting in behalf of German, and I eventually had to take a Vice-President-directed reprimand from a smiling Dr. Flys for not confining our strong protests to official channels—we directly approached legislators, the news media, and etc.), we were mysteriously authorized to hire an additional faculty member in 1976-7.

My goal was to get Dr. Awdziewicz's temporary position with us made permanent, but she was forced to enter again a national search for the position. This time Dr. Couch would be back, and she who had been chosen for her professional similarity to him was now at a disadvantage in a search to complement him with other aspects. In the end, with active opposition from Chairman Flys, I was unable to retain Dr. Awdziewicz beyond the following summer (1976). It was then that *Dr. Dora Burton* from the University of Washington joined our faculty. We were then unable to hire additional full-time faculty for more than a quarter century until Dr. Burton's retirement in 2003 brought Dr. Jeanette Owen here from Bryn Mawr College as a tenure-trial Assistant Professor of Russian. Dr. Martha Awdziewicz married a professor of mathematics who left ASU to take a position at U.S. International University (now Alliant University) in San Diego. He's a Dean there now and Martha works as a computer translation expert, first for Air Force Intelligence and then for the Systran Corporation (originators of the BABELFISH machine translator online) and as the full-time mother of ten-year-old twin boys (Dual childhood stars of a single role in the Tom Cruise movie, "Top Gun").

In 1972 while a graduate student at Cornell University, I had participated in a study abroad program in the Soviet Union run by the American Institute for Foreign Study (AIFS) of London, England, and Greenwich, Connecticut. The tour's Dean was a former US Army Intelligence Colonel James Wilmeth, who taught at the University of Texas at Arlington. On this program with me, studying together in the Soviet "INTOURIST summer school of the Russian Language and Soviet Culture," were several later notable professors in our field: Gerald Mayer of Fordham University, Liudmila Koehler of the University of Pittsburgh, young Steven Young, later a Professor of the University of Chicago, Ann Vinograde from Iowa State University (who subsequently sent her daughter Alice to be a Russian major at ASU), Bernard Roffman of Indiana University of Pennsylvania, Michael Naydan of Penn State University (he was then only 18 years old and encountered on this trip his recently freed Ukrainian Uncle), Carol Avins, then a graduate student at Yale University and later a professor at Northwestern University, and David Hart, later of the NSA (after my attempt to hire him failed) and now BYU. The Soviet Intourist people quartered us in the same residential corpus with a group of twenty-six young communists from North Vietnam…this at a time when our military was bombing Hanoi. At first, this group feared us and would only appear in our presence (at the cafeteria or the basement showers) in groups of four or more, lest we bigger Americans (as we found out in German conversation with them…they had been in Dresden, East Germany, for a year training to become governmental administrators in the soon anticipated "unified Vietnam.") "attack and kill them." As we gradually interacted with them, fanatical "hard-liners" intent on reforming their southern brethren who were, in their terms, living in "economic sin," we could foresee the woeful consequences that would ensue under their administration in South Vietnam should public protests in our society force us to abandon it to them. Unfortunately this is what happened in the next few years, but at that time, personally hearing these North Vietnamese youths' plans for their "bourgeouis" southern countrymen, some of our previous "doves" became "hawks" against them. My own views on the Vietnam conflict were heavily influenced by this contact.

Four years later from my faculty position at ASU, wanting to provide study abroad opportunities for my students, I contracted with the American Institute of Foreign Studies to lead a group of students to the Soviet Union in the U.S. bicentennial summer of 1976. In that very adventurous group were fourteen students, including James Glenn "Jim" O'Haver, now an attorney in Prescott, Bennett B. McCutcheon, Jr. ("Junior"), later a decorated USAF intelligence officer, ASU law graduate and international trade negotiator, Nina Bondarook, later a Colorado television news anchor, later teachers Susan Reibman, Debra Anderson Jaynes (and husband Rick), later NSA analyst Joyce Tilzey Keeler, later social science and business professors Eric Dittert and DeeDee Doyle, international business leaders Elizabeth "Dee Dee" Myers and Michael DiLucido, later Illinois Slavic librarian Suzanne Galvin, and ballerina/practical nurse Lila Roberts. Other groups in Russia under AIFS auspices that summer incuded the Rose-Hulman Institute group under Prof. Peter Priest, the Colgate University group under Profs. Anthony and Martha Brill Olcott (who marched their students out of a cafeteria singing of our national anthem on July 4, 1976 as a protest against what they saw as an interculturally insensitive act), the Edinboro State College group under Prof. Julius Blum (who disappeared for most of the term of the tour, inquired about by the KGB), and a group from the State University of New York at Purchase led by later legendary middle eastern dancer Carolina Varga Dinicu (known now as "Morocco"...see www.casbahdance.org). In the summer of 1977 my study-abroad duties expanded. Colonel Charles McDowell, another retired Army Intelligence officer teaching with James Wilmeth at U-Texas-Arlington, had taken over the AIFS Russian program deanship and, wanting a summer's break, recommended me for the job. Although I was appointed the overall AIFS Russian Dean, I nevertheless took another group of my own, including my wife Betty (children Cathy (11), Chris (9) and Billy (7) stayed in Montana with the grandparents and in-laws) and four ASU students, including Shirley Strunk, later a high-school Russian teacher at Shadow Mountain High in Paradise Valley, Arizona, Robert Holcombe, later an NSA international security analyst and Russian linguist, later Idaho Russian teacher Mary Jo Smith, and Eva Zukotynsky (of whom I've lost track). Together with this ASU contingent were six students from the University of Arizona, including Tammy Fannin, granddaughter of an Arizona Governor and Senator, Christine Kellogg, the daughter of UA History Professor Frederick Kellogg and UA football player Eric Peterson. The total AIFS group was over ninety in number, including groups from other institutions in the U.S., Canada, and England.

The 1976 and 1977 summer adventures in the Soviet Union led me to want to expand ASU's study abroad possibilities under the AIFS auspices. For 1978 I would not be the Soviet programs' Dean. Charles McDowell would return to that position. And I would not lead the ASU contingent myself, but would enlist Martha Awdziewicz to do it. In addition, I would arrange a tour to France under the ASU leadership of French section faculty member, Deborah Losse (now our Humanities Dean). But I had troubles. First was the new scrutiny the credit arrangements had come under, thanks to a scandal provoked by ASU Education Professor Roger Axford, who regularly took people at large to diverse points, granting them academic credit for the mere "experience," without classroom structure, etc. The cessation of this under examination led to the cessation as well of my own arrangements whereby AIFS programs were given ASU credit. I was trying to cope with this when Debby Losse announced that she would not be able to lead the French group after all because of her first pregnancy (she and her husband John now have a daughter Katie and a son Owen). She suggested I replace her with a French Teaching Assistant named Louise Couplan-Cashman as leader. But then the other members of the French Section felt slighted that they hadn't been asked. The French Coordinator, Dr. Owen Wollam (another fellow Montanan, from Valier), who had initially assented to the choice of Louise Couplan-Cashman, changed his mind under pressure from his section colleagues and rescinded his own assent to the appointment in a letter to Chair Michael Flys. In this climate of leadership uncertainty the student enrollment dropped off and the French tour was scuttled. In the end I cancelled the entire thing, scuttling the continuation of the Russian tour as well. In the years since I have continued strongly to advocate that students make every effort to study abroad. Professor Sandy Couch has also been a champion of this point of view, leading students to the Soviet Union and then to Russia under diverse auspices (CIEE, IREX, InterVarsity Christian Fellowship, and his own (1994-8) exchange agreement with Moscow State Linguistic University). Most recently I have been recommending to our ASU students that they participate in the "best in the universe" program, the University of Arizona Russia Abroad (UARA) program run by Professor Delbert Phillips which includes my 1977 joint ASU/U of A tour in its illustrious pre-history.

As far back as 1975 Dr. Couch began positions of national leadership in study abroad programs. When he was the CIEE leader from the summer of 1975 through the summer of 1976 (he took his wife Marge and children Mark and Christina (later an ASU Russian graduate) along with him), I replaced him as national Executive-Secretary of the honoraries DOBRO SLOVO (The National Slavic Studies Honorary for college and university students which Dr. Couch still administers, even in his retirement) and SLAVA (the national Slavic Studies Honorary for high-school students (the design of the logo and pin for which I designed in 1974) that is now headed by Marian Walters, an AATSEEL officer from Toledo, Ohio). Dr. Couch asked the figurehead national president of both these honoraries, Henry Ziegler of Princeton High School in New Jersey (whom I also knew from Leningrad as the leader of student tours to Russia), to appoint me to these posts and he did so. I was helped in this capacity by student aide W. Michael "Misha" Welsch who also contributed editorial work to the publication of my "first book" that year (1977): <u>Russian Symbolist Poetry: Verse Translations From the Silver Age</u> (Four Continents Bookstore, New York, 77 pages of bilingual poetry in translations by ASU Russian students Lin Abernathy, Terri Bowers, Linda Buhrig, Dee Dee Doyle, Suzanne Galvin, Mitch Green, Bob Kelley, Jim O'Haver, Anthony Parella, Barbara Rasnick, Catrien Ross, William M. Welsch himself, and U of A Graduate Teaching Assistant in Russian Dan Winters). The book's dedication said that it was "For Sanford C. Couch and Rolf Ekmanis, professors, colleagues, friends…" Dr. Couch subsequently functioned as the IREX (International Research and Exchanges Board) coordinator in Russia in the summers of 1980, 1982, and 1987. He ran cultural exchanges under the auspices of the Intervarsity Christian Fellowship in several Soviet cities from 1990-1992 and then developed his own exchange of ASU students with Moscow State Linguistics University from 1994 through 1998.

In Dr. Couch's 1975-6 absence the new Flys by-laws made the position of "Coordinator" a quasi-administrative reality (I write "quasi-" because the university does not officially recognize the position or pay for it's performance). The six section "Coordinators" were to be elected every other year and were to constitute the departmental board to assign merit increments of pay. They were responsible for submission of the section's teaching schedule and for a host of other representative matters. I was appointed to this position to start, in 1975-6, but was then elected to it in all subsequent years in which elections were held. The fact is that neither the by-law mandated coordinator election nor the by-law mandated sectional meetings ever took place after those first attempts, which served as good reasons not to try others (and after Dr. Flys' term as Chair was extended without the electoral mandate required by his own by-laws (I was a duped candidate in the aborted search to replace him), the by-laws quickly became unenforceable, though in many ways we continued to operate by our memory of them). For various complex interpersonal reasons, I was trapped forever in the Coordinatorship and on the Merit Board and as the "person of record" for Russian at ASU. And so this is the way we functioned administratively for the next three decades.

When I went up for tenure and promotion in 1978 I anticipated no trouble. But I got an unexpected call to appear before the college-level committee. With trepidation I appeared in Dean Guido Weigend's office only to find Dr. David William Foster of Spanish (whom I later nominated for the rank of Regents' Professor), our departmental representative on the college council, sitting in the lobby. He soberly told me that he had decided to absent himself from the council's hearing of "my case." When I faced the council, I could feel a certain hostility. First, they wanted to address my "rather modest" record of scholarly publication. I could only point out that I had, in fact, at that time, outpublished in their terms all the other professors of Russian Language and Literature (I exempted Dr. Ekmanis here as a Baltic specialist for obvious reasons) in the entire state combined. There was a long silence as they abandoned that direction of attack. Then a prominent scientist among them (now controversially embattled as the recently relieved head of ASU's Cancer Institute) got to the bottom line. "Dr. Croft," he said, "this council takes a dim view of faculty members who claim to have authored the works of others." I was stunned. He explained that they had looked up my article in The Journal of Biological Psychology/The Worm Runner's Digest from 1972 and discovered that I was only the translator of an article entitled "Synthetically Induced and Electrically Maintained Trance Glossolalia as a Method of Foreign Language Learning" which was written by "Academician Viacheslav Obmanov of the Moscow Psycholinguistics Institute." This was, in fact, a scientific hoax I had authored which used the precepts of molecular memory transfer to give the impression that the Soviets had found a method to transfer language fluency from one prison-camp inmate to another with injections of cerebro-spinal fluid. The hoax had received considerable attention, even in the local press after I made an ASU Honors Lecture out of it. But none of the council members were aware of this, and they had obviously "bought" the whole thing...and were angry at me for "stealing" such significant research from Academician Obmanov (whose name, based on the Russian word for "hoax" I had made up, along with other names like "Naprasov" (Futile) and even "Utkonosov" (Platypus)...which they, non-Russians, didn't pick up). As I listened to the college council lay out the case against me, I had the thought that, if I then explained the matter to them in the wrong way, the backlash of their embarrassment would bury me yet. So I tried to break it to them delicately, even pointing out to them that news-clippings about my earlier presentation of this hoax had been submitted to them apart from my vita in the file. There was another silence and more grim faces. But then a respected Professor of English (Dr. O. M. "Skip" Brack, still teaching at ASU) broke out laughing, and other nervous laughter quickly spread. I was given tenure and promotion to Associate Professor.

In the late 1970's and early 1980's the Department of Foreign Languages grappled with the transition from its operation by the crony system to a more democratic by-law system. Once, after the DFL Faculty meeting of December 3, 1981, faculty secretary Eugenia Tu recorded the following: "In the matter of the Dean's input into changes of our departmental by-laws, Prof. Croft stated his objection to a policy whereby we always act in anticipation of the way we think the Dean will think. *The matter of the accordance of our actions with the Dean's will was then discussed and it was proposed that the Dean be consulted. Acting Chair Horwath asked about the desirability of inviting the Dean to the department for a meeting...*" It really happened, although Dean Guido Weigend decided not to come discuss this matter with us. He had, however, come to see us on another matter...

In 1979, Dr. Michael Flys' term as Chair had, by the by-laws he had worked to create, expired. Initially, Dr. Flys decided not to seek an extension of his term by the by-law mechanism of departmental referendum. I was appointed by Dean Guido Weigend to the committee to find a replacement for him and attended this committee's first commissioning meetings with the Dean. But then Dr. Flys decided to stand departmental election to have his term as Chair extended for two years and I supported him in this. The by-laws specified that he needed an assenting vote of 75% of the faculty to have his term extended, but he did not get it, missing by a few votes. As a member of the search committee I then urged Dr. Flys to declare himself a candidate for the Chairmanship as if he were applying anew. There was no formal prohibition of this in the by-laws. But, dispirited by his lack of the specified electoral mandate, he told me, his Assistant Chair, that he would not serve in violation of either the letter or the spirit of his own by-laws and that he would support *my* candidacy for the chairmanship (others had nominated me to the search committee's consideration). This required that I resign from the search committee and declare my candidacy, which I did. At the next departmental meeting, the next week, I was, together with the other two internal candidates (Dr. Peter Horwath of German and Dr. Justo Alarcon of Spanish), to present my "plans" for the departmental operations to the faculty. But at this meeting, to my complete surprise, Dr. Flys, who was presiding, announced that he had agreed to accept a two-year extension of his term as Chair that was offered to him by Dean Weigend. I stood up and loudly opposed this on the grounds that we should not allow the Dean's interference into our democratic governance. Also, I felt stabbed in the back by Dr. Flys, who had had plenty of time to tell me of this decision before I withdrew from the search committee and declared my candidacy. I invited the other members of the faculty present to "stand up physically with me against this," but only two (Couch and Senner) of the thirty present did so. I then personally circulated a petition to the Dean in which the faculty asked for his appearance before us to discuss our protest of this situation. Almost all (over 90%) of the tenured faculty signed this petition and I took it to Dean Weigend's office myself. I remember in particular asking former DFL Head Douglas Sheppard to sign it. He was then resident in the office I now inhabit (currently LL-402D, the department's largest with a window on the mall...much contended for). I asked him whether he agreed with the petition and he said he did. But he said that he would not sign it UNLESS he saw that my name, the name of its author, was NOT on the petition that had, five years before, resulted in his own ouster from the departmental chairmanship. He quickly drew the former petition out of his desk drawer and consulted it. I confessed to him that I had, in agreement with it, wanted to sign it, but that my senior colleagues had not allowed me to. Nevertheless, because my name was NOT on this earlier petition that had ousted him, he did sign my petition asking for Chair selection redress from CLAS Dean Weigend.

Dean Guido Weigend came and confronted our faculty about the matter of his arbitrary extension of Chair Flys' term that spring 1979 semester. After much discussion about the process, the candidates, and such, one of our faculty members, Miriam Abdow-Morgan of French, made a formal motion to the assembly that we take the issue over the Dean's head to the university Vice President (Dr. Paige Mulholland at that time, I believe). This angered Dean Weigend (as he later told me when we were playing tennis together several years later) and he said, "I wouldn't take it kindly toward a department that would go over my head in such a way, and so I'm hoping that this motion will NOT be seconded by anyone." I, who was sitting in the front row (of LL-18 in the basement), immediately raised my hand and said, "I second the motion." So Dean Weigend said, as if he were presiding instead of testifying, "All in favor?" Even Miriam Abdow-Morgan did not vote for her own motion. Only I voted in favor. "All opposed?" Thirty people raised their hands in accordance with what they perceived to be the Dean's will. Flys continued as Chair for another two unfortunate years. I think that as he now looks back on it, he regrets it. After this I declined all nominations to be considered for leadership in my overall department.

In 1981, Dr. Dora Burton was being considered for tenure and promotion to Associate Professor. The matter of her teaching was not in

Dora Burton (with our ritual rose), Lee Croft, and Deborah Losse at Losses' Retirement Gathering for Dora in 2003. Photo by Lib Wong.

doubt. She was excellent. And she was regarded to be satisfactory also in service. But scholarly publication had, by that time, become the crucial factor in this consideration and, at that time (fall 1980) she had written three scholarly articles on early nineteenth-century poets and poetry, having one accepted (on Pushkin's "Bronze Horseman" by Slavic and East European Journal), but not yet out, and two others, including one on Boratynskii, in editorial process at good refereed journals. Chair Flys expressed to me his opinion that the three levels of personnel committees would see this as insufficient publication to merit promotion to Associate Professor and that even Dora's chances for tenure were doubtful. What was needed was some evidence that the quality of her scholarly work was especially meritorious. I remembered conversations I had had with Dr. Martha Awdziewicz, who had been his student, that the super scholar, Dr. Roman O. Jakobson (simultaneously Samuel Hazzard Cross Professor of Slavic Languages and Literatures at Harvard University and Institute

Professor of Linguistics at Massachusetts Institute of Technology...one of our field's most revered scholarly "Gods" and nearing the end of his illustrious career) was extraordinarily magnanimous when writing in support of colleagues, even colleagues he didn't know. So I proposed that we send copies of Dora's scholarly articles to him and ask that he assess them in regard to her case for tenure (the case for promotion to Associate Professor was withdrawn as was then sometimes done). At my urging, Dr. Flys sent the articles and the request to Dr. Jakobson at Harvard. The concise letter of assessment he promptly sent back got Dora tenure here, so did it impress the personnel committee people. I'm sure she has the letter framed somewhere.

When I first got to ASU in 1973 I immediately asked Drs. Couch and Ekmanis why we did not form some kind of faculty group together with colleagues in Russian/Soviet History, Political Science, or Economics. I knew there to be such people in the ASU faculty community, people like Prof. Frederick Giffin of History, Professor D. Douglas Dalgleish of Political Science (later Military Science), and Professor Marvin Jackson of Economics. I felt that such a group might not only encourage collegial scholarship but might add weight in the contention for our subject area's resources. But it soon became apparent that lack of leadership and certain personal frictions among these men discouraged any effort to form a group. But when we added Dr. Burton, and Economics added Dr. Josef Brada, and, especially, when History added Dr. Stephen Batalden, this situation changed. Dr. Batalden soon became the leader we needed to form into a unified group. His first effort to unify us was for the purpose of taking on a renowned editorial venture—the scholarly publications of Editor Charles Schlacks, Jr. then housed at the University of Pittsburgh. These publications included several well-regarded scholarly journals, including Canadian-American Slavic Studies (CASS), Russian History, Soviet Union, Southeastern Europe, East-Central Europe, and Byzantine Studies. Charles Schlacks wanted to leave the University of Pittsburgh with his journals and his publication enterprise and was seeking a new home. The presence of this enterprise at ASU would bring it not only scholarly visibility, but library acquisition of the exchange serials and the books intended for review. So, Dr. Batalden proposed this acquisition to the administration and the Schlacks' publication enterprise was moved to ASU. A seven-member board was formed to administer this enterprise. It was called the Russian and East European Publications Board (REEP) and it included: Profs. Lee Croft (me) and Rolfs Ekmanis of the Department of

Foreign Languages, Profs. Fred Giffin and Steve Batalden of the History Department, Profs. Marvin Jackson and Joe Brada of the Economics Department, and Beth Luey, a History Department expert on scholarly publications with Russian and East European training. Our task was to commence twenty-four-hour efforts in the new office on McAlister Avenue to make up, with newly appointed editorial boards, the lamentably long publication backlogs of all these journals. My Russian language students were hired on an hourly basis to aid in this, learning, as they did so, editorial make-up and production skills using the latest IBM electronic composing machine. All went well for about a year. But Charles Schlacks, Jr. was, and is, an eccentric individual and soon our problems with him became serious. I should have known problems were coming when I asked him to attend one of our Arizona State AATSEEL meetings in the ASU Memorial Union so that I could introduce him to statewide colleagues as "one of ours." He was sitting in the audience reading a newspaper as I began my introduction, but then, just as I swept my arm in his direction to introduce him, he got up and hurried out of the room, not to return. He offered no explanation for this later.

While he was with us, Charles Schlacks began a venture to publish a bilingual (Russian and English on facing pages) "History of the Russian/Soviet Law Codes" including every Russian law code since Prince Yaroslav the Wise's Great Russian Pravda of the 11th century. This was to comprise 25 volumes. Schlacks maintained that it would be a financial success since "every law library in the world would have to order one." I especially liked this project because my students were to be hired, on a royalty basis, to do the translations. So a local émigré named Yurii Blankov, alleged to be a former Soviet lawyer and chess champion, agreed to go to Europe on Schlacks' behalf to garner orders for the project from law library administrators of his acquaintance. He came back with several filled-out order forms and Schlacks was enthused enough about this "sample" of orders that he gave Blankov his credit card to return to Europe for more. But after Blankov left with the credit card, Schlacks discovered that the order forms were bogus. Blankov was a crook. He enjoyed himself on Schlacks' finances in Europe and did not soon return.

Soon after the "Blankov affair," our REEP meeting received a call from the ASU Vice President's office saying that the U.S. Secret Service had inquired with that office about an ASU official "making a deal with the Bulgarian secret police." At that time the Bulgarian government under Todor Zhivkov (1911-1998, head of state in Bulgaria from 1971 to 1989) was one of the most fanatic of the communist hard-line governments. It was alleged to have been involved in an attempted assassination of the Pope and in the killing of a Radio Free Europe/Radio Liberty correspondent (Georgi Markov) in London. Our committee was surprised, though Marvin Jackson had just related about how he had run into Charles Schlacks by coincidence in Bucharest, Romania, the past month. It turned out that Charles had signed in Sofia an agreement with Jusautor, the Bulgarian Publication and Censorship Administration, to produce for publication a Festschrift, an "honor volume" of essays by Bulgarian scholars "commemorating four hundred fifty years of autonomous Bulgarian rule." For this publication under the Arizona State University imprimature, the Bulgarian Jusautor was to pay us two thousand ($2000.00) dollars. When our board protested this agreement to him, pointing out that there was no such "four hundred fifty years of autonomous Bulgarian rule" (the questioning of Schlacks on this was comical) and that to support this fiction with an ASU publication was tantamount to ideological treason, he insisted that he "was the Director of this effort and could do what he wanted." So we took a vote on terminating his employment with us. Three of us (Ekmanis, Giffin, and I...thinking that I could "sway" Charles and not wanting to lose this valuable course of employment for my students) voted to retain him; three more (Batalden, Jackson, and Brada) voted to fire him—and Beth Luey broke the tie in favor of termination. As he prepared his offices to leave, Charles went to Hayden Library and, by a ruse, stole the list of serial exchange addresses and agreements that the library (Sandra Batalden) had vastly expanded. Steve Batalden, finding out about this, called the police to recapture the list. This took a search warrant and a break-in search of the McAlister offices to do. The office secretary there unfortunately lost her job. Schlacks went on to be housed with his publications at other universities, immediately the University of California at Irvine. From there, he sent to me alone (maybe because he knew I had voted to keep him) a copy of his "recognition medal" from the Bulgarian government for his "intercultural cooperation" and a copy of the $2000 check they sent in his name.

The most positive result of the "Schlacks' episode" was the unification of diverse subject-area faculty into a group. In 1984 Steve Batalden, together with Political Science Professor Bill Welsh (who subsequently departed ASU for an administrative post in South Carolina), Fred Giffin, and I signed a document requesting the initiation of a "Russian and East European Studies Consortium (REESC)." This request, coming at a time when the university had declared a moratorium on the creation of new "centers" (thus our title as a "consortium"), was granted (by Vice President for Academic Affairs Jack B. Kinsinger in February of 1984) without an accompanying budget or office space. But it was the seed of something very positive for us...a place to be together, an auspices for our activities. Gradually it grew to over thirty faculty members. It started to grant students a certificate of competence in Russian and East European Studies. It began a series of scholarly publications. It took over the academic exchange of faculty and graduate students with the Universitet Kiril i Metodij in Skopje, Macedonia (Yugoslavia initially), our host city of Tempe's first (and the country's first) "sister city." And, importantly, it provided a financial avenue under which we contended for external grants, including those supporting the Critical Languages Institute, especially after REESC took over the CLI in 1997-8. So, REESC became a major factor in our professional lives under the able direction of Steve Batalden. Recently, having received a major financial contribution ($1 million and the promise of more) from the family of Armenian Cultural leaders Gregor and Emma Melikian to support its global ventures, REESC has been renamed the Melikian Center for Russian, Eurasian, and East European Studies. It has a full suite of offices in the new Lattie Coor Building adjacent to the History Department.

Our section was composed in those years primarily of four tenure-track professors—Assistant Professor Dora Burton, Professor Sanford Couch (who in the mid-eighties changed his first name to "Snaford"), Associate Professor Lee B. Croft (me) and Professor Rolfs Ekmanis. These four were very different people, united only in a constant and persistent urge to mentor and potentiate our beloved students. But, different as we all were, we shared something else...we all suffered through divorces in that time. My own divorce from wife Betty was final in 1979, preceded, I think, by Dora's separation and subsequent divorce and followed by the divorces of Sandy and Rolfs. Rolfs and I have remarried (both his wife Shelly and my wife Lesley Hoyt were one-time Russian students of ours) and are now very happy, but Dora and Sandy remained, and remain, single (since I wrote this, Dora Burton has passed away...March 4, 2007). Over those years and those since, we have had several highlights as faculty members. For me it was winning the Dean's Quality Teaching Award (Guido Weigend was the Dean...1978), Honorary Membership in the Golden Key Honorary, and the Burlington Northern Foundation Distinguished Teaching Award (1985), the Dr. Joe Malik, Jr. Arizona Slavic Studies Award in

1993, and the Russian Academy of Natural Sciences "10 Years of RAEN" V. I. Vernadsky silver medal in 2005. Dr. Couch has been selected USSR Resident Director for both CIEE and IREX, succeeded Dr. Joe Malik, Jr. as National Executive-Secretary of AATSEEL (1986-9) and was awarded the Joe Malik, Jr. Arizona Slavic Studies Award in 1991. And Dr. Ekmanis was appointed senior Baltic Analyst in Munich for the Board of International Broadcasting's Radio Free Europe from which he has been instrumental in cementing the independence of the Baltic Republics (even set up an RFE news bureau in Riga in Summer 1989, earning a US congressional commendation). Dr. Burton was a winner of the CLAS Dean's Quality of Instruction Award in 1991. I termed her a "human treasure, the kind of person ASU should provide for contact to its students" in a newspaper article about her. In addition to these, Dr. Danko Šipka, a more recent senior appointment to our faculty (2005), has also won the CLAS Dean's Quality Teaching Award (2006) and won a "special recognition" in the ASU Parents' Association's 2007 "Professor of the Year" competition.

In 1984 I came upon an article in <u>Coop's Satellite Digest</u> describing the fabrication of the equipment necessary to track, intercept, and decode the Soviet domestic television signals from the polar-orbiting Molnija satellites. I realized that I could have the first academic program in the country to utilize Soviet Russian television broadcasts in classroom instruction. By that time I should have known better. Chairman Horwath was supportive as long as no funds would be necessary, the Dean's office sent me around on a "garnering of support" mission to fifteen other Chairs and Directors (not all of whom could see any worth in the project...one Associate Dean was quick to inform me proudly that she "never really watched any television"). At the university television station the head broadcast engineer put me through a four-month stall. By spring of 1985 when I revealed the idea to our state AATSEEL, I had already seen the effort start elsewhere (at Creighton and at Columbia), but I decided to pursue extra-institutional sources of support...the National Security Agency's Instructional Support Program. I had been the NSA's "contact person" for a developing Coop Program by that time and had, after all, sent them many a Russian competent intelligence analyst. The project was grand...a tracking satellite dish on the Language and Literature Building's roof, construction of adult-peep-show-like viewing booths with student-controlled repeat functions adjacent to the language laboratory, and etc.

46

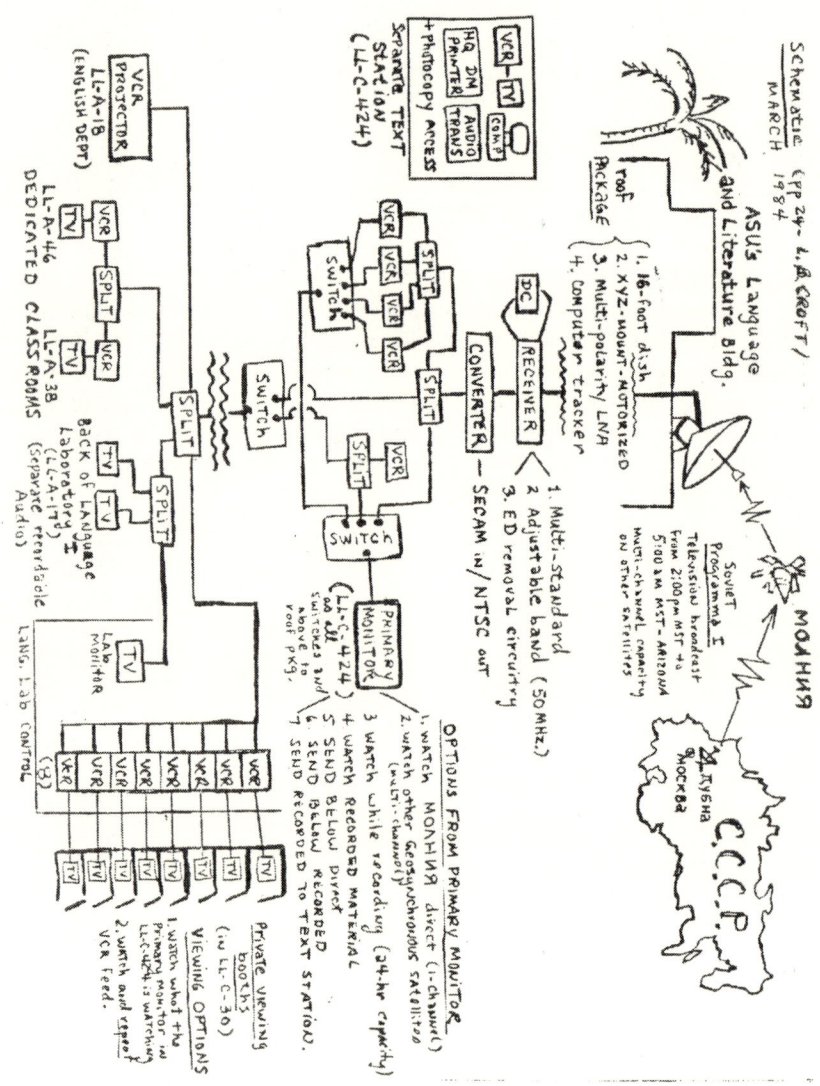

But I needed university design review board clearance, had to get competitive bids on the gear in hand, etc., etc…it took me another year. Meanwhile my U. of A. colleagues in Tucson (Dr. Adele Barker aided by her Dean's travel support and advised by an enthusiastic technician from their television station and listening to the flamboyant Ken Schaeffer, inventor of the cordless microphone and later mastermind of the post-Soviet BELKA telecommunications consortium in Russia, who aided in the more publicized Columbia University set-up) picked up on my idea and beat me to it. The grant proposal came through…over $130,000 earmarked for initial award…but disbursement was delayed by Gramm-Rudman-Hollings mandated stoppages of expenditures. Eventually the funding would have come, but in the meanwhile the Soviets removed their domestic broadcasting from the Molnija satellites. This happened very soon after the visit to ASU of a later-acknowledged Soviet KGB spy, Oleg Tumanov, who was more than casually curious about my plan, even taking a copy of my plan diagram off my office's exterior door (on this, see the May 2004 Barrett Honors College honors thesis by Kerry Pace (now Meyer) entitled "Russian Intelligence Activity in the Pre-perestroika Era: A Case Study" which I supervised). But even the Soviet transfer of signal to where I could not pick it up did not end what I now term "the television farce." I had expressed an interest to Fr. Lee Lubbers at Creighton in his nascent SCOLA network and, sometime in 1987 as I recall, he sent me a bill for ASU's charter subscription to it. I thought the SCOLA network would become an important university resource, and tried to get my university to pay the bill (which was a ridiculous fraction of what we later finally started paying them) and, moreover, to take an offered share of SCOLA equity. But no ASU administrators, from the Walter Cronkite School of Broadcast Journalism (very surprisingly…but I have the letter from Director Eldean Bennett to this effect), to the KAET television station (their satellite engineer stalled inexplicably to give technical advice and the Director gave no answer at all), to the University International Programs Office, wanted to add such an amount (I now recall it to have been in the hundreds of dollars) to their program's budget. Taking the matter up with then Vice President for Academic Affairs Jack B. Kinsinger elicited another "Good-idea/Keep-on-thinking" response. I finally quit trying. We do now, thanks to more recent (and costly) efforts by Associate Dean of Technology for the College of Liberal Arts and Sciences Dan Brink (subsequently and very unfortunately deceased), get SCOLA news broadcasts. But Dean Brink's path to get it here was not easy either (it was terminated once despite faculty petition to keep it, and now resources can't be found to make it accessible via the campus television network to most of the sites where it is desired...you can see what it has now become at www.scola.org). We're not liable soon to utilize translated teletexts of current foreign language news broadcasts in classroom efforts which labor under cut-rate blackboard chalk, paper allowances, photocopy moratoria, and the like. But, of course, our main resource is human...our faculty which did its best to serve human educational needs without currently available technology or administrative support. And a diverse bunch of humans we were, though all were constantly devoted to student welfare, each in his or her own way.

As for academic specialties in all those years (the twenty-seven years, 1976-2003—Burton, Couch, Croft and Ekmanis as the only tenured faculty) we were well balanced. Dr. Couch was clearly our pedagogy expert, focusing his expertise on the elementary levels of language teaching. He did, however, regularly teach RUS-424 Tolstoy, the subject of his Master's Thesis. I was the linguist. I added RUS-440 "History of the Russian Language" to the curriculum in my first years here and have, in recent years, taught the RUS-417, 8 "Applied Russian Phonetics." I also initiated and first taught the RUS-420 "Russian Poetry" course, even publishing an anthology out of its first offering. But I did, in more recent years surrender it to Dr. Burton, whose knowledge of Russian poetry was splendid. She was our "native speaker" and our literary classicist, teaching the nineteenth century period of the survey and the poetry, as well as RUS-425 Chekhov, and RUS-430 "The Short Story" which she initiated. Dr. Ekmanis was our Soviet period specialist, teaching the modern period of the survey and RUS-426 "Soviet Dissident Literature" and attracting considerable attention for his offering of RUS-494 (an omnibus listing for special topics) "Non-Russian Soviet Literatures." The 400-level courses (other than the 411-2 language series) are offered once each three years in rotation. They are all we can maintain in catalogue residence, given the size of our faculty and the university policy requiring catalogue-entry courses to be offered that often. And, in addition, we all taught the language: in recent years Burton (201-2, 211-2, 311-2, 411-2, and an occasional beginning section); Couch (101-2, 201-2, 303-4, 411-2); Croft (101-2, 201-2, 211-2, formerly 311-2, and 494 omnibus translation); and Ekmanis (101-2, 201-2, formerly 411-2).

In the 1980's our sectional enrollment essentially *tripled* while the general university population increased by one-and-a-half times (we grew at twice the university's already amazing rate). In that time our resources declined: travel money diminished, student aide money vanished, capital expenditure money evaporated...and increases of pay disappeared. We faced three budget cuts and two budget revertments. When I would apply for new faculty positions to meet the increased enrollment, I would instead

Dr. Nick Vontsolos, Don Livingston, and Tatiana Kazanina, a Russian guest teacher at Phoenix Central High. Dirk Willeford, back to camera, is in the background with ? Lee and Lesley Hoyt Croft's Phoenix home on McNeil with their 1936 Ford Model 68 Deluxe Phaeton car. Photo by Lesley Hoyt Croft, ca 1990.

get .25 Faculty Associate positions in exchange for faculty service (Dr. Couch's National AATSEEL Directorship got us one, his service on the grant-funded university "Writing Across the Curriculum" Committee got us another, etc.) until I had amassed seven of them (seven "quarters" at $2,000 of pay per 4 sem. hr. course). These positions were filled by very able "Faculty Associates." They mostly taught our high-energy, grading-intensive Russian language classes, 101 through 202. Here I can mention our own former students Dirk Willeford, Mark Preslar, and Andrew Reese, as well as my replacement during my 1979-80 sabbatical leave to Wichita, Kansas, Dr. Carl Goldberg (Carl later became the editor of the well-regarded local émigré newspaper, Аризонские новости). Drs. Nick Vontsolos and Don E. Livingston were also constantly outstanding. Summer teaching also was accomplished, especially after a change of the system of allocating pay to summer teachers in 1995-6, by Faculty Associates. Summer Faculty Associates who taught Russian at ASU include Justin Capin of Phoenix College, Joyce Story of Glendale

Community College, and, more than the others, Dirk Willeford, who also taught at Mesa Community College.

In the early days of my professorship here I was, by dint of my age and my simple concern, privvy to aspects of my students' lives to which many of my colleagues were oblivious. One of the most telling of these aspects was student use of psychoactive drugs (marijuana, cocaine, the opiates, the psychedelics, etc.), which had so gained in proportion in the sixties and seventies in our country. One day in 1976 or 1977 I realized that this problem (which had never been a part of my own too-busy-for-it life) was eliminating a full one-third of my talented students from eligibility for high-responsibility careers. That is, on NSA applications (as just one example) they were asked about their use of these substances, and their responses were checked by polygraph and by thorough personal investigation. So I spent my sabbatical year of 1979-80 investigating the "Drug Phenomenon" in this country. What I learned, principally about the biomedical effects of these substances and about all the dimensions of toxicomania in our society, scared me, and I returned to ASU determined to educate away the demand for drugs if I could. I asked Associate Dean of Liberal Arts for Instruction Paul Hubbard to let me teach a course called "Marijuana and Man." He formed an ad hoc committee of "experts" to interview me to see whether I knew the subject. I passed and was given upper-division listings for the course in both General Liberal Arts (LIA-494) and in Health Science (HES-494). Trying to be brief, I can simply say that this course, taught without any help and as a fifth or sixth course to 60-90 students at a time from 1981 to 1983, was the beginning of an ancillary career for me. Publicity was extreme, both local and national. I became known as "Dr. Anti-pot," and my telephone began to ring. The national Institute for Drug Abuse sent me on a lecture tour all over the country. My wife, Dr. Lesley Hoyt Croft (whom I married in 1981), and I started Croft Consultants, a Drug Education and Counseling company. We began the idea of a "Drug Offenders' Diversion School" in the jurisdiction of the Maricopa County Superior Court and its Justices-of-the-Peace. Our method was to drug test these first-offenders every other week of 16 weeks of class meetings to enforce substance abstinance (we never had a repeat offender). To that end we purchased and utilized the state's first EMIT immunoassay kit from the Syva Corporation, which then paid for us to make presentations around the country on "how to do it." After that, we won a VA contract to do "readjustment counseling" of Vietnam-era Vets, and, after that, a major contract with a consortium of Sheet-metal Workers'

Unions to provide substance and alcohol abuse counseling. All this anti-drug activity had begun when I decided to get ASU on the record against drug use...not at all the typical response of U.S. academia to the drug problem at the time, I can assure you. But ASU couldn't find a way to pay a Russian Professor to begin a Substance Abuse component...that was left to the Health Science Department, which promised to engage a qualified person to do it, but never really did. But by 1985, Croft Consultants was clearly doing well. Our drug testing by urinalysis in the diversion school had "grandfathered" us into this booming technology and our consulting services in industrial drug testing were in steady demand both nationally and locally. Now my wife is the President and Chief Executive Officer (I am listed as Vice President) of a successful national company, a pioneer (the first *Yellow Pages* listing for "Drug Testing" was made for us) in the field of workplace drug testing.

I relate all the above in order to explain the difficulty of my promotion case of 1987-8. The drug education, counseling, and testing work had, in the course of six years, added quite a sizeable number of citations to my curriculum vitae...lectures, articles, booklets, program designs, all kinds of consultantships, contracts, broadcasts on radio and television, a video program script and narration, and other such measures of professional achievement and stature. Since it had all started in association with ASU and since I always used my ASU affiliation to lend credibility (?) to all these activities, I did not imagine that I should not include them into my case for promotion to Full Professor in 1987-8. Chairman Peter Horwath took a daunting posture when I asked him about my promotion chances and suggested I compile it all up and show it to Dr. Ingeborg Carlson of German who had just completed a term of service on the college council. I showed the resultant 27-page vita to both Dr. Carlson and to closer-colleague and former Assistant Dean of the CLAS, Dr. Fred Giffin. They both agreed that I should proceed. Dr. Carlson gave me a hand-written note that the preparation "couldn't be better." So I embarked upon the process of promotion...but was denied. The first rejection came from my departmental colleagues. Strangely, the five senior voting members of our personnel committee who issued the non-supportive verdict even included Dr. Couch and the earlier consulted Dr. Carlson (?). But, this same committee had, for unfathomable reasons, also split on three other of the five promotion candidates that year...and it had approved the nomination for "Regents' Professor" rank of a new departmental faculty member that no one even knew. I was sure that Chair Horwath would, in his politic way, focus on my being a "wonderful teacher" (the kiss of death), but I had faith in the consideration of the higher college-level committee. After all, I could see why my Foreign Languages' colleagues had trouble understanding how all my drug education activities should count toward my being made a Professor of Russian (even though it made sense to me). Many thought that I was just moralizing or expiating my own problems (not true). The college and the university, however, were the units upon which my drug education activities had made a direct positive impact. But unfortunately the college council merely affirmed the departmental decision and asked me (and three of the others too, though not the same three others as above) if I wouldn't withdraw the application before it went to the university level. Two of the others (Debby Losse of French (who was promoted later and is now Dean of Humanities) and Laurel Rodd of Japanese (who then left here to find advancement in Colorado)) quit at this stage, but I requested an interview with Dean Samuel Kirkpatrick and Associate Dean (later Dean) Gary Krahenbuhl (who had been in and even chaired the Health Science Department during the time I contributed my efforts to it). I directly asked Dean Kirkpatrick to intercede in my behalf with a letter to the university committee about the wider significance of my professional activities (now, under ASU President Michael Crow, we would term this my activities' "transdisciplinary" significance). But Dean Kirkpatrick refused and Associate Dean Krahenbuhl would not stand up for me either, although he did admit when pressed that I had "helped them out" in Health Science. These deans told me in essence that, given my teaching and service record, if I had only two one-inch-thick books instead of all the other listed achievements of the past fourteen years I would be promoted…that this was the way of the university's future. They offered me a written "contract" to that effect, but I refused this idea. Dean Kirkpatrick added the patronizing comment that he was sure I "was smart enough" to be eventually promoted to Full Professor. "Избави Бог и нас от этаких судей." My reaction after getting the final letter from Acting Vice President for Academic Affairs and Provost C. Roland Haden ("I have decided that you shall not be promoted to Full Professor at this time") was to remove almost all vestiges of my drug education activities from my vita and to refocus on Russian-related publication projects, and to await a brighter regime.

So, under ever increased expectation of published research, we all continued three and four-course loads, and employed in addition highly qualified Faculty Associates at slaves' wages to help us out. By 1989, thanks to an "offer from without" (Chair Margaret B. Gibson of the University of Arizona's Department of Russian and Slavic), I managed to get Don Livingston elevated from Faculty Associate to salaried "Visiting Lecturer" ($26,000 for a three-course load instead of $16,000 for a four-course load). Livingston and the other academic-year Faculty Associates (Dr. Nick Vontsolos and Andrew Reese) were very fine teachers...low attrition rate, high student evaluations, quality students retained, etc. Our enrollment had topped 400 students by fall 1990. This was, by statistics published by the Modern Language Association (MLA), ONE FULL PERCENT of all the students taking Russian in the nation's colleges and universities. We were one of the nation's largest Russian BA programs, graduating over twenty student majors a year. Still we were not allowed to hire additional full-time faculty. But we were dreaming once again of participating in the creation of an interdisciplinary M.A. program in collaboration with the Russian and East European Studies Consortium (REESC) under Dr. Stephen Batalden's leadership. We began a self-study so that we could "apply (to the Arizona Board of Regents) for permission to apply" for such an M.A. program. But at this juncture (1991) the increased enrollment/decreased resource nexus reached critical mass—the university was forced to cancel all positions funded by "salary savings," i.e. the positions of Livingston, Vontsolos, and Reese, representing five of our sixteen course listings and a large share of our student enrollment. Especially in the case of Don Livingston, a person I had twice nominated for the outstanding teacher award, I tried to find some kind of exemption from the budget-revertment, going to see all relevant deans and even the Provost, at that time Dr. Jack B. Kinsinger (and then subsequently Elmer Gooding, Interim Provost), who told me in the course of refusing my request that I should publicize Don's plight and "bleed in public" so that the Arizona public would become aware of its university's financial quandary. Indeed I did this too, availing myself of the help of former students then in the field of journalism. But it was all to no avail. Lecturer Livingston and all our Faculty Associates were terminated. The only benefit to me was that I was then granted a transfer into my current office (now LL-402D in the G. Homer Durham Languages and Literatures Building)...previously that of Dr. Rolfs Ekmanis (he won it in 1979 coin flip I enforced over Dr. Carmello Virgillo of Romance Languages) but who had been on leave from ASU since 1986 (the longest leave ever granted an ASU professor—even longer than that granted to Dr. Lew Tambs of History who had been on President Ronald Reagan's National Security

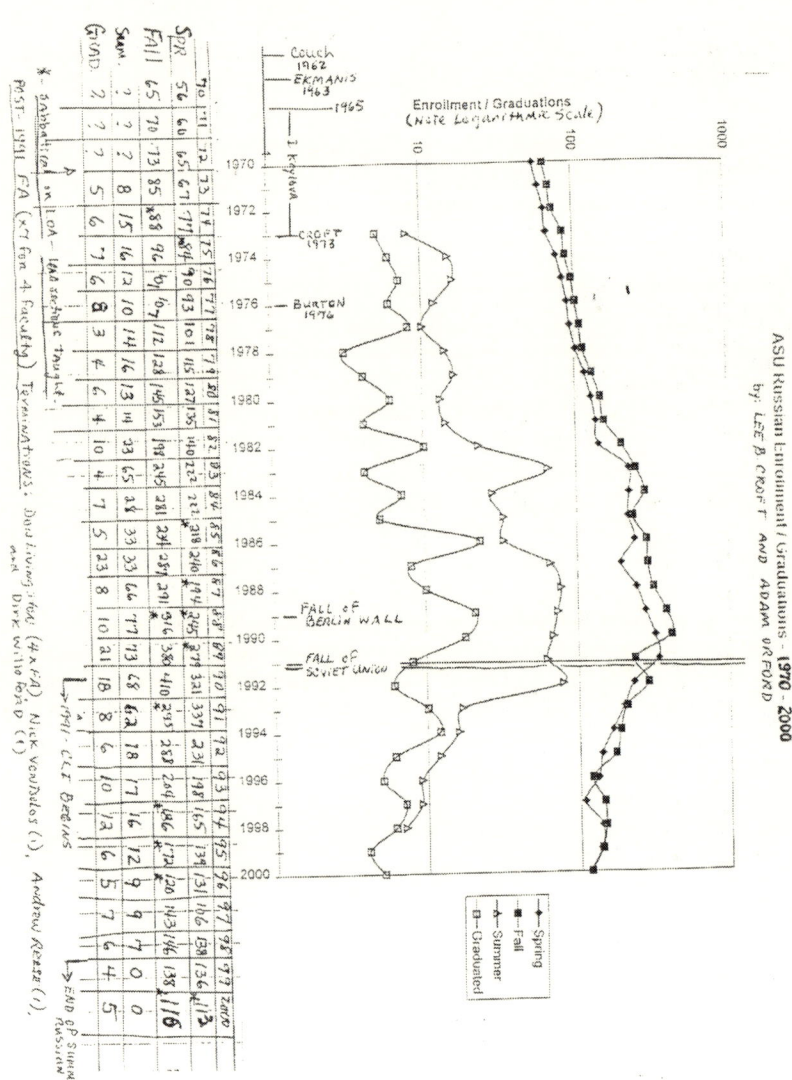

Council and had served as Ambassador to Columbia and to Costa Rica) allowing it to be inhabited by SIX Faculty Associates (all of whom were terminated). So, from my previous closet of an office (LL-424) I "moved up" when all these others had to "move out."

The next year circumstances drove me to write the following letter on ASU Department of Foreign Languages' stationery:

"October 22, 1992

To: Lattie Coor, President of ASU; Lonnie Ostrom, Director of Development at the ASU Foundation; Charles S. Harris, ASU Director of Athletics; and Frank J. Sackton, Professor of Public Affairs

Please add this to the number of expressions of dissatisfaction regarding the ASU Foundation's payment of $34,500 to effect the Harris' entry into the Phoenix Country Club. The proferred excuses for this that I have seen in the press and elsewhere are woefully lame. Try to think of it as I do...all during early 1991 I tried every way I knew how to protect the "salary-savings-funded" job of our Visiting Lecturer (earlier Faculty Associate) Don Livingston...a young man whom I had twice nominated for outstanding teaching honors for his sterling student-oriented work in our Russian Language Section. I pleaded for some extraordinary release from the budget stricture...letters to chair, dean, vice-president, interviews with local and state newspapers, appeared on two television channels...but all to no avail. Eventually I had to tell him: "No, Don...ASU can not afford your $26,000 salary. You'll have to go." And now, as our enrollment has dropped from 380 to 220, I can read where our president calls up the director of the ASU Foundation to find the resources to get our athletic director and his wife into the Phoenix Country Club. This, in my opinion, was a grievous error in judgment...demoralizing in its impact throughout the university community. Frankly, it "sticks in my craw" like few other of the administrative gaffs I've encountered here.

As an ASU alum, faculty member, and donor, I was proud of the growth and the administration of the ASU Foundation. I administer two small sub-accounts in it myself. Before this incident I was planning to work to increase these accounts. Now I'm thinking of withdrawing every dime. Surely we can do better than this in these tough times.

Sincerely,

Lee B. Croft, Ph.D., Associate Professor and Coordinator, Slavic Langs., DFL

xc: Pier R. Baldini, Chair DFL, Gary Krahenbuhl, Dean, CLAS, Milton Glick, ASU Provost" (1992-).

President Coor responded to this complaint forthrightly in a letter to me, taking responsibility for his actions in the interests of increasing possible donations to the university as a result of increased personal contact between Charles Harris and his wife and the wealthy members of the Phoenix Country Club. He did not address other of the putative reasons (wanting to get the African-American Harris's into the previously all-white PCC because the university administration favored a woman member of its board (Claire Sargent), who was running as a democrat to unseat republican Senator John McCain). The irony is that McCain, as universally expected, prevailed in the senatorial election, and, in the next year (1993) President Coor, ostensibly based on academic athletic department monitor Frank Sackton's advice, fired Charles Harris as university athletic director and Harris moved on to somewhere else, his membership in the Phoenix Country Club unused. I have wondered, however, about what role the matter of this "complaint" of mine to ASU President Coor in 1992 had with regard to my subsequent case for redress of my promotion case in 1993-4.

The budget revertment of 1991 was not, of course, the only problem to affect our enrollment in those years (say, 1989-1993). The dissolution of the Soviet Union in December of 1991 was clearly very impactful also as the motivations of students to take Russian changed from "know thy enemy" to business reasons (so, therefore, the reasoning changed to "If they want to do business with us, let'em learn English"). But there were other problems as well. Several positions in the greater Slavic Studies area at ASU were vacated for different reasons: Guido Weigend of Geography and Marvin Jackson of Economics retired, Bill Weidemeier of History was promoted to administration in the Honors College, Bill Welsh of Political Science moved to South Carolina and Douglas Dalgleish sued his way into promotion to full professor, but changed his department to Military Science. Joe Brada was given a teaching load reduction to help retain him under an "offer from without" response. Rolfs Ekmanis was absent in those years too on prolonged leave to advise the U.S. Congress' Bureau of International Broadcasting's Radio Free Europe/Radio Liberty surrogate broadcasting effort. With all these key area faculty members unreplaced, the effort to create an interdisciplinary M.A. program was indefinitely postponed (it has not been revived to date). I continued, and continue today, to send our talented Russian language students for graduate study to the University of Arizona's program in Tucson where I once studied. By now two generations of them have prospered thereby (I recall Misha Welsch, Mark Preslar, Dirk Willeford, Paul Kachur, Elisabeth Elliott, Aggie Bednarz Czerski, and others).

As I type this "History of ASU's Russian Section," I do NOT want the reader to conclude that the "adversarial relationship" I depict between the section's Russian program and the administration of the university means that I am not proud of ASU. I am proud of ASU, proud to be an alumnus of it and a faculty member in it. My daughter Cathy was an ASU student, son Bill an ASU Graduate, and son Hayden a current ASU freshman. It's just that the values I see to be positive at ASU are not always the values finding elevation in its administration. After I won the Burlington Northern Faculty Achievement in Teaching Award for 1985 (one of the first three), an article entitled "Award Winning Professor of Russian Nearly Went Underemployed" appeared in the ASU INSIGHT publication (Vol. 6, No. 3 from July 15, 1985). In this interview article I stated that "by and large, we teach as we were taught, and I was taught right here at ASU by some very noteworthy professors…such as Charles Wexler of Mathematics (after whom the Math wing of the Physical Sciences Center is now named), George Peek of Political Science (later CLAS Dean), William Wooten and Wallace Adams of History (after whom an award in the History Department is now endowed), Morris Starsky of Philosophy (whose termination for his radical views caused a two-decade censure by the AAUP), David Rasmussen of Zoology, George Herman of English, and Claude Olney of Business Law (later entrepreneur in educational motivation video tapes, including "Where there's a will, there's an 'A'" which earned him a fortune and in which he mentions me as the successful professor of his son James)….But of course I was mostly inspired by my current colleagues, Professor Sanford Couch, the designer of our Russian language program, and Professor Rolfs Ekmanis, our superb scholar of Baltic Literature…*Like others who were taught here and who then went elsewhere, I know that, as far as teaching is concerned, ASU is a world-class institution* (italics added)." Whenever I hired a Faculty Associate, and I hired over twenty of them over the years, not only in Russian, but in Serbo-Croatian, Macedonian, and Tatar, I would find a time to stress to them (note the 3X) "Teaching is first, teaching is first, teaching is first." Even our Full Professor Danko Šipka, a most prolific published scholar and grantsperson extraordinaire and a wonderful administrator too who was "regularized" to us in 2005, will remember being told this. In 1991, Assistant Vice President for Academic Personnel Alleen Pace Nilsen (wife of Linguist Don L. F. Nilsen of the English Department whom I helped bring here in 1976) asked for my written input as a "faculty member identified as a distinguished teacher" into an orientation booklet to be given to all incoming ASU faculty. On July 5, 1991, I wrote:

"WHY AM I HERE? When asked to prepare suggestions for new faculty on the theme: 'What do you know now that you wish you had known your first year,' I couldn't help thinking: 'I wish I had known how little being an 'outstanding teacher' would serve to advance me professionally here at ASU.' This, of course, is a sad thought, bearing upon the character of ASU, which in 26 years I've come to view as I would an eccentric family member...sometimes petty and irritating, but nevertheless unavoidably mine. I'm a part of it and it's a part of me, inextricably and forever. All I can do is to 'make the best of it' by 'making the best of me.' I do that by reflecting on WHY I'M HERE. I'm here to make myself immortal by investing the largest possible bits of myself into the lives of my students, who will then carry these bits into succeeding generations of our species. I'm here to attain heavenly reward by enriching the lives of others. I'm here to help others get what I already have and more. Now it would be nice if I could also get financial wealth and professional status along the way, BUT these are derivative benefits only indirectly related to the central rationale of our lives here in academia. Remember that. Try to stay a person-to-person, classroom teacher FIRST...it'll pay off in the long run (you might read Tolstoy's great short story 'God Sees the Truth, but Waits'). If it's money or status you're primarily after (as opposed to 'mere' immortality), you really ought to be doing something else anyway.

RESEARCH? In order to impart knowledge and wisdom to others, you simply have to have some yourself. And since we function at the upper edges of the educational process, we simply must involve ourselves in research. Our research involvement...pushing the frontiers of knowledge forward...is what distinguishes us as university professors from the larger numbers of six-seven-and-eight-classes-a-day teachers laboring mightily below us in support. To me, research is the indulgence of interest and curiosity...using my accumulated skill to find out this or that which interests me. Of course my interests are diverse, hardly even confined to the conventional bounds of my 'specialty.' I do not apologize for this, since my central mission is to SHARE my knowledge with others. And knowledge is its own reward. Ideally, I want to know, and want my students to know, everything. I don't countenance the question: 'Why do I have to know this?' Such a question perturbs me. We want to know everything...EVERYTHING...and that takes research.

CLASSROOM MANAGEMENT? If I've had success in classroom management, it's because of these two methods: I WORK them harder than they thought they could work, wasting not a second; and I PRAISE them lavishly for every personal or collective victory gained. The work front has two sides, of course. The harder you make them work, the harder you have to work yourself. I always grade all written work myself and return it to the students in the next class hour...no matter the class size or nature. This hasn't been easy through daily language classes with daily written homework, but it's become my hallmark. And, they must work as hard in the classroom as they are required to work outside of it. The fifty-minute hour must be highly structured to keep them busy at diverse learning tasks. If they're busy enough at a vital task, management is no problem. If you are more patient with that 'trouble-maker' than the rest of the class would be in your place, then you'll find that the rest of the class will exert the requisite peer-pressure to deal with the problem. All you have to do is to provide the necessary sense of camaraderie in the class environment...the sense of mutual involvement in something important. See yourself as a cheer-leader for their efforts, a catalyst to their teaching themselves. And the matter of constant praise is essential. I try to wear out the Russian word 'хорошо' ("Good/well") on their ears...even if I can't hear their response. For homework I write "Good," "Very Good," and "Superb." On daily declensions I jot personal encouragements. In my beginning class I make a 'big deal' of awarding the very top student a medal (a Russian значок), thus trying to involve them in celebrating each other's achievements. I'm always relating to them another 'success story' of a 'former student.' Hard work and lavish praise...those are the keys. Disparagement and negative criticism should have no place in academia...no place at all.

Respectfully Submitted...Lee B. Croft, Assoc. Prof. of Russian."

All through the 1990's Dr. Couch, Dr. Burton, and I labored under overloads to hold up the Bachelor's degree in Russian. Dr. Ekmanis returned to us from his RFE/RL leave-of-absence in Munich and resumed his overloads as well after 1994. In 1996 the BA in Ed in Russian was cancelled, however, and the training of high school teachers ceased in 1998. I had personally supervised the certification of almost all the high school teachers in Maricopa County (17 of the total 22), but, in the post-Soviet era of 'enrollment challenge' (our own program here lost an average of fifty students per semester for three years, then began to stabilize just above the level it was (ca. 80 students) when I came here in 1973) the high-school programs were reduced from 11 to 2 (Dr. Nick Vontsolos' program at Phoenix Central, originally funded by federal "magnet school" block grants prepared pursuant to a seminar we ran at ASU for high-school administrators, and Pat Barrett's program at Mesa Westwood) and finally to just one (Pat Barrett's after Nick Vontsolos retired in 2000). The flow of students from the diminishing high-school programs almost stopped. Our program was enduring a severe trial, a time of crisis.

In 1992 my book Жабы или объяснение токсикомании в американском обществе was published by Sintaksis Publishers in Moscow with the help of Prof. Delbert Phillips. I had written this book, a satire on the american use of drugs, while in Wichita, Kansas, on sabbatical leave in the 1979-80 year. I wrote it in Wichita State University's Ablah Library while waiting for my wife-to-be, family sociologist Dr. Lesley Hoyt Croft, to teach an evening class in the Sociology Department there (I was working days as a photocopier salesman after my application for a National Science Foundation grant to research linguistic iconicity was belatedly denied). I had been unable to find a publisher for this strange and unnerving work, which dealt with questions of drug-use motivation, media hypnosis, and the Faust myth. But Delbert Phillips found a translator (unnamed and unknown to me still) and a publisher for it, in Russian, in Moscow. The book sold well, I was told, in Moscow at a time when many people were selling their books in order to eat. The Russians liked the depiction of how a population could even be propagandized through the media hypnosis to practice the licking of bufo toads for hallucinogenic purposes…a process for which I coined the term "bufoglossation." The publisher reported that it was unable, given the crazy fluctuations in the exchange rate between the dollar and the ruble at the time, to pay me for the copies sold. They proposed to print ENGLISH copies of the book (titled TOADIES, the Explanation of Toxicomania in American Society), for which they disavowed copyright claim, and send them to me in a proportion (I never learned the exact proportion) to the number of Russian copies they sold. In time I received precisely 169 copies of the English version, replete with myriad typos on every page. This resulted in my being able to show my department TWO books, one published in Moscow in Russian, in addition to my other publications from 1988 on. The book's reviews were mostly positive, both from Americans and from Russians. In the December 1993 issue of Аризонские новости reviewer Irina Danielova wrote (in Russian, translation here is mine): "Reading this book you involuntarily marvel: actually the absence of a positive hero might frighten readers away from it, but the most important thing is to understand the author's conception, and then it becomes accessible. The author places a very important task before us, forcing us to ponder what could lead us to a fascination with drugs. The author gives us warning, even though we should make conclusions for ourselves. The book is written in what is, perhaps, a strange allegorical form, calling to mind Erasmus of Rotterdam's 'Praise of Folly,'... I recommend that you obtain and read this book, immerse yourself into the thought of what is written, and make the conclusions for yourself." The prominent M.I.T. Slavic Linguist, Catherine V. Chvany, assessed the work as follows: "I couldn't put it down and eagerly re-read it in Russian translation. It is a Swiftean satire, open to multiple interpretations, depending on the values one assigns to its symbolic figures. One immediately understands its relevance to ugly current fads—not only drugs but, say, the role of handguns in gang members' rites of passage, and to ugly earlier fads, such as snuff in the 18th century or chewing tobacco and ubiquitous spittoons in late 19th century America. Croft not only makes the toad cult a plausible horror, he makes one see more clearly just why Gogol associated snuff with the Devil...The book is gripping, terrible, witty, moving, it resonates with items in the English and Russian literary canons—and it would make a fine movie. Dr. Croft is to be congratulated. It is a major achievement backed by a profound understanding of several humanistic traditions, including our own popular culture." The literary "super-agent," Scott Meredith, in the course of rejecting it as a client work, wrote: "Disturbing material—a little on the bizarre side too—and it attempts satire through its allegorical framework to say nothing of its social commentary; it's a most unsettling little book indeed." Gabriel G. Nahas, M.D., pioneering researcher and writer on marijuana and a Professor at the Columbia University College of Physicians and Surgeons (and who is a backwardly named character (i.e. Dr. Sahan) in the book itself), wrote that TOADIES "...is a timely book which has the right approach in attempting to get a good laugh out of this tragi-comedy we are all witnessing today." Robert L. DuPont, M.D., the founding head of the National Institute for Drug Abuse (NIDA) wrote: "I've just read...TOADIES. What a delight! I think it's great. I wonder what high-school and college students think of it...Also I wonder about the characterizations of ***, ***, and ***. They seem almost too real-to-life. Is there not a risk of libel?" I did not fear libel suit. On the back of the title page I wrote (in the English version this text is badly mangled by typos): "Although this is a work of fiction, similarities to actual characters and past events *are strictly intentional.* The author is protected by the truth."

Despite the publication in both English and in Russian of what I thought was a significant book, a book touching not only my drug education efforts, but also my accrued understanding of (as Catherine Chvany wrote) "the English and Russian literary canons," my case for promotion to Full Professor, as presented in 1993, was rejected. My Chair at the time, Pier Baldini, was supportive of my case. But the departmental personnel committee issued a non-supportive verdict based, as Baldini told me, on their assessment (reinforced by half the four exterior evaluators they had chosen from my list (half were apparently supportive)) that I still had an insufficient record of research published in the Russian area. This rejection caused me to write the following letter:

"October 21, 1993

To: DFL Chair Pier Baldini and DFL Personnel Committee Professors John Alexander, Mark Curran, David Foster, Deborah Losse and Teresa Valdivieso.

Re: Recent DFL Personnel Committee decision on the promotion of Lee Croft

Colleagues,

Chairman Baldini has informed me of your collective (though split) decision to recommend that I not be promoted to full professor and to the accompanying senior status in our profession. Although some of you may have made this decision based on your perception of particular aspects of my candidacy, the consequences to me represent a lack of sanction of the totality of my professional activities here…activities which include most forceful work to get most of you teaching awards, raises in pay, and even promotion. This is why your decision seems so picomental to me. I would clearly have done better by any of you. Is your place at the top so inaccessible by other paths? Are my professional achievements really so much less than your own (see attached)?

I have only begun to fight.

In disgust,

Lee Croft

xc: ASU President Lattie Coor, Provost Milton Glick, CLAS Dean Gary Krahenbuhl"

The attachment included a statistical break-down of the "NUMBER OF CITATIONS, and specifically the number of citations in the category of "PUBLICATIONS/CREATIVE WORKS" that were listed in the previous five years' <u>ASU ANNUAL REPORT OF THE FACULTY</u>, that is, the number of scholarly publications listed for Full Professors Alexander (1), Curran (9), Foster (48), Losse (9), Valdivieso (15), and me (Croft...19). In addition I provided the data on grant activity for the past two years published in the <u>ASU REPORT OF SPONSORED PROJECTS</u> listing me among the four top "grantspeople" in the department. AND, from the 1991 "DFL Market Inequity Adjustment Committee" (which I chaired) I cited data stating that in terms of considered merit-pay allocations I was ranked "5th of our 44 DFL faculty." Finally I asked: "According to these institutional data, does not Croft belong among these DFL 'leaders'?"

But this was the start of a two-year fight...long and ugly. To this day I have in my office an entire file cabinet filled with petitions to various administrators for redress. I tried to avail myself of several avenues of appeal. First was the CLAS Dean's advisory council, but this council (under Prof. Ned Grace of Mathematics) refused to hear the matter. When I did receive the official university rejection letter from Provost Milton Glick I tried to arrange a conference with him as I was entitled to by the terms of the ASU ACD Policy Manual. Several times I was told by his office staff that I should have my post-rejection interview with the CLAS Dean or my departmental Chair. The more I insisted on my policy-manual-specified right to meet with the Provost about it, the more avoidance I encountered. Even personal visits to the Provost's office did not help. I just could not see him, I was told. So I sought the aid of the University Ombudsperson, Architecture Professor Michael Nielsen. Believe it or not, he shared with me after several inquiries that Provost Glick's office had mistaken me for my colleague, Prof. Sandy Couch, who had recently endured an interview with Associate Dean of Liberal Arts Gretchen Bataille about the university's cancelation of his exchange program with Moscow State Linguistic University due to some disagreements about his hosting of the MSLU exchangees (one exchangee, in an effort to stay in the US, had caused us real trouble, eventually requiring the university to pay for the visa-forced return to Russia of both him and his wife). In this interview with Dean Bataille (who soon after left ASU), Sandy Couch, a truly Godly man with a strong belief in the value of prayer (I recall his immediate request that we pray together when I told him, in 1984, of my wife's emergency hospitalization in Louisiana for a life-threatening ectopic pregnancy) asked her to get on her knees and pray with him for the successful transition to a democratic society of the Russians. This caused her to telephone REESC Director Steve Batalden and ask whether she, or he, should not initiate "committal procedings" on Sandy Couch. And so Provost Glick, confusing our single-syllable names (Couch, Croft...?) and our similar subject affiliation (Russian), apparently thought that I (Couch) would likely ask HIM to pray for the Russians as well. It sounds like something out of the works of Nikolai Gogol, but I swear it's true. After Ombudsperson Nielsen, however, "deconfused" the Provost's office about which Russian professor was seeking redress for what, a conference with Provost Glick was finally held. Glick decided to have his Associate Provost Harris investigate the matter, but nothing was done. So, receiving no redress from department, college or university, I hired an outside lawyer. At the recommendation of attorney Nadia Axford (daughter of the Education Professor Roger Axford whose tours abroad had eliminated my AIFS programs' credit in 1977), I engaged the services of Scottsdale Attorney Sally Clifford Shanley. This was, in my later estimation, a good move, mostly because Sally allowed me to make my case on her letterhead, which clearly earned considered responses from ASU's chief counsel, Mary Stevens, and ASU administrators. For the most part, CLAS Dean Gary Krahenbuhl was the "point person" for the administration. In the course of the next 18 months I came to admire the way he could issue detailed responses in kind to my frequent memos. At one point, after a very contentious conference that I recapitulated in my terms to him in a memo, he wrote (January 18, 1994): "Your memorandum is so detailed it suggests that the meeting was surreptitiously tape recorded. I remind you that such action would be a serious breach of professional ethics. If your memo was constructed entirely from your notes and memory of the meeting, I am impressed and apologize for suggesting otherwise..." He then issued a "gag order" on Chair Baldini or other DFL members whom I had asked to express an opinion as to whether I had or had not been given the DFL by-law-specified avenue of appeal of a personnel committee's judgment (the by-laws clearly stated that a faculty member had right of appeal to the DFL advisory committee, but I was not so informed). During this time I resigned my position as sectional coordinator, turning it over temporarily to Rolfs Ekmanis and I declined to be considered for two important teaching awards because I was simply too busy dealing almost daily with these promotion matters.

As the case continued to evolve in 1993 and 1994, my grounds for redress were several: 1) that my record as a teacher and service provider were outstanding enough to compensate for insufficient publication; 2) that my record of publication was: a) equal to that of those considering me and not, therefore, insufficient at all; and b) not capable of being properly understood by colleagues outside my area (because no one on the committee read Russian and because of the concept of "differential publicational resistance" of a small-section member operating in an adversarial ideological publicational environment (i.e. USSR did not allow and opposed US scholar's publications); and that 3) documentarily specified avenues of appeal had been denied to me. These grounds were just, but they would never have prevailed had I not had a most formidable "internal champion." This champion was Dr. Stephen Batalden of the Russian and East European Studies Consortium (REESC). He wrote letter after letter of protest. He went to see people, enlisting them in the effort to find me redress. Letters of protest began to come in from both inside and outside the university. Poor ASU President Lattie Coor must have tired indeed of seeing each day's mail requiring that he answer another letter elaborating the injustice done by his subordinates to Professor Croft. Throughout 1993 and most of 1994 he got letters from (as I am now leafing through a pile of them in apparent chronological order...mostly the ones I received copies of only, of course, though some are only names on a list... tears of gratitude come to my eyes and I fear only that I will omit someone here): Prof. Steve Batalden, Prof. Rolfs Ekmanis, Prof. Walter Comins-Richmond, Dr. Don Livingston, Peggy Walker, Carl Sergeant, Brian J. Thomas, Stacy Maugans, Thomas Bonifield, Tracy West Klenk, Dan Tappan, Annette Fettig, Aggie Czerski, James Bade, Daniel Meahl, Michael Galope, Brian Fitzgerald, Prof. Chad Menning, Michael Phillips, Myna Frestedt, Prof. Walter Vladimir Tuman, Phil Dunihue, J. Scott Christian, Margaret Dower Foley, Andrew Reese, Prof. Margaret B. Gibson, Miodrag Cedic, Ella Krasnova-Douglas, Dr. Nick Vontsolos, Dr. Maria Budisavljevic-Oparnica, Prof. Joe Malik, Jr. (whose letter now read reveals signs of the Alzheimer's Disease that contributed to his death five years later), Prof. Delbert Phillips, Prof. Marge E. Landsberg, Gary Walker, Jay Davis, and Prof. Wayne M. Senner. Once Dean Krahenbuhl called me and asked that I cease requesting people to send letters on my behalf. I told him that I was not so requesting (mostly true, I admit to asking the U. of A. colleagues and AGSIM-Thunderbird colleague Walter Tuman to write, and perhaps Nick Vontsolos) and that I had, in fact, restrained some people from writing (also true...one émigré blamed the

Pope and the "Trilateral Commission" for my misfortune and was going to inform President Coor of this personally). At last I got word from my attorney that the university had a proposition for me. I was to go see Dean Gary Krahebuhl about it.

Dean Krahenbuhl took the position that I had not prepared my case "properly" in 1993. I had not established any specific niche in my field's scholarship by which I was renowned. I protested that my program needs (ASU's undergraduate-only program in Russian) required that I be a "jack-of-all-skills" and that I not focus my scholarly efforts into any particular "niche" at all. I stated that parochial people made parochial programs and that I had, on the contrary, endeavored all my time here to "transcend the boundaries of my subject area" with my personal and scholarly impact. But Dean Krahenbuhl insisted that I "would be allowed" to go through the promotion process again in 1995, this time with "proper preparation." This "proper preparation" would include the letter of publication acceptance I had received from Hermitage Publishers of New Jersey for my long-in-process textbook <u>**RUSSIAN THROUGH POEMS AND SONGS**</u> (subsequently, I withdrew this from Hermitage in copyright disagreements and have published it locally...though it is used in other universities (U of A, U. of the South) and in Russia at Moscow's GRINT institute). My exterior evaluators were to be encouraged to define for me specific labels to describe the "scholarly niche" I particularly inhabited. These exterior evaluators were: Dr. Catherine V. Chvany of M.I.T. (who had been one of the 1993 evaluators), Dr. George Gutsche of the University of Arizona, Dr. Walter Vladimir Tuman of the American Graduate School of International Management-Thunderbird Campus, and Dr. Michael K. Launer of Florida State University. It was Dr. Tuman who came up with the sobriquet appropriate to Dean Krahenbuhl's required "niche." I was, Tuman said, a "mnemonotactician" in the teaching of Russian, a claim based primarily upon my well-regarded article in Slavic and East European Journal entitled "The Mnemonic Use of Linguistic Iconicity in Teaching Language and Literature" (Vol. 22, No. 4 (Winter 1978), pp. 509-19). Also, Dean Krahenbuhl was prepared to have all levels of committee consider the input of the REESC Personnel Committee that Dr. Batalden had composed for just this purpose (this was, in fact, the nascence of the REESC Personnel Committee I later chaired in behalf of junior professors in other departments like Religious Studies and Sociology). This committee was composed of esteemed senior subject-area scholars like Joe Brada of Economics, Fred Giffin of History, and Emil Volek of the DFL's Spanish section, who were willing to put their reputations on the line for me in opposition to the earlier opinion of my DFL personnel committee. This time, with the aid of all these good people, I did prevail and was recommended for promotion to the rank of full professor...the realization of a long-time dream (especially have I relished signing recommendation letters for my students with the "weightier" title "Professor and Coordinator of Slavic Langs/Lits."). Only my lawyer insisted that my full professor's appointment be listed retroactively to 1994 because of the "obvious injustice done" me, and that I receive in financial settlement the appropriate one-year's increment of promotion pay. This was done. On the ASU rolls I have been a Full Professor of Russian since 1994.

At this writing in 2007, I have served another thirteen years at ASU as Full Professor and Coordinator of the Slavic Languages and Literatures Section of the Department of Languages and Literatures. In 2002 Sandy Couch retired. He continues to run the DOBRO SLOVO honorary nationally and occasionally inhabits his emeritus office on the first floor. He still travels often to Russia and always remembers to send to me and to Lesley some kind of postcard, always with humorous commentary. In 2005 he claimed to have found remnants of the "great hydrogen balloon" my current biography subject, George Anton Schaeffer, helped to construct on the Vorontsovo estate of Prince Repnin-Volkonsky during the invasion of Napoleon's "Grand Armee" in 1812, but somehow these remnants were lost, perhaps confiscated by airport security. Dora Burton retired in 2003. I helped her pack her books and move them...all twenty-five boxes of them...to her Scottsdale apartment. Then I saw her only twice in the next four years, until she was admitted by her daughter to Scottsdale's Hospice of the Valley's Eckstein Center. I visited her twice there before she passed away on March 4 of this year. I attended the nice memorial service for her and helped tell stories about her twenty-seven-year service with us at a wake dinner put on by her daughter Irene and son-in-law Stan Bassin. Now it has been proposed that we institute a teaching award in her name in the new School of International Letters and Cultures. I think it is a good idea.

When Dora Burton retired, our section was allowed to search to find a replacement...i.e. a tenure-track Assistant Professor of Russian Language and Literature. We advertised for a second-language acquisition person with subspecialty in literature to come to ASU to teach THREE language courses per semester. I chaired the search committee of Profs. Barbara Lafford, Gail Gunterman, Rolfs Ekmanis, and Danko Šipka, who was at that time still Associate Director of the CLI for REESC). Our goal was to find "the world's best" teacher of Russian. And after much consideration and candidate interview by telephone and in person here, selected for the

Russian Faculty Associate Tatyana Dhaliwal and Dr. Jeanette Owen at Crofts' pool, Spring 2006. Photo by Lee Croft

job *Dr. Jeanette Owen* of Bryn Mawr College. Dr. Owen began in the fall of 2003. I remember asking her to replace me for a single Friday so that I could attend the funeral of my father that November. The only other day that I have not met my scheduled classes was the day of son Hayden's birth, October 5th of 1987. Jeanette taught admirably here for six semesters (one semester was a research leave in the interests of bolstering tenure chances), playing ice hockey on the same team (Anger Management) that includes my wife. Her service was well beyond expectations and she participated in grant efforts successfully as well. The students loved her. But, in December of 2006, she announced that she had accepted an administrative job with the American Councils for International Education in Washington, DC and, because of this organization's immediate need for her, she left before the beginning of the Spring 2007 semester. We miss her.

In the years 2002-5 Steve Batalden and I cooperated in various ways to get *Dr. Danko Šipka* a regular faculty appointment as Full Professor of Slavic Languages and Literatures in the Department of Languages and Literatures. This multifarious effort, bolstered by Danko's clearly manifest excellence in all spheres—teaching, research, service, grants, etc., was rewarded in 2005 with the requested regularization. Danko has taught Russian here (RUS-311/2 in a team effort with Faculty Associate Tatyana Dhaliwal), but he has primarily been engaged in building minors in Bosnian-Serbian-Croatian (BCS) and in Polish (PLC). He has also

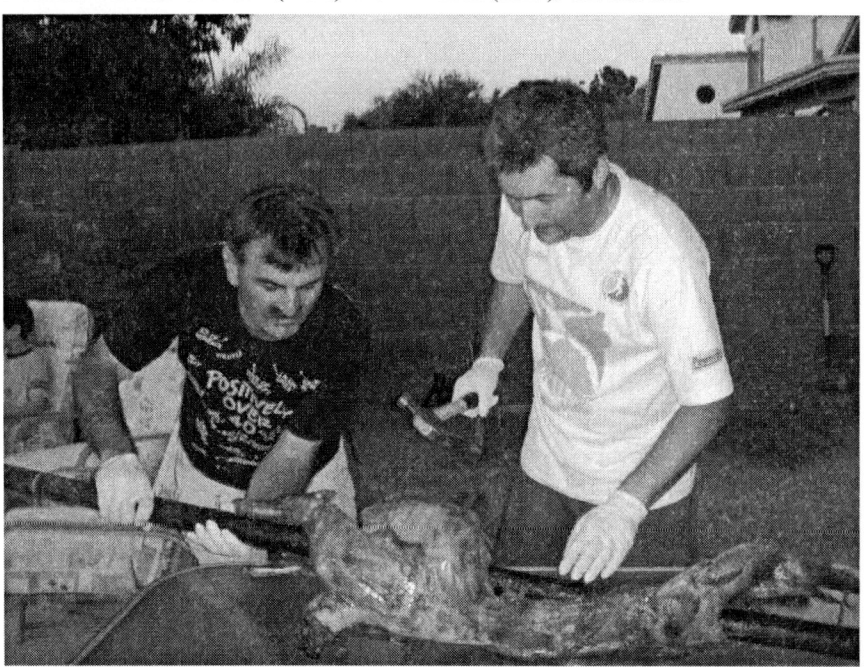

Dr. Danko Šipka (R.) with friend Mario Filipovic at work on a spitted lamb. Entertaining the students at Orthodox Easter. Photo by Ljiljana Šipka, spring of 2005.

established a course series called SLV (general "Slavic" studies), one course of which (SLV-304 Computational Linguistics of the Slavic Languages) satisfies, thanks to his able petitioning of university committees, university general studies requirements in applied mathematics/computer studies (a 6,000 student/semester constituency...a real enrollment hope for us).

Now I (Croft) am the only tenured professor left in the section teaching Russian, where only a short time ago were four (Burton, Couch, Croft and Ekmanis). Danko Šipka is teaching BCS, PLC, and SLV courses in semesterly amounts that a mule could not carry. We have Faculty Associates Danuta Kalisz (teaching Polish courses), Dr. Don Livingston (teaching Russian language courses, 101-202), Russian poet and SRP Electrical Engineer Tatyana Dhaliwal (teaching upper-division Russian courses in diverse areas and in summer too), Public Programs Doctoral Candidate David Mashuri (teaching RUS-411/2), and Prof. Emeritus Rolfs Ekmanis (teaching a literature "person" course per semester for us as a Faculty Associate). Current requests for additional benefitted faculty (a "Principal Lecturer in Russian") have not been granted by our administration. And so, like always, we soldier on "for the good of the cause" doing more and more with less and less.

Lee B. Croft

Who Has Taught Russian in the State of Arizona?

Here we attempt to list, institution by institution, EVERYONE who has ever taught Russian in the State of Arizona. Memory is the obvious limitation to this, as is the definition of what "teaching" means. This list, however, very likely includes those who have taught in a paid academic environment 99% or more of all the students of Russian in Arizona State history. We regret anyone's omission.

At **Arizona State University (ASU)** in Tempe, Arizona (roughly in chronological order): Dr. George Portnoff (1946-48), Mrs. Anna Wall

(1948-1962), Dr. Sanford (later Snaford) C. Couch (1962-2002), Dr. Rolfs Ekmanis (1963-2004 and subsequently as a Faculty Associate (FA)), Mrs. Irina Borisovna Krylova (1965-1973), Brian Dulley (1968-1969), Dr. Lee B. Croft (1973-), Dr. Martha Awdziewicz (1975-1977), Dr. Dora Burton (1976-2002), Dr. Carl Goldberg (1979-80 as sabbatical leave replacement for Dr. Croft and 1982-1985 as FA), Dr. (subsequently) Mark Preslar (1985-1986), Dr. (subsequently) Don E. Livingston (1987-91 as FA and Instructor, and 2003- as FA), Andrew Reese (1991-1992), Dr. Nicholas Vontsolos (1991-1995), Justin Capin (summer 1990 FA), Dr. Joyce Story (summer 1991 FA), Dirk Willeford (some academic year and intermittent summers 1992-2002), Ella Krasnova-Douglas (replacement and FA, 1993-2000), Dr. Danko Šipka (2000—with Russian in 2002), Tatyana Dhaliwal (2002—as FA), Tamara McKane (now J.D., 2002-4), Dr. Jeanette Owen (2003-2006), Tatiana Keeling (2005, 2006 FA), and David Mashuri (2005 as aide, 2006—as FA). That's 24 people for Russian to this date. In addition, the section has also taught Macedonian in the normal academic year. Instructors have been Violeta Milenkovska (1975), Evica Konecni (1976-7, 1981-2), Mihailo Popovski (1984) and Eleni Buzarovska (1996-7). We are now teaching Bosnian-Serbian-Croatian and Polish in the academic year as well. Dr. Danko Šipka is doing this, aided by FA Danuta Kalisz (Polish). Also, the summer intensive Critical Languages Institute (CLI) founded by Dr. Croft in 1991 taught Macedonian, Serbo-Croatian and Tatar in summers until Dr. Stephen Batalden of REESC (now the Melikian Center for REEES) took over administration of it in 1997. Instructors were: Dr. Evica Konecni, Dr. Eleni Buzarovska, Dr. Liljana Mitkovska, Dr. Maria Kusevska and ASU doctoral candidate in English, Lupco Spasovski, for Macedonian, Dr. Maria Budisavljevic-Oparnica (an ASU Russian alumna and USC Ph.D.) for Bosnian-Serbo-Croatian (then we called it "Serbo-Croatian"), and Agnès Kefeli Clay, Goljihan Kashaeva and Hafiza Andreeva for Tatar. These and other CLI instructors (including, for example, Dr. Danko Šipka (in the CLI BCS, 2000-5), have continued under Melikian Center for REEES auspices, currently administered by Dr. Ariann Stern-Gottschalk (a University of Arizona M.A. alumna and UCLA Ph.D. who plans to teach Russian herself intensively in the summer 2007 CLI offerings).

Ancillary to the teaching of RUSSIAN at ASU is the work of faculty in related areas. In Russian History at ASU I must mention Dr. Frederick Giffin, Dr. Bill Weidemeier, Dr. Stephen Batalden, and Dr. Laurie Manchester. In Russian/Soviet Political Science Dr. Douglas Dalgleish should be mentioned. In economics Dr. Marvin Jackson (now deceased) and Dr. Josef Brada have represented their field well in our sphere. In Religious Studies it has been Dr. Eugene Clay, in Sociology Dr. Victor Agadjanian, and in Music Dr. Robert Oldani. In Architecture and Design it is Dr. K. Paulius Zygas, who once taught me his native Lithuanian at Cornell. Also, our university library staff in the Slavic area deserves mention: Dr. Vladimir Borovansky of the Noble Science Library, and Sandra Batalden, Molly Malloy, and Michael Markiw of Hayden Library, who were, successively, in charge of Slavic acquisitions and cataloging all these many years.

At the **American Graduate School of International Management-Thunderbird Campus (AGSIM-T-Bird)** in Glendale, Arizona: ASU's Dr. Croft agitated for years with AGSIM-T-Bird VP Jorge Valdivieso (an ASU-DFL faculty husband) to begin Russian instruction at that institution. But Dr. Croft provided from ASU the required proficiency examination services for their students until approximately 1985 when Dr. Leon Kenman, a Russian-speaking faculty member of English there, got a Russian "key man" program installed, which began on-site Russian instruction that he (Dr. Kenman) provided. Soon (1990--) the demand for Russian increased there to the point where Dr. Walter Vladimir Tuman was hired away from Louisiana State University to come and teach Russian full-time. Dr. Tuman almost immediately won a large federal grant to aid in the establishment of "Business Aid Centers" at multiple sites in transitional Russia, and this effort involved many AGSIM-T-BIRD students, including several who had been ASU Russian graduates, for example David Lorti and Aggie Bednarz Czerski (also a UA MA alumna). Dr. Tuman subsequently hired native speaker instructors Liudmila McIntyre (Russian wife of an ASU Russian alumnus, Sean McIntyre) and Julia Arzumanova. Dr. Tuman retired in 2004, however, effectively ending Russian instruction at AGSIM-T-Bird. He remains a consultant to them for Russian-related business instruction. AGSIM-T-Bird has hosted conferences of the Arizona State AATSEEL (as well as AZLA and the RMMLA) and the yearly RUSSIAN BUSINESS COLLOQUIUM initiated thirteen years ago by the University of Arizona's Roza Simkhovich. The ASU Russian program has sent many students to AGSIM-T-Bird, including: Mirjana Baich, Loren Krebs, Anna Krajewski, Marianne Bohl, Susan Coady, Tami Shahar, David Lorti, Aggie Bednarz Czerski, and Russell Van Der Werf.

At **Honeywell Commercial Flight Systems Group**, of Phoenix, Arizona: Honeywell had a large commercial interaction with Russian aircraft manufacturers (Tupolev and Ilyushin) in the early 1990's, and so they began Russian language instruction there of their Russian-contact staff. Don E. Livingston was involved in this in 1991 and 1992, as was Russian native instructor Julia Demkova.

At **Prescott High School,** Prescott, Arizona: a man named Don Rogers taught Russian there from 1965-ca 1974. He attended an AATSEEL meeting or two and I met him only once. His daughter was an ASU student of textiles in the 1970's and she came to my office a time or two, but I can't remember her name.

At **Prescott College**, Prescott, Arizona. Prescott College, a private liberal arts institution, has gone through several financial closings and reincarnations over the years. When Russian interest was high in the late 1960's it may have engaged Don Rogers from Prescott High School to initiate Russian instruction there, but in 1969 the Liberal Arts Dean at Prescott College, Dr. Peter Horwath (later ASU DFL Chair) hired Brian Dulley to teach Russian there. This Dulley did, until dying of a brain hemorrhage in front of his class in 1974. Prescott College closed for a time soon after this and Russian was discontinued.

At **Northern Arizona University** in Flagstaff, Arizona: Anne Slobodchikoff, who has been teaching the Russian at NAU since January of 1985 (in addition to teaching French) and is responsible for getting a Russian minor approved there in addition to an exchange with a university in Barnaul, Russia, reports that Russian was taught before her there at NAU by "a gentleman of the old school," a Mr. Victor Kobylin. This was in the late 1960's. Anne has hosted an AzAATSEEL meeting at NAU, invites us all to her yearly "Russian meal," and has traveled to Russia with the U. of A.'s Dr. Del Phillips (see below photo).

At **Mesa Community College (MCC)**, in Mesa, Arizona: MCC's Russian program is the most contiguous CC program in the state. Russian was begun there upon the petition for interest circulated by ASU's Dr. Lee Croft and Dr. Sandy Couch in 1979-80 with the approval of Foreign Language Chair Martin Durant (an ASU Spanish alum who had previously been Chair at Phoenix College as well). The first instructor was native speaker Janna Malkina, whom Dr. Croft aided in getting certified. But

A 1989 "mini-tour" of the UARA St. Petersburg facilities (e.g. the CHAIKA dorm) by a number of academic and travel professionals. Del Phillips is on the left in the fur hat. Also in the picture are Marla Wycoff (Mesa College, San Diego), Olga Shashkevich (New Mexico State U.), Pierre Hart (Louisiana State), Lee and Lesley Hoyt Croft (ASU...in back center), and Anne Slobodchikoff (NAU) (fourth from right).

Janna Malkina soon gave up and the Russian instruction was taken over by ASU and UA graduate Dirk Willeford, who has largely sustained Russian instruction there since the mid 1980's. Dirk has been helped by Alena Cheppel (1990-1996), by Ella Krasnova-Douglas (1992-2000), and by Liudmila Derizemlya (2002-2006). The MCC Russian program has contributed to ASU many good Russian students, including James Rogers, Ezra Ziegler, Erin Traeger, and others.

At **Scottsdale Community College (SCC)**, in Scottsdale, Arizona: Since the 1970's Russian has "been on the books" at SCC, but has been irregularly taught, mostly 101 only, by native Russian Vera Dunn.

At **Phoenix College (PC)** in Phoenix, Arizona: Phoenix College is the state's oldest "junior" or community college, and the first of the prominent

Maricopa County Community College District (MCCCD) which now administers ten community colleges. In the late 1960's Russian language instruction began there under Justin Capin, a military Defense Language Institute-trained Russian linguist. Justin's program was rigorous and sent many students on to university study of Russian. He was a leading local individual teacher of Russian too, earning money on a per-hour basis for his instruction. One summer he taught RUS-101 at ASU as a Faculty Associate as well. After he retired in the early 1990's Phoenix College tried to replace him with native speaker Marina Romazanova, but the program faltered and has not been revived.

At **Glendale Community College (GCC)** in Glendale, Arizona: Here the whole story (no pun intended) is Dr. Joyce Story, who has been teaching what Russian would "justify" there (in addition to teaching Spanish) since 1987 and continues the struggle to this day. Dr. Story is very active in our professional organizations (RMMLA, AATSEEL, AZLA), in the state-wide effort to set proficiency standards for our foreign language graduates, and in mentoring her Russian students (e.g. Charles Sketch, Kevin Torrey, Charles White, and others) on to become Russian language students at ASU. She also taught Russian as a summer Faculty Associate at ASU in 1991. Also affiliated (now, perhaps, loosely) with GCC is Andrew Conovaloff, a long-time student of Russian and of the Molokan religion of his personal heritage (one of this originally Russian religion's largest populations in to be found in the Glendale area). Andrew has not, to my knowledge, taught Russian in any institutionally paid way, but he is married to a Russian and he has made it his business for years to provide information to the local Russian émigré community by internet postings and email lists. This has caused him some troubles with some of the emigres, and some of his associated ventures (a Russian radio station, a planned TV offering, a website on the GCC server) have not "worked out." But Andrew Conovaloff provides "information central" for the Phoenix-area Russian and Slavic Community and certainly deserves mention in this history of <u>RUSSIAN IN ARIZONA</u>.

At the Phoenix, Arizona **Berlitz School of Foreign Languages**: Berlitz offers Russian instruction to individuals periodically by maintaining a file of eligible Russian native instructors who are then equipped with the Berlitz materials when a request comes in. For a decade or more, starting approximately 1975 (Dr. Croft recommended him) Russophone architectural draftsman Alex Kislik was the Berlitz "go-to guy," and was successful when (occasionally only) he received a teaching assignment. There was a long gap in Berlitz' Russian offering after Kislik's retirement in the late 1980's and people who inquired there were told that they had no Russian instruction. But now (2006-) Tatiana Korovina (a talented poet/translator and mother of ASU student Lev Korovin) has earned the designation as Berlitz Russian teacher by her sound instruction, and ASU Russian French TA Tatiana Farbishel is registered as a possible instructor.

At the **Arizona Foreign Language Institute,** Mesa, Arizona: Here was an attempt to teach individuals certain languages upon demand, beginning in the mid-1990's and continuing (?) today. Several times the Director would call me (Lee Croft) to find a Russian instructor appropriate for some inquirer's needs, but to my knowledge, despite my giving them several names across several years, no such instruction (at least no regular instruction) occurred. If an individual called me at ASU and asked me for a recommendation of someone who could teach or tutor them in Russian, I gave them SEVERAL names from a long list of eligibles whose names, phone numbers and (in recent years) email addresses I kept. For years and years I have been giving such referrals at the rate of at least one per month and DO NOT CHARGE for this referral or for advice to the refered-to instructor/tutor either. For that reason I am actually a competitor of the Arizona Foreign Language Institute, which does charge an individual for finding them a Russian language instructor. The instructors are often the same, the same ones whose names I gave to the AFLI. It's just that if a person calls me, the referral is free.

At **Paradise Valley Community College (PVCC)** and at **Rio Salado Community College (RSCC)**-Paradise Valley Site, in Paradise Valley, Arizona: Here for a brief time (1988-9?) was instructor Michael (Michelle) Blackwell, who left a high-school position at Shadow Mountain High to teach Russian at more than one site in the MCCCD district, but then left that position too.

At **Phoenix area (Maricopa and Pinal Counties) High Schools:** Ruth George at Camelback High School (1966-74), Helen Lenz at Phoenix Country Day School and at Greenway High School (1975-1992), then

Heather Lambert Frackiewicz (both she and her husband were ASU Russian students, 1993--) at Greenway High School, Shirley Strunk (ASU Russian student/Spanish combination, ASU/UA tour to USSR, 1977, 1977-86 ?), then Michael Blackwell (1986-8 ?) at Paradise Valley's Shadow Mountain High School, Glendon Bergfalk at Scottsdale's Saguaro High School (1968-9), Ron Bodiroga at Coolidge High School (1981-5), Sue Farbarik Fry at Gilbert High School (1994-8), Pat Barrett at Mesa's Westwood High School (1987-- and continuing, aided in broadcast project by Dan Secklin, Janna Malkina and Katia Avedisian), Robert Bordwell at Mesa High School and at Dobson High School (he commuted to offer courses in Russian and German, 1985-1998), Dr. Nicholas Vontsolos at Phoenix Central High School (1993-2003 with aid from Russian teachers on exchange, Tatiana Kazanina and Sergei Petrosian--one academic year each), Lyudmila Derizemlya at the Echo Tech Charter School in Chandler, Arizona (1997-1998), and Roxanne Nelson (1996-1997) and William "Billy" Gunn (1997-1999) at the Heritage Academy Charter School in Mesa, Arizona. Other certified teachers of Russian (i.e. supervised through the ASU Dept. of Education by Dr. Croft and supervised by "master teachers" already in place, mostly Helen Lenz, Nick Vontsolos, and Pat Barrett) who did not find permanent high-school positions here, but went elsewhere to teach, taught something else, or did not teach, are: Michael Turek, Deborah Anderson Jaynes, Debra Carnes, Lois Calo, James Donnelly, Kathy Pate, Susan Moore, and Kristina Efimenko. They all (in addition to me, Lee Croft) "student taught" Russian in the Arizona high schools. Also, in 1974 Sandy Couch, Lee Croft, and ASU student Timothy Korb taught Russian for six weeks to sixth-graders at Supai Elementary School in Scottsdale, and, in 2001 Natalia Bor founded a Russian child-care/pre-school in Phoenix near the "Russian Grocery" at 19th Avenue and Northern.

At the **University of Arizona (UA or U. of A.)**, in Tucson, Arizona: Martha Breger (wife of Rabbi Marcus Breger of Anshei Israel congregation, 1939-1970) (part-time nights, 1958-62), Dr. Joe Malik, Jr. (1960-1989 and until 1994 part time), Paul I. Macura (1961-1964 with whom Malik wrote the <u>Supplementary Russian Reader</u>, University of Arizona Press, 1965), Savel Kliachko (1964-1965), Dr. Boriss Roberts (1964-1992), Dr. (subsequently) Gerard L. Ervin (as TA or instructor 1965-1967), Dr. Nicholas Vontsolos (1969-1974), Dr. (after 1977) Delbert Phillips (1969—and continuing), Dr. Alex Dunkel (1973—and continuing),

Dr. (after 1978) Margaret Gibson (1972-7 and 1978-1999, Head, 1988-1991), Dr. Roger Hagglund (1976-1983), Dr. Adele Barker (1979—and continuing, with a 1990-1993 "gap" at U. of Washington-Seattle, after which she returned to the U. of A., affiliated with the Russian program from the Graduate Program in Comparative Cultural and Literary Studies), Dr. John Garrard (1986—and continuing, 1986-1988 Head), Dr. Alex de Jonge (1987-1989), Valerian Golovskoi (1987-1990), Dr. Teresa Polowy (1990—and continuing, Head, 2005--), Galina DeRoeck (1990-1999), Dr. George Gutsche (1991—and continuing, 1992-2004 as Acting Head or Head), Instructor Ron Mastaler (1990-1992), Dr. Grace Fielder (1992—and continuing), Roza Simkhovich (1995--? and continuing), Dr. John Leafgren (1994— and continuing), Dr. Olga Ovtchinnikova (as Visiting Professor, 1999-2000), Dr. Lisa Wakamiya (2002-2003), Dr. Meghan Murphy-Lee (2003-2006), and now Dr. Romy Taylor (2006-7 Visiting). That's 25 people for Russian. Also, the Teaching Assistants in the M.A. program have all taught Russian in Arizona, and well. But here sources and memory are more limited and regretable omissions are more possible: Lee Croft, Louis Prazma, Paul Weadon, Dan Winters, Rick Ruth (a USIA exhibit guide and now diplomat), Al Cannon, Walter Vassiliev, Richard Holmes (a USIA exhibit guide), W. Michael Welsch (an ASU graduate), Dirk Willeford (ASU graduate, now teaching Russian at Mesa Community College), Herman Schiller (ASU graduate), Mark Preslar (an ASU graduate, now a Professor at the University of the South in Sewanee, Tennessee), Alan Anderson (a chess champion ASU graduate and USIA Exhibit guide) Don Livingston (now a Faculty Associate at ASU), Karrie Gonnerman (an ASU graduate), Annette Fettig (an ASU Russian graduate), Suzanne Thompson (now Eanes), John Lee and others...

I (Lee Croft) interject here an email message I received from John Lee after I sent an early draft of this to him, helping me out in this regard:

"Lee,

Nice of you to include me on the list of prominent TA's at the U. of A.

However, there are at least a couple of other TA's closer to my day who should be on that list: Michael Brewer completed his M.A. in the U. of A. Russian program and is now the Slavic and German Librarian at the U. of A. Library; Dr. Phillip Hammonds completed his M.A. in 1994 in Russian there, then went on to complete a Ph.D. in Second Language Acquisition at the U. of A. (he is now Program Manager for Northrup Grumman IT at Fort Huachuca); Cary Piper completed his M.A. at U. of A. in the early

1990's and went on to do doctoral-level work at the University of North Carolina (but never completed it—unfortunately, Cary died last month); Elisabeth Elliott (also an ASU Russian graduate) completed her M.A. at the U. of A. in 1995, then went on to complete a Ph.D. in Slavic Linguistics at the University of Toronto and is now a Lecturer at Northwestern University. Dr. Hammonds, my wife (Dr. Meghan Murphy-Lee), and various others (e.g. Dr. Don Livingston, now of ASU) led at least one (and in my case 2) groups of students on the U of A Study Abroad Program.

There are probably others, but those are the most prominent and noteworthy that I myself can recall—and that's not to mention my beautiful, skinny, genius wife, who was a TA at U. of A. from 1993-1995, then went on to complete her Ph.D. at the University of Kansas in 2003, return as faculty to the U. of A. from 2003 to 2006, and is now an Assistant Professor of Russian at the US Military Academy at West Point.

All the best,

John Lee"

In addition to this substantial help from John Lee, I have received additions from others as well, mentioning: Mary Jo Smith (an ASU grad and joint ASU/UA summer tour participant, 1977), Ron Mastaler, Venita Polechla, Guy Velgos, Paul Kachur (an ASU Russian graduate), Aggie Bednarz Czerski (also an ASU graduate), Dr. Ariann Stern-Gottschalk (now of ASU's Melikian Center for Russian, Eurasian, and East European Studies as the Director of the Critical Languages Institute), Cindy Seaborg Humphries, as well as more recent AzAATSEEL presenters James Romanesko (cf. http://russian.arizona.edu/awardshonors.htm) and Tom Brixius. Current University of Arizona Graduate Teaching Assistants in Russian include Natalia Samokhina, Glen Grover, and Suzanne Stringfield, former UA Russian Drama Troupe actress and current (2007) UA College of Humanities "Outstanding Graduate Teaching Assistant" awardee.

Ancillary faculty members at the University of Arizona include Dr. Robert Browder, Dr. Frederick Kellogg, and Dr. Douglas Weiner of Russian History, as well as Dr. Gregory Oswald of Political Science. The University of Arizona Library's Slavic holdings were managed for years by Andrew Makuk. Then Michael Markiw of ASU commuted to UA for a time to help in this regard. But now Michael Brewer (former Russian/Slavic Dept. TA) serves in this capacity.

Natalia Samokhina, Suzanne Stringfield, Glen Grover, and Tom Brixius.
U of A Graduate Students.   2007 Photo by Lee B. Croft

At **Pima College**, in Tucson, Arizona: having taught Russian at Pima College in Tucson are Lydia and Vera Alexander.

At **Tucson Area High Schools:** Here we have Jeanine Alexander (Marana High School ?), Guy Velgos (University High School and Tucson High School), Richard McNabb (who was in my M.A. cohort at U. of A., ca. 1969), and Cindy Seaborg Humphries.

Some Statistical Ruminations

From the above data we may statistically conclude that in sixty one years (since 1946) several thousand Arizonans (permanent or temporary) have been taught Russian by approximately 120 instructors in approximately 35 educational institutions…mostly, though, at ASU and the U. of A. My own gradebooks across thirty-three years of teaching (1973-2006) reveal that I have taught in 83 semesters or summer sessions 4382 student enrollments in 289 courses worth 961 semester credit hours. I have taught the daily, grading-intensive RUS-101 thirty-one times at ASU to classes averaging almost 20 students per class (maximum was 47 students). Multiplying the total number of my student enrollments by the total (not individual) number of credit hours by a thirty-three-year average of $100 per credit hour equals over 420 MILLION dollars. But this nearly-half-billion-dollar sum is illusory, since it implies that every one of the 4382 students took every one of the 961 credit hours. But, more appropriately, if each of these students (majors and non majors) took, as I reckon, an average of 6.25 credit hours from me in their academic career, then the sum to ASU was (6.25X4382X100) $2,738,750, during which time ASU has paid me a total of 1.3 million (my salary averaging $42k/ay for 33 yrs)). Allowing for student overlap year to year, our 1970-2004 enrollment data at ASU gives an estimate of almost 7,000 students. Extrapolating backwards to 1946 using a declining scale raises the TOTAL ASU estimate to 9,000. The high-school students, in their aggregate, may add 1000...the community colleges 500...with NAU and U. of A. providing the rest in estimated respective proportions (i.e. NAU a 500 maximum, but U. of A. 7,000 since 1958). All that totals 18,000 students in sixty-one years...an overall average of 295 per year statewide. In that time ASU produced 300 B.A. graduates in Russian. I think it likely that the U. of A. produced a similar number, perhaps more if the Russian and Area Studies (RASS) count is included, say 350 (my very limited data on the ratio of "majors" to total enrollment indicates that the U. of A. has a higher ratio than ASU). And an estimate of the U. of A.'s M.A. production, figuring an average of 3 per year since 1968 would be 114. This means that the Russian-language-teaching degree "enterprise" in the State of Arizona turned out 650 B.A.'s and 114 M.A.'s in its history, mostly since the late 1960's. And, as you will see as you read on into the student-oriented sections, these Russian-trained Arizonans became and are becoming very productive and positively contributing American citizens indeed.

From the above list of Russian teachers, however, it is our intent to feature several of the prominent figures in a more elaborate way with the following "profiles."

RUSSIAN TEACHER PROFILES

ASU Faculty Profiles

Burton, Dora, MD, Ph.D., Assistant Professor Emerita of Russian, ASU:

Dora Burton (1921-2007) by Lib Wong

Born in Russia, Professor Dora Burton came to ASU in 1976 from the University of Washington in Seattle, where she earned her M.A. and Ph.D. in Slavic Languages and Literatures. Professor Burton had previously received an M.D. degree in Russia, studying mostly in Leningrad at the First LMI-I.P. Pavlov and completing in Kazan. In the course of gaining her Ph.D., she taught for twelve years as an instructor of the Russian language and literature at the University of Washington. At ASU she teaches all levels of the Russian language, focusing primarily upon the intermediate composition and conversation series as well as advanced specialty courses in the literature, taught in both English and in Russian. Her specialization is in 19th-century Russian literature and poetry. Her scholarly publications and numerous presentations, in even international fora, have established her as an insightful interpreter of the poetry of Pushkin and a pioneering scholar of Boratynsky's verse as well as the works of Chekhov. In the Spring of 1991 she was awarded ASU's College of Liberal Arts and Science's Quality Teaching Award.

Addendum: (a March 5, 2007 email notice to DLL faculty)

"Dear Colleagues,

I have the sad duty to inform you that Dora Burton, who taught Russian with us here in this department from 1976 to 2003 and who, in 1991, won the CLAS Dean's Quality Teaching Award here (in the newspaper I termed her a "human treasure") passed away last night in Scottsdale's Hospice of the Valley's Eckstein Center. A memorial service for her is to be held at Sinai Mortuary, 4538 N. 16th St (just off the 51 south of Camelback), at 4:00 pm on Thursday afternoon. A gathering of close ones after the service is being arranged by her daughter Irene and son-in-law Stan Bassin.

Dora, as you may not know (she was pretty sensitive in life about revealing her age) was born on June 26, 1921, was educated as a medical doctor (at the prestigious I. Pavlov Leningrad Medical Institute), overcoming personally the disappearance of her beloved father into Stalin's purges and the Soviet Union's anti-Semitism, and she served in a medical capacity during the terrible three-year Nazi siege of Leningrad, one of the twentieth century's most tragic dramas of human suffering. Evacuated to Tashkent in 1944, she then made her way to Kazan where she completed her M.D. degree. After WWII she made her way out of the Soviet Union and, after enduring displaced person's camps in Poland and then Italy, she came to the United States. Here she married and had a daughter, Irene. Settling in Seattle with her pharmacist husband and daughter, she rejected the notion of finding employment in medicine or pharmacology, wanting to involve herself in "the positive side of life" at last. She enrolled in the University of Washington's program in Russian Language and Literature and earned her Ph.D. in 19th Century Russian Literature, teaching meanwhile as an Instructor of the Russian language there for twelve years. We hired her as an Assistant Professor in 1976 and she taught heavy loads (always three courses of more) of our Russian language and literature courses for twenty-seven years, retiring at the age of 81 in 2003.

I recall that on her last day here she came to my office and, to her amazement, heard, for the first time in sixty years, the actual voice of the Russian poet Anna Akhmatova reading her poem "Courage" over the computer at www.russianpoetry.net. Akhmatova's poetry had consoled the Leningrad populace during the blockade and Dora had been inspired by the line "We will preserve thee, Russian speech," a logo we once had on a Russian Club T-shirt. Dora reads the poem herself on the audiotape <u>A READING OF GREAT RUSSIAN POETRY</u> by Lee B. Croft and Dora Burton (ASU-DLL-Slavic Section Audio Resources, 1996). Her student legacy is large and in this section she will be missed. –Lee Croft."

Couch, Snaford C., B.A., M.A., Ph.D., Professor Emeritus of Russian:

Our senior Professor, Snaford Couch, came to ASU from the University of Wisconsin, Madison, in 1962. He is the primary designer of our program and the initiator of most of our courses. As a specialist in foreign language pedagogy, he is the author of six of our program's course texts and most of its language laboratory resources. He led the section through its accreditation of the Bachelor's Degree program, which gave its first degree in 1965. Professor Couch has spent a great deal of time in Russia and in diverse areas of the former Soviet Union, and he remains active in exchange work. He has been the National Executive-Secretary of the American Association of Teachers of Slavic and East European Languages (AATSEEL) as well as DOBRO SLOVO, the National Slavic Honor Society. He is a curriculum advisor to the Ukraine Ministry of Education. He is one of seven recipients of the Joe Malik, Jr. Arizona Slavic Studies Award for his outstanding contributions to the advancement of Slavic Studies in the State of Arizona. (He retired from ASU in 2002 in his 40th year of service).

Here I am adding the text of the April 13, 1991 <u>NEWS RELEASE</u> from Tucson, Arizona about Dr. Couch's award:

"Dr. Snaford C. Couch, the senior Professor of Russian at Arizona State University in Tempe, has been named as the third recipient of the prestigious Joe Malik, Jr. Arizona Slavic Studies Award. The award, founded in 1987 in honor of Joe Malik, Jr., long-time Head of the University of Arizona's Department of Russian and Slavic Languages, is given 'by the judgment of peers for sustained outstanding achievement in

This sketch of (L.) Mark Preslar and (R.) Sandy Couch was made in only seconds by renowned Russian cartoonist and caricaturist Vladimir Mochalov of the satire magazine Крокодил who visited ASU with a delegation of humorists in April of 1987. The inscription says: "To my wonderful American friends, Mark Preslar and Sandy Couch, in friendly memory of our meeting!" Notice that Mochalov renders Mark's "11th Annual New Times 10K Run" T-shirt (November 1986 in which I (LBC) ran with Mark) and places an ASU Sun Devil's pitchfork in the hands of a "Krokodil" ("Crocodile") on Sandy Couch's shirt shoulder.

the advancement of Slavic Studies in the State of Arizona.' The award was previously given to Dr. Boriss Roberts and to Dr. Margaret Gibson, both of the University of Arizona.

The announcement of the award and the presentation of the associated plaque came at the semi-annual meeting of the Arizona Chapter of the American Association of Teachers of Slavic and East European Languages (AATSEEL) held on Saturday, April 13, in Tucson. Dr. Couch was congratulated at the meeting by his colleagues and by several generations of his students who now fill professional positions in various areas of academia, government and private service. The award is the highest honor given to Arizonans in the Slavic Studies field.

Dr. Snaford Couch, 61, a U.S. Navy veteran, received his B.A., M.A., and his Ph.D. in Russian Language Pedagogy at the University of Wisconsin, Madison, in 1962, having been a participant in the first U.S.-U.S.S.R. academic exchange the previous year. In 1962 he accepted a professorship at Arizona State University where he has been teaching these 28 academic years since. At ASU he designed the Russian Language curriculum, writing into the ASU General Catalogue over 90 percent of the courses at all levels taught there today. He authored a unique set of textual materials for the first two years of Russian Language instruction—two pioneering first-year texts now in their ninth published editions, two accompanying laboratory manuals with the associated tape programs now in their fourth published editions, and two second-year texts now in their fourth editions. In addition, he is the author of two textbooks in Scientific Russian.

With tremendous effort put into the teaching of Russian, Dr. Couch managed to attract and sustain the student enrollment necessary to justify faculty expansion. By 1965 ASU's Russian Language Section had three faculty members and had issued its first Bachelor's Degree in the language.

Now, in this 1990-91 academic year, Dr. Couch advises six instructional faculty in Russian at ASU who teach over 400 students—51 of whom are Russian Language majors and who now graduate to enviable career placement at the rate of 15 per year. Indeed two of these ASU graduates, Andrew Reese and Dr. Lee Croft, who presented the award plaque to Dr. Couch, are now themselves ASU Russian Language instructors, using Dr. Couch's materials daily.

Dr. Couch has been professionally active throughout his career as a champion of student advancement. For many years he has been the National Executive-Secretary of <u>Dobro Slovo,</u> the National Slavic Studies Honorary for university students. In addition, he is the founding Executive-Secretary of <u>Slava,</u> the National Slavic Studies Honorary for high-school students. A former National Executive-Secretary of AATSEEL, he has long worked to establish programs of academic exchange between institutions of the U.S. and the U.S.S.R.

Today as Arizona's budgetary crisis and ASU's institutional priorities threaten the integrity of the Russian Language program he struggled to build, Dr. Couch continues to volunteer to teach ever more, to travel more in advocacy of academic exchange, to mentor more in support of his third generation of Russian Language students. The Joe Malik, Jr. Arizona Slavic Studies Award appropriately recognizes his inspirational efforts."

In a late interview, Sandy Couch expressed to this author his dislike of being referred to by the title "Dr." He strongly prefers "Prof.," pointing out with a smile that whereas professors at major universities without an academic doctorate are rare, "doctors who are not professors" are "all over the place." He asked to have a Russian poem that he has composed in the past three years included:

Жизнь продолжается	Life Goes On
Когда жизнь кончается	When life ends
Родственники собираются	Relatives gather
Гроб открывается	The casket is opened
Цветы покупаются	Flowers are bought
Могила вырывается	The grave is excavated
Слёзы проливаются	Tears flow
Водка выпивается	Vodka is drunk
И блины съедаются	And bliny are eaten
Родственники расползаются	Relatives creep away

Всё забывается	All is forgotten
И жизнь продолжается	And life goes on
А внизу труп разлагается	Below the corpse rots
Но душа поднимается	But the soul ascends
И с Богом встречается	And meets with God
Prof. Sandy Couch (Царь)	Transl. by Lee Croft

Croft, Lee B., B.S., M.A., Ph.D. (Cornell University), Professor of Russian:

Lee Croft with wife Lesley (L.) and daughter Cathy (R.) at a Montana Family Reunion in summer of 1992. From www.public.asu.edu/~iclbc.

A native of Cut Bank, Montana, Professor Lee B. Croft came to ASU as a faculty member from Cornell University, where he earned his Ph.D. in 1973. He had been a student of both Professor Couch and Professor Ekmanis in the 1960's as he pursued Bachelor's and Master's degrees in Mathematics at ASU. He completed his Master's Degree in Russian, however, at the University of Arizona in Tucson before going on to doctoral work and his first professorship at Cornell. His professional specialty is Slavic Linguistics. He was a participant of the first Joint Soviet-American Conference on the Russian Language in 1974, and he served as the Dean of Soviet Programs for the American Institute for Foreign Study in 1977. Since 1975 he has served as Coordinator of the

Slavic Languages Section of the Department of Languages and Literatures, which he has also served as Assistant Chair and as Faculty Senator. He has been active in the development of ASU's academic exchange with Universitet Kiril i Metodij (UKIM) in Skopje, Macedonia and is one of the founding members of ASU's Russian and East European Studies Consortium (REESC). Professor Croft's professional publications focus on linguistic iconicity, on the formal aspects of poetry and poetic translation, and on the mnemonotactics of language learning. He is one of the department's leading grantspersons and has won several awards for excellence in teaching and student mentorship: CLAS Dean's Quality Teaching Award (1978), Golden Key Honorary Student Mentorship Award (1985), the Burlington Northern Foundation National Distinguished Teaching Award (1985) and others. Like Professor Couch, he is a recipient (1993), as well as the fund founder and supervisor, of the Joe Malik, Jr. Arizona Slavic Studies Award. In November of 2005 he was awarded the prestigious (cf. www.raen.ru/en/award) V. I. Vernadsky-10 Years of RAEN silver medal for more than thirty years of professional achievement and collaborative Russian research by the Russian Academy of Natural Sciences (RAEN).

Prof. Croft has been married since 1981 to Dr. Lesley Hoyt Croft, the President of Croft Consultants, a national company designing and implementing workplace drug programs. He has four children (Cathy, Chris, Bill, and Hayden) and claims, through them, ten grandchildren at this writing, with a great grandchild expected.

Sample Publications of Lee B. Croft:

Nikolai Ivanovich Kibalchich: Terrorist Rocket Pioneer. Institute for Issues in the History of Science (IIHS) Biography Series, Tempe, AZ/Perm', Russia, 2006, 163 pp./il., ISBN 9-781411-623811. www.lulu.com/328860.

Slavic and East European Journal, "The Method to Madness in a Poem by Chinnov" (17:4, Winter 1973, pp. 408-14) and "The Mnemonic Use of Linguistic Iconicity in Teaching Language and Literature" (22:4, Winter 1978, pp. 509-18).

CLA Journal (Journal of the College Language Association), "Charlie Chaplin and Olesha's Envy," (Vol. XXI, No. 4 (June 1978), pp. 525-37 and reprinted online at www.enotes.com/twentieth_century_criticism in 2006) and "Spontaneous Human Combustion in Literature: Some Literary Uses of Popular Mythology" (Vol. XXXVII, No. 3 (March 1989), pp. 335-47).

(L-R) Prof. Fred Giffin and Prof. Valentin F. Olontsev of the Perm', Russia, Division of RAEN, who presented Dr. Croft's silver medal...at the REESC ceremony in December, 2005. Photo by Lesley Hoyt Croft.

Sample Publications of Lee B. Croft (continued):

Rocky Mountain Review "People in Threes Going Up in Smoke and Other Triplicities in Russian Literature and Culture," Vol. 59, No. 2 (Fall 2005), pp. 29-49 and also reprinted online at www.threes.com (2006).

"Mnemonotactics and Linguistic Iconicity," in The Learning and Teaching of Slavic Languages and Cultures in the 21st Century, Benjamin Rifkin and Olga Kagan, eds., Slavica Publications, Indiana University, Bloomington, IN., 2000, pp. 135-145. (cf. www.slavica.com/teaching/contents.html). This collection of essays won a national scholarly prize in 2001.

THREE Russian articles (one co-authored with Patricia Bailey Cossette) on the mnemonics of iconicity in language teaching in Методика преподавания русского языка и литературы в Америке, Д. Филлипс, ред., Синтаксис, Москва, Россия, том 2, 1996, стр. 113-127, 127-140, и 141-146.

Dean's Quality Teaching Award
in Memory of Zebulon Pearce

College of Liberal Arts
Arizona State University

1978

JEANIE R. BRINK

LEE B. CROFT

LEE B. CROFT

Ph.D., Cornell University, 1973
Assistant Professor of Russian, Arizona State University, 1973

The several characteristics which make a great teacher are perfectly combined in Dr. Lee Croft. Letters from his students and faculty colleagues and course evaluations attest to his truly extraordinary talents. Knowledge of the subject, imagination in presenting the material, ability to relate to students so they are inspired to learn, energy to teach thoroughly while still producing scholarly work and service — these are some of the marks of a great teacher. A few passages from among many show how students and faculty feel Dr. Croft reaches these standards: "Dr. Croft has taken a normally difficult subject and through an energetic and concerned approach has made it understandable to all." "classes are very exciting and fill students with love for the Russian language." "a creative flair for teaching that is indeed rare." "his rapport with his students makes it a joy to go to class every day." "the most accessible professor I have ever known."

The College of Liberal Arts is fortunate indeed to have a person of Dr. Croft's exceptional effectiveness on its faculty and takes pride in honoring him with the Dean's Quality Teaching Award.

EFFECTIVE TEACHING: NEW WAYS TO REMEMBER

Linguistics or Foreign Language, when taught by Professor Lee B. Croft, can be a fascinating experience. Co-winner of the College of Liberal Arts Distinguished Teacher Award in 1978, Dr. Croft is able to demonstrate to students that they know a great deal more about a language than they thought they did.

For instance — suppose you are shown a kidney-bean shape and a

star shape. Then you are asked which word applies to which shape, "ooloomu" or "taakaate". Eighty-five percent of students asked connected the kidney bean shape with "ooloomu" and the star shape with "taakaate". They easily associated the smooth sound of "ooloomu" with the roundness of the kidney bean, and the sharper-sounding "taakaate" with the points of the star.

As an Associate Professor of Russian in the Department of Foreign Languages, Dr. Croft has many other language tricks up his sleeve. If your language has but two words, "ping" and "pong", to represent an elephant and a mouse — which word would you pick for each animal? The majority of people, regardless of cultural origins, will choose "pong" for the elephant, and "ping" for the mouse, because they sense the association of magnitudinal impression and sound. Researchers have noted this tie between vowels and impressions of magnitude. The "i" connotes smallness ("itsy", "little") and the "o" or "a" connotes largeness ("grand", "awesome").

"Sound, then," says Dr. Croft, "is capable of conveying sense not just by conventional semantic assignment, but by *iconicity*, the sound's inherent relation to external reality. This capacity has been called the 'naturalness' or 'expressivity' of language. It is also this capacity of sound to convey increments of meaning apart from conventional semantic assignment that is used by poets to distinguish their special art form from ordinary discourse."

One important aspect of Dr. Croft's sound-sense association is its use in facilitating recall in the mind of students trying to memorize a new language. "How best can we present material to our students," he asks, "so that they can bring it forth when they need it? It follows that the best teaching method is the one which enables the student to 'file' the material to be recalled in the greatest number of ways. An especially effective family of mnemonic (memory) tags is related to this linguistic concept of iconicity, because they provide a ready-made connection between the worlds of sense and sound." These are tricks for remembering, in other words.

Another sound relationship used by Dr. Croft to prove his point is use of the word "shtanga". He asks his class to repeat the word several times and then asks them the following questions: Heavy or light? Shallow or deep? Masculine or feminine? Most students quickly choose "heavy", "deep" and "masculine". (No student was aware of the word's lexical meaning, "barbell"). Dr. Croft believes it is common sense to make use of these sound ties in teaching whenever possible. "Once a student is told," he says, "about the iconicity of the Russian word *pushka* 'cannon', how it starts with an explosion ("p") and has a rush of smoke ("sh") and then an impact ("k"), he never forgets it."

A more complex mnemonic tag is used by Dr. Croft in the classroom. Relational or "horizontal" iconicities, for example, abound in language. In this case, opposite phonological order signifies opposite meaning — such as *kar*, meaning *wise*, and *rak*, meaning *foolish*. Or *mer*, meaning *right hand*, and *rem*, meaning *left hand*, and *mes*, meaning *darkness*, and *sem*, meaning *to become visible*. Students find that when they are on the lookout for this "opposite sound/opposite meaning" tag, their vocabulary recall is greatly facilitated.

Dr. Croft's research on effective teaching methods has resulted in one book, *Russian Symbolist Poetry*, a *Bibliography of Linguistic Works on Modality*, and many articles, reviews and translations. He has led student tours to Moscow and Leningrad as United States Dean of the *American Institute for Foreign Study*, to study the Russian Language and Soviet Culture. Besides serving as Assistant Chair, Department of Foreign Languages, Dr. Croft has held the office of President of the Arizona State Chapter of the *American Association of Teachers of Slavic and East European Languages*. Some of his research has been supported by an ASU Faculty Grant-in-Aid.

Unusual teaching methods help Dr. Lee Croft's students learn foreign languages and linguistics. His sound-sense association is used to facilitate recall in the minds of students trying to memorize a new language.

FROM: ARIZONA REPUBLIC
SOUTHEAST EXTRA
FRIDAY, July 12, 1985
pp. SE-1, 4.

ASU professor of Russian hopes more learn language

By CATHRYN P. SHAFFER
Southeast Valley Bureau

Lee Croft, who recently won a Burlington Northern Foundation Faculty Achievement Award for outstanding teaching, would like to see more Americans gain a working knowledge of Russian.

TEMPE — There are as many teachers of English in the Soviet Union as college students of Russian in the United States, according to an award-winning Arizona State University professor who hopes to change that trend.

About 30,000 Americans are college students, study Russian, while about the same number of Soviet teachers instruct "hundreds of thousands" of students in English, said Lee Croft, who teaches many of ASU's 90 Russian language students.

"Russian is the third most spoken language in the world next to Chinese and English, and of course there is an official status of Russian as a second language of our major adversary," Croft said. "Yet there is a critical shortage of Russian-competent people in the United States."

Croft, who recently won a Burlington Northern Foundation Faculty Achievement Award for outstanding teaching, would like to see more Americans gain a working knowledge of Russian.

"I want students to be able to read, write, speak and understand Russian so they can make their own judgments based on primary information, not interpretations," he said.

Although many college students might believe they are too old to become fluent in a second language, Croft said he was an ASU student when he enrolled in his first Russian class.

"I was trying to become a mathematician and struggling at it," he said. "I took Russian as an elective and really enjoyed it."

While a student teaching at Saguaro High School in Scottsdale, Croft discovered he enjoyed teaching Russian more than math.

So, after earning a bachelor's degree in mathematics from ASU in 1969, Croft enrolled in the University of Arizona's graduate program in Russian. He then earned a doctorate in linguistics from Cornell University and returned to teach at ASU in 1975.

Croft said he has never regretted the switch.

"I have always been infatuated with the learning process, and I think I would have found a way to become a professor one way or another," he said.

Croft's goal now is to help more Americans get jobs with the federal government as interpreters and translators of Soviet newspapers and radio programs. He pointed out that the government looks

— Russian, Extra 4

Russian
Continued from Extra 1

Russian-speaking employees because it cannot employ many native speakers.

"If you have relatives behind the Iron Curtain, the government can't use you because you're a security risk," he said.

Croft said this mission also has made him an "anti-drug crusader" because he has seen several former students rejected by the government because they had used illegal drugs.

Three years ago, Croft developed a special course, "Marijuana and Man," in which he and students explored the reasons people abuse drugs.

"Today, I still tell students that it's time to shun the drug culture," he said. "I want to help students realize their personal potential and make sure they don't close doors in front of them."

Unlike some of his colleagues, Croft is not idealistic about the chances of eliminating the arms race simply by talking to the Soviets.

"I don't think all our problems will be solved by talking to the Soviets," he said. "I don't think the Soviets are simply misunderstood. They are in fact liars, and their government in fact is in conflict with human nature.

"We might be able to deal with them using logic and reason, but at the same time we must defend ourselves."

Croft said that although he is flattered to have won the teaching award, he does not find teaching Russian difficult because the students who study the language usually are hard workers.

"You get the very bright and the very strange," he said. "It's interesting."

Croft added that he encourages students who have no desire for a career in Russian to study the language because it leads to good mental discipline.

Students in his classes must learn the Cyrillic alphabet and practice reading and writing Russian daily, he said. Some students end up writing more in Russian than they do for other classes in English, he added.

"I think it would benefit anyone to learn Russian, whether they use it or not," Croft said. "It gives you a different perspective on the world.

"In Russian they say 'If you learn another language, you gain another soul,' and I believe that's true."

ASU teacher's work extends beyond language classroom

By Ben Winton
Staff writer

You name it, Lee Croft has done it or nearly done it. But not because he wanted to.

It was more a matter of necessity for awhile.

He was once about to become the only guy in the Ithaca, N.Y., sanitation department with a doctorate in Russian.

The Central Intelligence Agency nearly offered him the job of teaching Russian to Apollo astronauts for a linkup with a Soviet spaceship. But they turned him down at the last minute with no explanation after an interview in Washington, D.C.

Fortunately, he says, Arizona State University offered him a job and culminated his 10-year struggle of working on Montana drilling rigs, managing apartments and raising three kids to reach a position in life none of his relatives had ever reached — a university educator.

For that matter, he was the first in three generations with a college degree. In 1966, he received a bachelor's degree in mathematics from ASU.

He's keeping the tradition in the family, too. His wife, Leslie Hoyt-Croft, is an ASU sociology professor. A daughter, Kathy, is an ASU undergraduate.

This year he reached another milestone. He became one

Please turn to Croft, A14

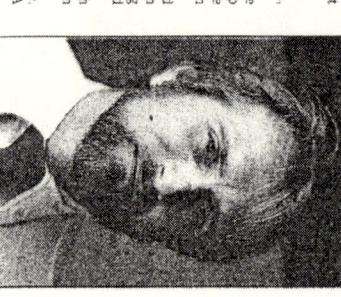

Lee Croft

Croft

Continued from page A1

of three ASU professors to win an award as one of the nation's top university educators. He received the Burlington Northern Foundation Faculty Achievement Award for excellence in the classroom. The other two professors are Ken Morrison, a religious studies professor, and Edward Friedman, a foreign languages professor.

Croft would like to think his work extends beyond the classroom.

"Many of my colleagues have no idea what happens to their graduates," Croft says.

He said he invests a lot of time into seeing what problems his graduates face after college.

In 1979 and 1980, he spent a sabbatical studying drug abuse because he had feared many Russian graduates could not get security clearances with the federal government because "they had smoked marijuana when they were 13."

He developed and taught a drug education course in 1981 and 1982 called "Marijuana and Man." It met a lot of controversy from colleagues, but the class accomplished its purpose.

"The person who gets involved in drugs does it in ignorance. They don't know what (career) doors they are shutting," he says.

Croft has other plans for his students. He has proposed that a satellite dish be set up on the roof of the ASU College of Liberal Arts to bring Soviet television into the classroom. The dish is far from reality. For one thing, it's too expensive.

But many of his students have said he does just fine without the fancy technology.

At medal award ceremony, ASU/REESC, December 2005. Awarder, Academician Valentin F. Olontsev, Awardee Lee Croft (wearing medal), and REESC Director, Stephen K. Batalden. Lesley Hoyt Croft, Photo.

Also at the medal ceremony: (L-R: Hayden L. Croft, Dr. Lee B. Croft, Kathyrn B. Hoyt (mother-in-law) and Dr. Lesley Hoyt Croft). Photo by Jeanette Owen, who acted as interpreter for Academician Olontsev.

Professor and Academician Valentin Fyodorovich Olontsev came to ASU from the Perm', Russia, Division of the Russian Academy of Natural Sciences (RAEN) to present the medal to Professor Lee Croft, with whom he had collaborated in publishing the biography in Russian of 1932 Nobel-laureate chemist, Irving Langmuir. The presentation was in Russian, interpreted by ASU Assistant Professor of Russian, Jeanette Owen. It began with these words: "В науке нет широкой, столбовой дороги, и только тот может достичь до сияющих вершин, кто, не страшась усталости, карабкается по её камнистым тропам." ("In science there is no wide, well-marked road, and only that one can reach its shining heights who, undaunted by fatigue, scrambles over its rocky paths"). These words, attributed to Karl Marx, were used by Academician Olontsev to introduce the citation accompanying the presentation of the Russian Academy of Natural Science's "V.I. Vernadsky 'Ten Years of RAEN'" silver medal to Prof. Croft. The citation mentioned Prof. Croft's "more than thirty years of TEACHING the Russian language, literature, and culture, his collaborative publication of RESEARCH on Nobel-laureate U.S. scientists Irving Langmuir and Linus Pauling, and his ADMINISTRATION of the Slavic Languages and Literatures Section of a prominent U.S. university (ASU)." The medal was initially given at a reception following the Arizona State AATSEEL convention at ASU in Tempe, Arizona, on November 19, 2005. But the ceremony was repeated at ASU's Russian and East European Center (now the Melikian Center for Russian, Eurasian, and East European Studies) in the new Lattie Coor Building, fourth floor, on Thursday, December 1st, 2005.

In every educational institution, and in other institutions and workplaces at large, there are basically TWO types of people: there are the "gate-keepers" and the "doormen." The gate-keepers' philosophy toward students is "I've had hell getting to where I am, and I'm going to see that it's even tougher on you," so as to "raise the standards" of the institution. The doormen's philosophy is "I've had hell getting to where I am, and I'm going to use my experience to make it easier on you to get to where I am...and I'm going to try to enable you to get even further still," so as to "raise the productivity" of the institution. I (LBC) am a "doorman," and not a "gate-keeper." Every day I try to think of how I can "put another ahead of myself," the door-posted motto of English Dept. colleague, Mark Lussier, a 2007 ASU Parents' Association "Prof. Of the Year" nominee.

Dhaliwal, Tatyana Len, B.S.E.E. (Arizona State University), Faculty Associate in Russian:

Tatyana Dhaliwal at the blackboard, 2007 photo.

    Tatyana Dhaliwal is a graduate of ASU's Bachelor's Degree program in Electrical Engineering, Power Engineering option. She has also completed all the coursework for the Master's Degree in Electrical Power Engineering. She has worked full-time as an Electrical Engineer for Arizona's Salt River Project (SRP) utility for 13 years, currently serving as a Senior Engineer/Analyst in Corporate Pricing. She is currently a Ph.D. student in Russian Philology at Vilnius University in Lithuania. She works as a Consultant to Spector Studio in Kiev, Ukraine, in the production and distribution of educational video games in the Slavic languages. She serves as a volunteer translator of Russian/Ukrainian/French/Hindi/Punjabi for the SRP call center.

    Tatyana's primary qualification for teaching Russian at ASU is her outstanding knowledge of the Russian language, literature, cinema, and culture, in which she has been involved since her birth into a family of Russian academics and intellectuals. And, very importantly, she is a widely known Russian poet, having published original poetry and translations of poetry in a number of languages (e.g. English, French, German...), including, of course, Russian. Many of her works, together with reviews and commentary by a wide variety of readers and fans, can be found on www.stihi.ru (now alleged to be the number one place for poetry publication in the world) under the English nom "Athena." From this most impressive corpus I (LBC) would point out her amazing verse (i.e. preserving the form: meter, rhyme, alliteration, and even the initial "acrostic" encoding of the theme) translation of Gavriil Derzhavin's "River of Times" (1816) at http://www.stihi.ru/poems/2002/04/16-250.html. Also, it is through her wonderful verse translations that great numbers of Russian poetry lovers know the subtleties of such extremely difficult English masterpieces as Gerard Manley Hopkins' (said to be "untranslatable") "God's Grandeur," and Dylan Thomas' touching "Do Not Go Gentle into That Good Night." See http://www.stihi.ru/poems/2003/02/28-388.html for the first of these, and http://www.stihi.ru/poems/2002/04/10-172.html for the second. Tatyana's work is also published in a number of poetry almanacs and magazines, in the US, Russia, and Great Britain. A feature about her is to be found at http://www.poetrymagazine.com/archives/2003/May03/dhaliwal.htm.

Tatyana Dhaliwal is the current President of the Arizona State AATSEEL (2006-8 term), and is a frequent contributor to this organization of scholarly papers and presentations of her humorous original Russian skits by her students. At ASU she has been teaching since 2001 everything that could reasonably be scheduled during the evenings or lunch hour when she isn't working as an SRP Senior Electrical Engineer. This includes: RUS-311/2 Intermediate Russian Composition and Conversation, RUS-394 Business Russian, and a number of RUS-494 Special Topics courses, including "Culture Shock and Inter-cultural Communication," "Russian Science Fiction and Fantasy," "Russian Literature in Cinema," and "Russian Children's Literature." She is a member of the ASU Epsilon Epsilon chapter of DOBRO SLOVO and a member of Eta Kappa Nu, the Electrical Engineering Honor Society, and she has recently been named an "Honors Disciplinary Advisor" for ASU's Barrett, the Honors College. She is a single mother, living in Tempe with her young son David.

Ekmanis, Rolfs, B.A., M.A. (University of Wisconsin-Madison), Ph.D. (University of Indiana at Bloomington), Professor Emeritus of Slavic Lang/Lit:

A native of Riga, Latvia, Professor Rolfs Ekmanis came to ASU in 1963 from a teaching position at Florida State University. After finishing his doctoral work at the University of Indiana, Bloomington, he set about to establish our university's scholarly credibility in the field of Baltic literature, publishing numerous books, articles, and reviews, and working as a bibliographer for the Modern Language Association's yearly compilations of scholarly contributions. It was he who began and sustained the growth of ASU's library holdings in Russian and East European languages and literatures until their dimensions merited dedicated in-house management in the mid-1970's. He has attained much international visibility in the years since the break-up of the Soviet Union as a long-time contributor (pseudonymously before 1992 as "Maris Rauda") to the Radio Free Europe/Radio Liberty broadcasts. His work as Director of the RFE Latvian Broadcasting Department in Munich and his setting up of the first RFE/RL News Bureau on former Soviet territory in Riga in 1992 earned him important commendations. His teaching at ASU focuses on the literature of the Soviet Period and on the literatures of the former-Soviet minority nationalities.

In his career at ASU, Prof. Ekmanis inspired the students by his personal commitment to the Soviet citizens' "great change of mind," and to the dissolution of the Soviet Union itself. As a boy in Latvia he was there when the Soviet Union annexed his country. He was there when the Germans' Nazi government militarily occupied it and he had to leave his country to be educated in Germany. When he made his way to the United States after WWII and continued his education, the idea of freeing his native land, Latvia, from Soviet domination was always paramount in his mind. The following page is an article about Dr. Ekmanis' government broadcasting activities by John Mathews in the ASU Insight publication.

PROFILE

Voice of ASU's Ekmanis reaches into Latvia

By John Matthews

An ASU faculty member has been on the cutting edge of the independence movement that began sweeping through Eastern Europe in 1986.

Rolf Ekmanis, a specialist in Slavic studies in the Department of Languages and Literatures, has played a key role in advancing freedom and democracy in Latvia through his involvement in Radio Free Europe/Radio Liberty (RFE/RL) headquartered in Munich, Germany.

William W. Marsh, executive vice president of RFE/RL, said recently that Ekmanis guided the Latvian Broadcast Service through its most difficult years — those leading up to and during Latvia's break with the Soviet Union.

"His brand of leadership and intellectual guidance was exemplary in the history of our organization," Marsh said. "Counting free-lance work dating back to the founding of the RFE/RL Latvian service in 1975, Rolf has been a significant contributor to the success of our broadcasting service to the Latvian people."

In 1986, the new Soviet policy of perestroika (rebuilding) had radio officials concerned. They appointed Ekmanis to the post of senior editor.

"They knew me because I had been affiliated with the RFE/RL since the launching of the Baltic broadcasts," he said. "I prepared literary programs, mostly reviews of books published behind the Iron Curtain. I have a good recorder, taped the programs in my office and mailed them. I published some of the material later in English as a book of reviews or articles."

Soon, Ekmanis was named director of Latvian Broadcasting and headed the services until 1993.

"I had no time for boredom during those years," he said. "I arrived right after the Chernobyl nuclear disaster. The following year (1987), all sorts of dissident movements erupted in Estonia, Latvia and Lithuania."

In 1989, Ekmanis returned to ASU to resume his teaching career, but not for long.

"I did not intend to go back, but could not foresee the rejection of communism in Hungary and Poland or the dismantling of the Berlin Wall. I agreed to serve another three years."

He assisted in establishing a bureau in Riga, Latvia, the first of its kind in the former Soviet Union, and also spent time in Estonia, Lithuania and Russia.

A visit to the Moscow McDonald's was a highlight of one Russian trip.

"In October 1992, I was in Moscow and went to the Latvian Embassy to meet the ambassador. I offered to buy dinner and suggested he choose the place. He selected McDonald's." Ekmanis said. "I was looking forward to dining in a not Russian restaurant. McDonald's menu was the same, and the food tasted the same as here. It's a huge place in a two-story building without the familiar arches."

Ekmanis said that RFE/RL has been broadcasting to the former Soviet Union and countries of Eastern Europe since the earliest days of the Cold War.

"Until the Soviet Union and its allied bloc dissolved, RFE/RL was one of the few honest, reliable information sources for the people of these countries," he said. "Many former listeners including current heads of state have

Professor Rolf Ekmanis has broadcast Latvian news to Latvians since 1975.

credited RFE/RL with accelerating the fall of communism and helping to eliminate totalitarian dictatorships in Eastern Europe."

He said that in 1991, when Soviet leader Mikhail Gorbachev was under house arrest near the Black Sea following the Russian coup, his little Sony radio provided his only link with the outside world.

"Gorbachev said later that he listened to Radio Liberty to keep abreast of the latest developments," Ekmanis said. "After August 1991, the Russians gave Radio Liberty permission to operate a Moscow bureau."

During Ekmanis' tenure, first as deputy director, then as director of the Latvian Broadcasting Department, the years 1986-1992 were fraught with danger, particularly during the massive demonstrations against Soviet rule. Attacks on the Riga Press Center and Latvian Interior Ministry by Soviet special forces resulted in bloodshed.

"The situation could have easily been worse if a foreign station tried to incite its listeners through inflammatory broadcasts," he said. "We strived to exert a calming influence, which ultimately led to the triumph of Latvian patriots and a relatively smooth transition to democracy."

During this period, a survey commissioned by RFE/RL found that the Latvian Broadcast Service had a regular audience of 21 percent, which at that time was the highest listenership rating at RFE/RL broadcast services.

"Indeed, we did have audience ratings in Europe. Our station was the most listened to in Latvia," he said. "The Voice of America had about 15 percent and there was some competition from the BBC (British Broadcasting Corporation), Radio Sweden, Germany, Vatican Radio and other stations broadcasting in Russian and Baltic languages."

Ekmanis said RFE/RL programming was similar to that offered by Cable News Network in the United States.

"News, interviews, commentaries, analysis and some cultural programs were the main fare," he said. "The original goal focused on providing truth to those living behind the Iron Curtain."

Ekmanis is frequently asked to explain the difference between Radio Free Europe and other services such as the Voice of America, Radio Sweden, Deutsche Welle (German Wave) and Vatican Radio.

"Basically, those and some others are government stations," he said. "The main purpose of stations like the Voice of America focuses on broadcasting in various languages from Washington about U.S. policies."

The Voice of America presents American viewpoints about such subjects as abortion, gays in the military and other national concerns. Radio Free Europe and Radio Liberty, on the other hand, report and analyze domestic and international events of the most immediate concern to their listeners in Eastern Europe and the former Soviet Union.

So, when the Voice of America broadcasts in the Georgian language it is really an American radio station broadcasting in Georgian.

"The RFE/RL service offers a truly Georgian station broadcasting from outside Georgia," he said. "There is a difference because the RFE/RL service stresses foreign and domestic news strictly pertaining to Georgia."

Radio Liberty's history begins in the late 1950s and until the early 1970s was supported by the CIA. Then Congress intervened.

"Several senators were concerned about the depth of CIA control. The operation did not complement the past journalism and was not as effective as open communication," Ekmanis said. "This year's budget is down about $80 million. Radio Liberty may move to Prague because the Czech president has offered the use of a castle rent-free."

Ekmanis said that according to information he has received, most broadcasting departments of Radio Free Europe will be phased out by October 1995. However, Radio Liberty will continue broadcasts in Russian, Ukrainian, Belorussian, Georgian, Armenian, Azerbaijanian, Tatar and five Central Asian languages.

"I believe it is important to continue broadcasting to the former Soviet Union because it can still play a key role in the whole democratization process," Ekmanis said. "The media is relatively free in the Baltic states, but others like the Ukraine, Belorussia, and Georgia are not so free."

Ekmanis said he hopes the day will come when the stations are no longer needed, but believes the broadcasts are more important today than ever. He pointed out that the former Yugoslavia would benefit from the service but funds to support it are not there.

Although he was never in serious danger during his years with RFE/RL, perils were near.

"Broadcasters and writers have been assassinated, and in 1981 terrorists tried to blow up the station," he said. "German guards closely watch those who enter and leave, and in some respects the station is like a walled camp. Because it is located near a huge municipal park, German police warned us to be alert when walking especially at night."

He said a particularly bizarre incident occurred in 1977. Georgi Markov, a Bulgarian writer and free-lancer for Radio Free Europe, was struck on the thigh by an umbrella tip on London's Waterloo Bridge. He died four days later, poisoned by a pellet that had been inserted in the back of his thigh.

Ekmanis has now come full circle. He was just a kid when he boarded a ship bound for America in 1950. After more than 30 years as an American citizen, the Latvian-born professor returned to Europe to facilitate the independence movements of countries that were behind the Iron Curtain for four decades.

> *'I believe it is important to continue broadcasting to the former Soviet Union because it can still play a key role in the whole democratization process. The media is relatively free in the Baltic states, but others like the Ukraine, Belorussia, and Georgia are not so free.' — Rolf Ekmanis*

Livingston, Donald E., B.A., M.A., Ph.D. (University of Washington), Lecturer in Russian: (Interviewed here by James C. Nielsen)

Dr. Don Livingston, 2006. Photographer unknown.

Donald Livingston was born in Tucson to a father who was a Geology professor and a mother who was a Math teacher. Livingston's interest in the Russian language came about during high school while living in Grand Junction, Colorado as a senior. Intending to become an electrical engineer, he began pursuing his college education at the University of Arizona in Tucson. He switched to Russian studies after a bad experience with a professor in the engineering department. He proceeded to earn his B.A. and M.A degrees in Russian from the University of Arizona in Tucson. During his Masters program he taught Russian at the U of A from August of 1984 until May of 1987. After receiving his Masters he found out about an opening at Arizona State University and taught Russian there from August of 1987 to August of 1991. When the state budget was cut, he found himself out of a job and moved on to work for Honeywell in the flight systems group. He was a translator and taught upper-level engineers who were developing American frames for Russian aircraft, namely the Tupolev and Ilyushin models. He recalls an experience in which 20 Russian translators were brought in and he was the only American. During this time, his Russian became better than ever before, and he attributes his success to his scientific upbringing. Typing classes helped as well since he had the Russian keyboard layout memorized during his first year at the U of A. Livingston says that his typing skills brought him more money than anything else because it gave him insight into the *Word Perfect* Russian Module. After having worked there from October of 1991 until August of 1992, Livingston left Honeywell and relocated to Seattle, Washington to earn his Ph.D. from the University of Washington where he studied from January of 1993 until August of 1997. He ran a translating business called *Voskhod,* which fed him through his doctorate. At the University of Washington, Don also taught some Russian language classes. After 2000, Dr. Livingston left the field for 5 years, working as an executive in a national drug testing company, but he returned to the teaching of Russian at ASU in Jan 2005 and has been teaching here since. He is a talented singer and a computer wizard, and he teaches yoga as well.

Since receiving his Masters Degree, Don Livingston has been to Russia 7 times: In the summer of 1986 he went with IREX and subsequently he went 5 times with U. of A. "Russian Abroad" program director, Dr. Delbert Phillips, as Assistant Director. In the summer of 1995 he headed the CIEE Russian Language Exchange in St. Petersburg. Other people of note that Livingston worked with at the U. of A. were: Joe Malik Jr., John Garrard, and Margaret Gibson.

Mashuri, David, B.A., M.P.A. (Pepperdine University), Faculty Associate in Russian.

David Mashuri

David Mashuri was born and raised in Kazakhstan in a small town, Jarkent, near the Kazakhstan-China border. He received his BA degree in Linguistics, Russian Language and Literature in 1995 at the Russian People's Friendship University in Moscow, Russia, where he also studied the Arabic Language. This led to his first employment opportunity as a Russian-into-Arabic interpreter in the Yemen Republic. In 1996 he immigrated to the US and lived in Los Angeles, California, until 2004. He received his Master's Degree in Public Policy at Pepperdine University the same year and moved to Phoenix, Arizona, to be with his wife Nargiza who attended Arizona State University. David Mashuri has been teaching Russian at ASU since August 2004, sharing two first-level classes with Dr. Jeanette Owen. He also assisted Dr. Danko Šipka in an Arizona Board of

Regents (ABOR)-funded project researching in Russian language and troubleshooting in the *Russian Tagger*, a software program designed to translate, cut, and paste Russian texts into English on-line. Currently, David Mashuri is teaching fourth-level Russian Composition and Conversation (RUS-411/2) in a class called "Russian in Central Asia," where students learn about the former Soviet Republics of Central Asia, their geography, economy, politics, culture and current events through the use of the Russian language.

Šipka, Danko, B.A., M.A., Ph.D., Habilitation, Ph.D.: Professor of Slavic Langs/Lits:

Prof. Danko Šipka in a photograph by Thomas Story, 2006

Danko Šipka is a Professor of Slavic Languages at Arizona State University, where he teaches Bosnian-Croatian-Serbian (BCS-), Polish (PLC-), Russian (RUS-), and general Slavic Linguistics (SLV-). He was instrumental in establishing the BCS-, PLC-, and SLV- courses into the

Slavic Section's curriculum. For his program building in the Polish area he received in 2006 an award of merit from the Polish-American Congress of Arizona and a certificate of recognition from the U.S. Consul General of Poland in Los Angeles. Dr. Šipka first came to ASU in 2000 to teach BCS in the intensive summer session of the Critical Languages Institute, advanced to a position of administration of the CLI, and, in 2005, was "regularized" as a tenured professor in the Department of Languages and Literatures (soon to become the School of International Letters and Cultures). He holds a Ph.D. and a Habilitation in Slavic Linguistics, an M.A. in Russian, as well as a doctorate in Political Psychology. In the course of his academic career, he has taught and researched at twelve different universities in Bosnia, Serbia, Germany, Poland, and the United States. He has served as a consultant for numerous corporate and academic entities, such as Microsoft Corporation, Inxight, McNeil Technologies, Tranexp, Multilingual Solutions, Glyph, New Mexico State University, and the University of Illinois. He has been a principal investigator on various research projects funded by several U.S. governmental agencies.

Dr. Šipka is widely published in the field of Slavic Linguistics. His publications include eighteen books and over 150 papers and reviews in English, Bosnian-Croatian-Serbian, German, and Polish. His most recent books comprise a Serbo-Croatian-English Colloquial Dictionary, a Dictionary of New Bosnian, Croatian, and Serbian Words, an Introduction to Lexicology and Neighboring Disciplines (in Bosnian-Croatian-Serbian), and The Concepts of Democracy and National Interest (in Polish). His major fields of specialization encompass computational linguistics, traditional and electronic lexicography, morphology and comparative linguistics of the Slavic languages.

In addition to being an amazing polyglot (Bosnian-Croatian-Serbian, Polish, Russian, German and English…and he's now studying Chinese too), a superb scholar, an enterprising grantsperson, and a competent administrator, Dr. Šipka is a fine teacher and student mentor. He still directs theses and dissertations from his former academic position in Poland, serves frequently on our university's NSEP and Fulbright juries, and works tirelessly to advance our students to important positions of employment or further study. In 2006 he was awarded the College of Liberal Arts and Sciences Dean's Quality Teaching Award, and in 2007 he earned a Certificate of Special Recognition in the contest of the ASU Parents' Association to name a Professor of the Year.

GLENDALE COMMUNITY COLLEGE, Glendale, Arizona:

Story, Joyce, B.A., M.A., Ph.D., Professor of Foreign Languages: (Interviewed here by Katherine Lutz)

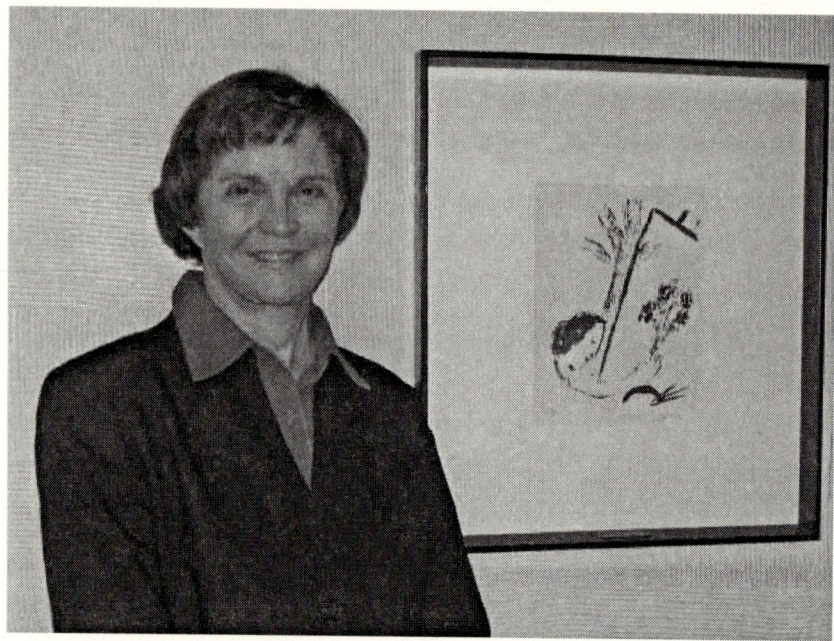

Dr. Joyce Story of GCC with a sketch by Marc Chagall, ca. 2005.

Dr. Joyce Story, a Floridian of English-Irish descent, and with a charming southern accent, keeps Russian alive at Glendale Community College in Glendale, Arizona. For the last 20 years Dr. Story has kept the Russian language afire with her passion for the Slavic tongue. Since her undergraduate study at Florida State University the language has been an integral part of her life. Dr. Story says, "It was curiosity first," that triggered her interest in the Russian language. She remembers a Russian textbook suddenly appearing in the campus bookstore, so she immediately enrolled in a class while majoring in French, and has not relinquished her interest in the Russian language since. It has not been an easy task for Dr.

Story to keep Russian course enrollment from "telescoping down," but she perseveres.

Dr. Story's interest in the language has taken her to the former Soviet Union numerous times between the years of 1964 and 1990. She lived and studied there; 1 year in Leningrad, 5 weeks in Moscow, and 5-week study programs in Kiev, Sochi, Krasnodar, and Volgograd. She has not been back to Russia since the fall of communism.

Dr. Story graduated from Florida State University and then went on to Indiana University where she received her Ph.D. in Slavic Languages and Literatures; her first language in the program was Russian (as was everyone else's) and her second was Polish. She used her Polish when she lived in Warsaw for a year. At some point after that she went to Ohio State University where she taught Russian and Polish. For a time, she also taught a cultural course at Park College Residence Center at Luke Air Force Base called, "Russia in the 20th Century." Marriage and motherhood found her in Alaska where she spent about 10 years; took a break from teaching before ending up back in the "lower 48." She ended up in Arizona and "didn't hear any Russian or any Polish, but heard a lot of Spanish," so she started learning Spanish, just because she was hearing it. She chuckles, "that's the way we students of languages are...we like to do that crazy sort of thing." In 1987, Dr. Story was hired part-time at Glendale Community College to teach Russian. Then in 1990 she was hired full time to teach Russian and Spanish. She has remained there ever since as a full-time faculty member.

Unfortunately, teaching Russian has become an arduous undertaking for Dr. Story, but she has not let it immobilize her efforts to keep it alive at the college. Dr. Story frankly shares, "We've had a number of problems here at the Community College... with the subsequent courses making because the enrollment "telescopes down." I'm sure that's true anywhere, but at a community college where you don't have the large enrollment to begin with, it becomes problematic. So I have been primarily a teacher of Spanish much to my surprise, and for years I would, and still do sometimes find myself in front of the Spanish class saying to myself, are you really doing this? How did this happen?"

Dr. Story has experienced enrollment problems, especially in transfer courses. She found that she could get students into Russian 101, but Russian 102 could not "make" because of enrollment; classes are cancelled

Dr. Joyce Story at the Crofts' post-AzAATSEEL reception, Nov. 2005. Photo by Lesley Hoyt Croft.

or as on one occasion she had to teach a class with reduced pay, i.e. paid for 2 credits instead of the standard 5.

Story has tried everything she could imagine to motivate, stimulate and support her students. She said she has "gone from offering during the day to offering at night so that it opens it up for the community." Then, she ran into a different problem; "meeting twice a week instead of four times a week and I'm of the opinion that any language ought to be meeting as many times a week as possible and two is problematic." Then she thought it would help to slow down the pace, she added "if I can slow down in Spanish, I can sure slow down in Russian, so I slowed it down, and so, sure enough, 102 makes, but then in order to finish that third section of the book, 201 didn't make. There's no way, it seems, to avoid this telescoping down no matter what you do. Then I had one student that needed the language requirement, so he had to go over to Mesa Community College, and it's doable, but the thing is that he was behind because I had slowed the pace down, and I said, ok, I'm not doing that again. We have this obligation… these are transfer courses, we're obligated to send students over prepared." The Russian program seems to be in this incessant spiraling-down cycle; students get into preliminary classes, build up interest, and finally the program deadlocks after students complete Russian 102. She has taught second-year Russian at the college only once, and that was the one with reduced pay. One summer in the early 1990's she was hired to teach beginning Russian as a "Faculty Associate" at ASU as well, and did so very successfully.

Dr. Story then got the idea to offer a course at Glendale Community College using an approach developed by Dr. Zev bar-Lev, a professor in the Department of Linguistics and Oriental Languages at San Diego State University. His approach is called "Sheltered Initiation Language Learning." Dr. Story incorporates this approach into a course called "Speak Russian," which is divided into two 8-week/1-credit courses: Russian 095 and 096. Dr. Story's interest was in "getting students' feet wet with Russian because Russian 101 was just such a brutal course for them." These two classes were intended to be not necessarily a degree-progress course, but a way to "introduce them (the students) to Russian in this gentle, friendly, user-friendly way." It has definitely served its purpose by opening the door for many students to further their Russian studies. Unfortunately, just like before, at some point the cycle recurs and she comes back to the invariable problem of courses being cancelled due to low enrollment. Dr. Story stresses, "I've tried that (referring to "Speak Russian"), I've tried teaching it at night, I've tried slowing the pace down, I've tried maintaining regular pace, I've tried everything I know to try and it just seems like, for Americans, Russian is so difficult." She adds, "Most Americans don't have exposure to a second language as a child, which I think is a criminal thing that we do to our children in school, and they're just like thrown to the wolves if they enroll in Russian." She has struggled with things like what book to use (she uses Marita Nummikoski's text, <u>Troika: A Communicative Approach to Russian Language, Life, and Culture</u>, John Wiley and Sons, NY et. al, 1996) because, at that time, Arizona State University and University of Arizona used two different books (i.e. ASU used Dr. Couch's <u>Практический курс русского языка</u>, and the University of Arizona used Vitalii G. Kostomarev, et.al's <u>Русский язык для всех</u>...though now both ASU and U. of A use the ACTR/Kendall-Hunt set <u>Live From Moscow</u>, Stages 1 for first year and Stage 2 for second year, complete with workbooks, audiotapes, and videotapes) but she finally decided to forget that and just concentrate on doing anything it took to just "keep Russian alive."

Dr. Story has tried various approaches to keeping it alive. In 1993, Dr. Story started the College's Russian Club. She says she "wrote the constitution, got it going, and served as the faculty advisor for several years." Various other people served for years, but today the club is "defunct." While the club was operating, Dr. Story got some much appreciated help from a local Molokan descendant, Andy Conovaloff, who "created a web-page for the club which absolutely blew the socks off everybody on this campus involved in club web-pages." (Story) Even with the club no longer existing at the school, Conovaloff has maintained this now online club, which has evolved into a club called the "Global Community Russian Club, Arizona" (http://www.russianaz.org/GCCRussianClub/index.html). Dr. Story imparts that his site presents to the people of Arizona, "everything that is going on in Arizona that concerns Russian." Story commends Conovaloff for his marvelous efforts in starting the website and to this day, doing "an absolutely fantastic job of keeping everyone informed of Russian activities in the state of Arizona." (Story) The home page for his site is <www.russianaz.org/GCCRussianClub> or one can get there by simply going to <www.russianaz.org>. (This organization is "temporarily independent of the Glendale Community College" as of November, 2004)

Dr. Story has also contributed to Russian language and literary scholarship in Arizona with some printed and oral works. She has written papers for AATSEEL (American Association of Teachers of Slavic and Eastern European Languages), published reviews, and given talks as contributions to Arizona's and the nation's Russian Language focus. For AATSEEL, Story has written a paper on "Extended-word Songs of the Molokans" and one on the Russian 'skazka', "Sister Alyonushka and Brother Ivanusha." As for publications, Story reviewed Victor Weintraub's book, A Russian Looks at America: The journey of Aleksandr Borisovich Lakier in 1857 for Slavic and East European Journal (Winter, 1976). She also wrote a review for The Doukhobor Century in Canada in Social Science Journal (Vol. 38, Number 2, 2001). Story contributed to Del Phillip's book, Методика преподавания русского языка и литературы в Америке (Синтаксис, Москва, 1995). Story wrote an article in the Arizona Language Association Newsletter (summer 2001), called "Why Study Russian?" In 2000, she gave a talk at the "Rocky Mountain/Western Slavic Association Annual Conference" in San Diego, California. This talk was on the folktale, "Sister Alyonushka and Brother Ivanushka." She also gave a talk in 2005 on Dr. Zev bar-Lev's previously mentioned method, "Sheltered Initiation Language Learning" at the Southwest Conference on Language Teaching (SWCOLT). This presentation was named, "Best of Arizona" at an AZLA (Arizona Language Association) conference the year prior.

Story was President of AZLA from 2003-2004 and on the executive board for 5 years. When Story left the board, she was cited and officially remembered for her contribution to "promoting the study of the critical languages in the state of Arizona." Dr. Story has been a member of other language associations such as AATSEEL and AAASS (American Association for the Advancement of Slavic Studies).

Dr. Story loves to share her passion for the Russian language and is completely devoted to preserving Russian at Glendale Community College, even if it means sacrificing some transfer courses temporarily. She now plans to simply "let some interest build up…build up a 'zapas'" (a 'reserve' in Russian). She suggests this because many students take courses not planning to move on and this way her "Speak Russian" conversation course could build up a 'reserve' of students over a couple of years who will be eager to dive into more Russian. All in all she keeps Russian alive, even if it is "going, but just hardly." She emphasizes that the College has been a remarkable buttress in all of her efforts to keep Russian alive. She says, "The College has been tremendously supportive. They've let classes go sometimes when I've been surprised they let them go. They bend over backwards to help Russian." With support like that, all Story needs is to sustain her continued dedication to Russian at Glendale Community College and her confidence in prospective Russian students of Arizona.

MESA COMMUNITY COLLEGE, Mesa, Arizona

Willeford, Dirk, B.A. (ASU), M.A. (U. of A.), Instructor of Russian. Interview by Lee B. Croft.

Dirk Willeford was a student of Profs. Couch, Croft, and Ekmanis at ASU in the 1970s. He graduated with honors in 1977, having been inducted into DOBRO SLOVO in 1976. He then went to the University of Arizona in Tucson where he taught as a Graduate Teaching Assistant in 1980-81 and earned his M.A. degree. Among his professors at the U. of A., he mentioned Dr. Roger Hagglund as exemplary for him, noting that he "last saw Hagglund in Russia in 1984 and would like to see him again." Dirk has traveled often to Russia—eight times while it was still part of the U.S.S.R. and nine times since. He has participated in the study-abroad programs of the Council on International Educational Exchange (CIEE) and of the Pushkin Institute of the Russian Language. Once he was acting as an interpreter for a group of opthalmologists who visited the Moscow Eye Institute operated by the famous Russian eye-surgeon, Sviatoslav Fyodorov—widely alleged to be U.S.S.R.'s richest man for popularizing in his insititute the radial keratotomy worldwide (one of his students was Dr. Leo Bores of Scottsdale, who then fought to gain medical approval for the RK here in the U.S...Bores and his wife Leara and daughter were Russian students of Dirk's and also at ASU). Fyodorov was then running for the

Dirk Willeford (L.) "advising" Mikhail Gorbachev (R.) at a Phoenix Conference in 2000. Photographer and others unknown.

Russian presidency against Boris Yeltsin. At about that time, Dirk married a Russian woman (later they divorced) and became a father to a son who is now a Russian-speaking young man, an outstanding baseball player. Dirk is athletic himself, an active tennis player, and, like Profs Batalden, Couch, Ekmanis, Croft, and Šipka, is a more-than-competent table-tennis competitor. He was hired as a Faculty Associate in Russian at ASU in the spring of 1992 and continued thereafter, mostly in the summers, until 2002.

Beginning in the fall of 1994, however, he began teaching Russian at Mesa Community College in Mesa, Arizona, one of the nation's largest community colleges. His success at growing the program there into second-year offerings meant that other instructors could be hired: Alena Cheppel, Ella Krasnova-Douglas, and Lyudmila Derizemlya all helped him for a few years each. But at this writing he is alone sustaining the program in Russian at MCC. A good number of Dirk's students go on to study Russian at ASU. Recent students from his program include Ezra Ziegler, now a car salesman at ABC Nissan who sold a car in Russian to a *Phoenix Coyotes'* hockey player, and Erin Traeger, who now, having graduated from ASU, has received a Fulbright Fellowship to send her to do graduate study in Macedonia.

Dirk has taught from several sets of materials in his career. It was he that consulted in the decision at ASU to begin using the ACTR/Kendall set, <u>Russian Stage One...</u> when Prof. Couch's retirement in spring of 2002 made his former materials unavailable. And he was the first to use these materials at ASU that summer. Now, at MCC, Dirk is using the <u>Nachalo: When in Russia...</u> text set by Sophia Lubensky, Gerard Ervin (also a U. of A. graduate and Arizona retiree), Don Jarvis, et. al.

HIGH-SCHOOL RUSSIAN LANGUAGE PROGRAMS:

In this section we profile our State's leading high-school teachers of Russian. At one time in Maricopa County (the Phoenix metropolitan area) there were more than ten high-school Russian language programs, but at this writing there is only ONE, Pat Barrett's program, from which he soon plans to retire, at Mesa, Arizona's Westwood High. We profile Dr. Nicholas Vontsolos in this section too since his program at Phoenix Central High until his retirement in 2000 was so important to our State's efforts to impart Russian-language facility and intercultural confidence to its high-school students. Dr. Vontsolos was given Ford Foundation supported scholar-teachers from Russia (Tatiana Kazanina in 1991-2 and Sergei Petrosian in 1994-5) to train with him in foreign language pedagogy and to help him. Both Pat Barrett and Dr. Nick Vontsolos were responsible as State-designated "Master Teachers" for the training of many of the State's other credentialed high-school teachers of Russian.

WESTWOOD HIGH SCHOOL, Mesa, Arizona:

Barrett, Pat: B.A., M.A., Master Teacher. (Interviewed here by James C. Nielsen)

Pat Barrett

Pat Barrett for most of his life has always had a fascination for languages. His first exposure to Russian was in college when he took it from a Ukrainian lady named Mrs. Anna Wall who taught strictly grammar. He quit after three semesters to study German, during which a friend of his took some Russian classes from Dr. Couch at ASU. His interest in Russian was renewed and he dug up his old textbooks and began studying the language. Barrett's fascination with languages continued over the years. His Russian studies never really became serious until the early 1970's, however. This was around the time when he met Dr. Lee Croft. He says he took a few classes here and there and had never really considered teaching. In 1975 he became a member of Dobro Slovo and he headed the Arizona State AATSEEL organization from 2000 to 2002. In February 1987, he was hired to teach Russian at Westwood High School and, due to the recent Helsinki Accords, there was an influx of Russian Students. This was a very exciting time for him. According to Barrett about 95 percent of the students were from the Church of Jesus Christ of Latter-day Saints due to the Gorbachev impetus and the Church's drive to get missionaries there with the collapse of communism. He describes the program as being pretty gung-ho with lessons he designed being broadcast via television to different classrooms in Maricopa County. ASU student Dan Secklin and Russian natives Janna Malkina and Katia Avedisian helped as site aides. He says that the program was enjoyed by the students. For 4 years, 1997-2001, there was no Russian taught at Westwood High. It was revived mostly because of a Russian Club that existed during that time. While Barrett taught Russian, his colleague Melissa Gamble, a social studies teacher, taught Russian History. Mr. Barrett mentioned his preference for the "Communicative Competence" method of teaching language over the "Proficiency Method" advocated by others. In 2002 Pat Barrett was recognized by the Arizona Language Association (AZLA) as its TEACHER OF THE YEAR, an honor applauded by all who know him. At this writing (March 2007), Mr. Barrett is currently teaching Russian at Westwood High School, but he is soon retiring and there are currently no replacements planned, meaning, that with his retirement, Mesa Westwood High School's Russian Language program, the State's only remaining one, will end.

Here follows the text of an email message the authors received from Pat Barrett:

"RE: RUSSIAN IN ARIZONA

Entering ASU in 1959 (it had just gotten university status, previously having been called "Arizona State College"), I found an unusual language, Russian, being taught by Anna Wall or "Mrs. OOal," who lived in "Scottsdailye." Around 1975 or earlier, I started hanging around the Russian department as an unofficial stalker because my buddy had taken some courses with Dr. Couch and I realized I wanted to know more Russian. Over the next ten years or so I took courses in Russian Poetry, Comp and Conv, History of Russian…all from Dr. Croft. I even sent him a student from the mental health center I was working at. I'm not sure how that ever worked out…"

I (Lee Croft) interject here the explanation that Pat Barrett was working at that time as a psychiatric social worker in the heavily African-American neighborhoods of central Phoenix. There he counseled a troubled patient named Arthur Adair, then quite obese and afflicted with unmanaged diabetes among other physical and psychological problems. But as a younger man "Art Adair" had been a noted AAU and "Golden Gloves" boxer, taking matches at Phoenix Madison Square Garden, the McDowell Street Sportatorium, Celebrity Theater and other venues. In the late 1960's he trained at a gym on the northwest corner of 18th Street and Washington (it was burned out during the race riots in summer 1968 and subsequently demolished) where I also was in training as a boxer. Since we were in the same weight class (156 lbs., light middle) we were frequently paired as sparring opponents in the ring there. How we did hammer each other in many a round, trying to establish ourselves in the tough company of professional boxers who also trained there! So, when, a decade later, I encountered him, clearly not the typical university student, sitting in my ASU classroom waiting for instruction in Russian 101, I did not recognize him. He had changed more than I had, I think it fair to say, and so he only "seemed somehow familiar to me" in the class's first week or so. He said nothing to me during this time, and he performed creditably in the class. But, finally I asked him, "How do I know you?" He said, holding up his fist, "You probably remember this right hand. I still remember your left. You had the best left jab I ever faced." Of course I then recognized him as Art Adair, my oft-times ring opponent, and I was stunned to see him in that context, such another world from the one we had shared. And it was Pat Barrett who had sent him there, getting his way paid somehow, as a kind of "escape therapy." As I recall, Art stuck it out in the RUS-101 and even earned a "B" grade. But then he did not return to ASU classes, and we did not really stay in touch. A few years later, Pat Barrett told me that he had suffered the amputation of a leg and was walking on a prosthetic limb.

(resuming Pat Barrett's email) "In 1987 I switched careers and began teaching social studies in Mesa where the LDS Church realized that missionaries were going to be let into Russia. Suddenly my dabblings in Russian catapulted me to star status in the district and I began a program that has continued to this day, but will end with my retirement this year (there was a four-year hiatus when Russian bottomed out in the 1990's, but it bounced back). All during this time, from the 1970's on, I was a member of AATSEEL, even serving gloriously as president for a time.

Let me cite several people and institutions who stimulated and supported my interest in keeping this program going (the last in the State, I believe):

first and foremost, Dr. Lee Croft, providing scholarship with humor, along with doughnuts at the AATSEEL meetings; the whole AATSEEL membership in AZ who put up with my hectoring them to join in the 'communicative competence' movement in language teaching; Dr. Phillips, whose program at the U. of A. sent me off to Russia for 5 weeks to discover so much about the country; Cindy Seaborg Humphries encouraged me greatly that first year as did Dr. Steve Batalden. The Critical Languages Institute gave me that 8-week Macedonian course with Eleni Buzarovska, one of the best language classes I ever took; Dr. Joyce Story has been my colleague in both AATSEEL and AZLA and has been president of AZLA and put me forth for Teacher of the Year for AZLA. She and I constantly represented Russian to the rest of the foreign language teaching community in AZ. As AZLA president last year I put on a regional conference (SWCOLT) where we again made the presence of Russian felt.

I've enjoyed the ride. Thanks to all. Pbarrett@cox.net."

PHOENIX CENTRAL HIGH SCHOOL, PHOENIX, ARIZONA

Vontsolos, Nicholas, B.A., M.A., Ph.D. (Ohio State University), Faculty Associate in Russian at ASU and Master Teacher, International Magnet School Program. Interview by Barry Boosman.

Dr. Nicholas Vontsolos has taught Russian in Arizona for more than two decades, but his total time teaching Russian was more than forty years. Though an American citizen, he spent a significant part of his youth in Greece. He first began to study Russian as an undergraduate in International Studies at Ohio State University, where he enrolled in

Dr. Nicholas "Nick" Vontsolos

Russian classes to fulfill the language requirement. He received his BA in 1960, and did some post-graduate work there over the next year. After that, he studied Russian in the U.S. Army at the Defense Language Institute, and completed the course with honors in 1962. Over the next few years, he earned his MA in Slavic Linguistics and Literature, with a focus on Russian literature (his thesis was on the perspective presented of the Decembrist Uprising in Soviet fiction), from Ohio State University, supporting himself there as a Graduate Teaching Assistant. He taught Scientific Russian at Battelle Memorial Institute, and visited Russia for the first time in summer of 1964 as an assistant to the program coordinator. In 1965, he led the program. That same year, he won a National Defense Education Act fellowship. In 1967, Dr. Vontsolos participated in an Inter-

University Committee on Travel Grants (IUCTG) program to study at Moscow State University, and spent the next year there.

In 1969, Dr. Vontsolos received a position as a lecturer in Russian at the University of Arizona, and taught there for five years. In 1974, he went to teach at Pars College in Teheran, Iran, but left in 1975 due to the political climate. From Iran, he went to Athens, Greece, where he had relatives and taught at the American College of Greece (Deree) for the next eight years. His Ph.D. in Slavic Linguistics and Literature from Ohio State University was completed while he was in Greece, in 1978. He returned to the US in 1984 and taught as a visiting professor at the State University of New York in Albany for one year. In 1986, he returned to Arizona, where he taught Russian as a Faculty Associate at Arizona State University until 1991, and taught Russian at Phoenix Central High School until 2004, authoring his own textual materials. While at Central High School, he served as the Chairman of the Department of Foreign Languages and initiated a student exchange with Russian schools. Since 1995, he has also served as an adjunct professor for Western International University (though he did not teach Russian there, but Humanities).

Over the course of his career, Dr. Vontsolos has taught Russian language courses, courses in Russian translation, numerous courses in Russian literature (including seminars on Tolstoy, Dostoevsky, and Soviet Literature), Slavic Linguistics (Old Church Slavic, History of Russian, Comparative Slavic Linguistics, and the Structure of Modern Russian), and Russian, Soviet, and Balkan History. In addition to the courses about or relating to Russian, Dr. Vontsolos has taught a number of other courses in various fields. In literature, he has taught comparative literature and the genre of the short story. In linguistics, he has taught introduction to linguistics, applied linguistics, historical linguistics, and contrastive structures. In History, he has taught world history, 18th century European history, and European history. He has also taught US Government, International Relations, western thought as reflected in art and literature from Homeric and Biblical times to the present, survey of philosophy, survey of world religions, the etymology of English words with Latin and Greek origins, Greek, English, and English as a second language.

Dr. Vontsolos has also published a number of scholarly works, including conference papers, critical reviews and books; and has a number of works in progress. He has also been active with AATSEEL (the American Association of Teachers of Slavic and Eastern European Languages), the MLA (Modern Language Association), and the Modern Greek Studies

Association. Dr. Vontsolos is fluent in English, Russian, and Greek; and has a working knowledge of French, German, Polish, and Serbo-Croatian. He is also widely traveled. Currently, at Arizona State University, there is a student award, the **Dr. Nick Vontsolos "Я НЕ СДАМСЯ" ("I WILL NOT GIVE UP") Perseverance Award**, endowed in his name. The first awardee, Enrique Canales (2002), the first native speaker of Spanish to receive a degree in Russian at ASU, was once a student in Dr. Vontsolos' classes.

When I (Barry Boosman) spoke with Dr. Vontsolos he expressed some of his ideas regarding education. He stressed the importance of a broad education, the importance of Greek and classical education in general, and the importance of travel in order to experience diverse cultures (all things which are reflected in his own experiences).

I (Lee Croft) want to interject here a relation of how, this past December 22, 2006 during the Christmas season, Nick's wife Cathy surprised him at a friend's home with a party on the occasion of his seventieth birthday. People from all over the country and indeed the world came to fete him, and all had some tale to tell about his wonderful knowledge and his sense of humor. The guests included all three of his sons (George, Alexei, and Michael), his three granddaughters (Melina, Alexi, and Nicole (named after Nick) of George and Lourdes), and his grandson Lucas (of Alexei and Lisa). His son Michael and my son Hayden are life-long friends. Hayden, who could not be at the gathering, sent a token gift of chocolate, something he had often received as a gift from Nick, who was reprising the days of his childhood during WWII in Greece when soldiers of both sides would gift the native children with chocolate. So Hayden received a thank you note on this (including a poem Nick had once written about chocolate) from that old sage, "Salokhin Solostnov," Nick's backwardsly spelled humorous personna. Like the other teachers of <u>RUSSIAN IN ARIZONA</u>, he is a very special person.

NORTHERN ARIZONA UNIVERSITY IN FLAGSTAFF

Anne Slobodchikoff, B.A., M.A. (University of California at Berkeley), Senior Lecturer in Modern Languages (French and Russian).

Anne Slobodchikoff from
http://www.cal.nau.edu/languages/people/slobodchikoff.html

Anne Slobodchikoff came to Northern Arizona University in January of 1985 and revived instruction there in Russian that was initiated in the late 1960s by Victor Kobylin, who retired to Santa Barbara, California in 1974. In the next decade, Anne built the Russian course offerings and the enrollment at NAU to the point where a Russian minor was approved for its students. By herself, and in addition to her duties teaching French, she offers three-years of Russian language courses, with a fourth year of independent study possible. In 1989, along with Lee and Lesley Hoyt Croft of the ASU community (and others, see photo on pp. 74), she went to Leningrad (as it was then still called) to inspect U. of A. Prof. Del Phillips' study-abroad program facilities (e.g. the "Chaika" residence on the Baltic Sea strand) as a possibility for her Russian students. Subsequently she took the position of Assistant Director of the UARA program as her students participated. But in the 1990s she developed her own study-abroad program in Russia in a locale far from the ordinary Russian study-abroad sites and culturally more "akin" to her Flagstaff, Arizona, environment. This unique program is centered in the city of Barnaul, Siberia, and the offering there gives students the opportunity for home-stays and for travel on the Trans-Siberian Railway. Anne helps the students pay for their study abroad experience by arranging a yearly "Russian meal" in Flagstaff, which is now eagerly anticipated by Russophiles throughout the state. She has hosted at NAU at least one conference of the Arizona Chapter of AATSEEL and represents her university well as a key teacher of RUSSIAN IN ARIZONA.

Anne writes in a recent email to me (LBC) that her "older son Michael and his Russian wife Tanya are living in Tucson. She is getting a Ph.D. in the Linguistics Program there and he is getting one in Political Science. They have a 1-year old son named Nikolay."

THE UNIVERSITY OF ARIZONA IN TUCSON

This history of <u>RUSSIAN IN ARIZONA</u> is clearly biased in favor of the role of Arizona State University, presently the bigger university in the bigger city with the bigger Russian enrollment. But, of course, the University of Arizona in Tucson was our state's FIRST university. It had, and still has, the ONLY solely dedicated academic Department of Russian in the state (at ASU we have always been and are still a "Section" of something larger…DFL, DLL, SILC, whatever). And the University of Arizona has the state's only GRADUATE program in Russian, the M.A. program from which I (Lee Croft) once graduated into a fully supported Cornell University Ph.D. program. Now I, the lead author of this book, as a faculty member at ASU, focus its content on the role of ASU (and my role) in the history of the teaching of Russian in Arizona, relatively slighting in this focus the role of the University of Arizona. The two institutions have their rivalries, and our two Russian progams have had their rivalries also, but, as an alumnus of BOTH programs and as a forty-year student and teacher of Russian in this country, I believe that if you can compare your program in any positive way to the University of Arizona's program you are indeed doing well. They are in all ways, and especially in student potentiation, superb. Check them out at http://russian.arizona.edu. On that website you will find the following depiction of the current University of Arizona Russian faculty (I'm adding other information to the entries here and subtracting the office addresses and telephone numbers):

UA Dept. of Russian and Slavic faculty and staff Retreat: (L-R) John Leafgren, Delbert Phillips, Judi Greil, Sarah Monks, Head Teresa Polowy behind Roza Simkhovich, Romy Taylor, Grace Fielder, Michael Brewer, and John Garrard. Photo from www.russian.arizona.edu.

Adele Barker (PhD). Professor *affiliated with the department.* Soviet literature and popular culture and Soviet and post-Soviet women's writing and cultural studies.

Alexander Dunkel (PhD, New York University). Associate Professor. 20th Century Russian literature; 20th Century Russian culture; problems of Russian idiomatic translation. Founder of the *Critical Languages Program.*

Grace Fielder (PhD, UCLA). Professor. Slavic Balkan Linguistics; syntax and semantics; discourse analysis.

John Garrard (PhD, Columbia University). Professor and former Head of the Department. 19th and 20th Century Russian literature and culture.

George Gutsche (PhD, University of Wisconsin). Professor and former Head of the Department. Former National Executive-Secretary of AATSEEL. Russian literature (19th and 20th Century); literary criticism; Russian culture; Balkan cultures; Russian language, technology and language instruction.

John Leafgren (PhD, University of Virginia). Associate Professor. Graduate Advisor. Former President of Arizona State AATSEEL. Russian, Polish, and Bulgarian linguistics; morphosyntax, phonology, discourse analysis.

Delbert Phillips (PhD, New York University). Professor, University Distinguished Teaching Professor. Pedagogy, Russian language, Russian literature. Former President of Arizona State AATSEEL. Director of the University of Arizona Russian Abroad Program (UARA) since 1987.

Teresa Polowy (PhD, University of British Columbia). Associate Professor and current HEAD of the Department. 20th Century Russian literature; contemporary Russian women's prose fiction; social and literary reflections of alcohol use; Russian language; Ukrainian literature and language.

Roza Simkhovich (MA, University of Arizona). Senior Lecturer. Native speaker, Russian language and conversation. Faculty DOBRO SLOVO honorary advisor. Producer and director of Russian-language plays. Founder and Director of the yearly *Arizona Russian Business Forum*, now arranging its 14th session.

Romy Taylor (PhD, USC). Visiting Assistant Professor. Genre theory, poetics, 19th Century poetry, 19th Century women writers, Black intellectuals, Black Americans in the USSR in the 1930s.

STAFF:

Judi Greil. Administrative Associate. Graduate Coordinator.

Sarah Monks. Administrative Assistant, Assistant Director of the *Arizona Russian Business Forum.*

Here is a historical chronology of the University of Arizona's Department of Russian and Slavic Languages and Literatures. It was prepared by former Chair George Gutsche and given to Aimee M. Raymer during his interview with her in March, 2006.

History of the Department

1960-61: Joe Malik, Jr. was hired to develop a full Russian program at UA; he had been Head of the Slavic Department at the University of Texas. First courses in Russian were offered in the German Department in 1958-59. Joe joined this department as an Associate Professor.

1961-2: The Department of German was renamed the Department of German and Russian.

1962-63: The Arizona chapter of AATSEEL was organized. The U. of A. Russian Club was organized by Joe.

1963-64: A Russian major (BA in Russian) was available for the first time.

1964-65: A local chapter of the National Slavic Studies Honorary, Dobro Slovo was established.

1967-68: Joe Malik was chosen Executive Secretary-Treasurer of national AATSEEL; headquarters were moved to UA.

1968-69: The M.A. degree in Russian became available.

1970-71: The Russian Section of the Department of German and Russian became independent as the Department of Russian.

1971-72: The name of the Department was changed to the Department of Russian and Slavic Languages. 45 Russian majors.

1984: Joe Malik retired as Executive Secretary-Treasurer of AATSEEL, (succeeded by Prof. Sanford C. Couch of ASU, headquarters moved)

1986: Joe Malik retired as Head of the Department of Russian and Slavic, succeeded by Dr. John Garrard, who came from the University of Virginia. Malik continues to teach in the department.

1987: Dr. Delbert Phillips initiates the University of Arizona Russia Abroad Program.

1989: Joe Malik retired from the University of Arizona, becomes a Professor Emeritus, Dr. Garrard is succeeded as Head by Dr. Margaret B. Gibson.

1993: Dr. George Gutsche comes from Northern Illinois University, becomes Acting Head, then Head, 1994-2004. Roza Simkhovich begins the Arizona Russian Business Forum.

2004--: Dr. Teresa Polowy becomes the Head of the Department. The faculty is composed of nine full-time faculty members: Professors Grace Fielder, John Garrard, George Gutsche and (Distinguished Teaching Associate, then 2006-, Full Professor) Delbert Phillips; Associate Professors Alexander Dunkel, John Leafgren and (Head) Teresa Polowy; Senior Lecturer Roza Simkhovich; and, in a single tenure-trial Assistant Professor's position there have been, since 2004: Lisa Wakamiya (who left to take a position in Florida), then Meghan Murphy-Lee (who left to take a position at the Military Academy at West Point), and now (2006-7) there is Visiting Assistant Professor Romy Taylor. Undergraduate Russian language enrollment is approximately 100 students, with the MA program enrolling another 10. In addition, the Russian Literature in Translation courses offered through Comparative Literature add significantly to the subject-area enrollment. Teaching these courses are George Gutsche and also a departmentally "affiliated" faculty member, Professor Adele Barker. Essentially, this means that the U. of A. has TEN faculty members teaching approximately 200 students per semester Russian Language and Literature at undergraduate and graduate levels. In addition, they offer periodic instruction in other Slavic languages (Czech was offered in Malik's day, and Bulgarian by Profs. Fielder and Leafgren). Prof. Dunkel has founded a "Critical Languages Program" with exterior funding that offers instruction and credit in a large number of less-commonly taught languages as well.

We will start the "faculty profiles" of the University of Arizona faculty with reminiscences of Joe Malik, Jr. and some material relevant to his AATSEEL functions.

Reminiscences of Joe Malik, Jr. (1920-1998)

by:

Lee B. Croft

In the spring semester of 1969 I was student-teaching Russian at Saguaro High School in Scottsdale, Arizona, and thinking about what I wanted to do next. At Sandy Couch's suggestion, I applied for admission to the University of Arizona's MA program in Russian. Sandy thought that "Joe Malik" might be able to give me a "teaching assistantship" based on my positive experience at Saguaro High. At the time I didn't even know what a teaching assistantship was. But, of course, I got one and I found out.

I remember my first meeting with Joe Malik in the central Russian Department office in the University of Arizona's Modern Languages Building. He looked physically fit. His dark hair was slicked back trimly. And he was well dressed, wearing a complete suit and tie. He spoke forcefully, stressing that Russian programs are "built from the ground up," that RUS-1A was the "basis upon which everything else rests," "the place where we create the audience for our own expertise." That is why we Graduate Teaching Assistants were "so important" to the effort...the effort to prevail over the Soviet Russians in the space race, the bomb race, the WHOLE race...because we were to "teach the 1A's." Our students, if we served them well, would become the next generation of diplomats, intelligence analysts, foreign service officers, foreign broadcasters, foreign news correspondents...and, of course and most importantly, TEACHERS. Certainly Malik imparted into us a grand sense of mission. And to see that we learned method too, he gave us into the teaching supervision of Delbert Phillips, a doctoral candidate in Russian literature at New York University, who had just come into the department as well. Russian would be taught to us, he said, by "Bor-EEss," meaning Dr. Boriss Roberts, a Russophone Latvian who had studied with Malik at the University of Pennsylvania. Boriss was truly a pedagogue "of the old school." He slowly read his lectures in Russian for us to copy longhand, and he used to paraphrase one of Gogol's characters in characterizing his teaching: "Rigor, Rigor, Rigor" ((3x) "строгость, строгость, строгость"). In addition, we were to avail ourselves of the opportunity to learn of the recent advances in linguistics from new Lecturer Nicholas "Nick" Vontsolos, who had come there that year too from Ohio State University. Malik also gave us a talk about the need to keep the central office clean and neat, and about how the first person into the office every day was expected to "make the coffee." "Anyone who thinks that cleaning the office and making the coffee is beneath them...I'll mop up the office with," he threatened. We (TA's Louis Prazma, Paul Weadon and I) were awed. Since I was assigned the earliest section of RUS-1A...the 7:40 AM section...I made the coffee.

Large Figures in the history of <u>RUSSIAN IN ARIZONA</u>: Prof. Snaford Couch (ASU, 1962-2002) and Prof. Joe Malik, Jr. (U. of A., 1960-1989). Photo by Valerie Hathaway at ASU, 1991.

Joe Malik wanted us all to dress up professionally in suit jackets and ties. He said that to be a professional you had to look like a professional. And Joe Malik was an "organization" man. He was the Executive-Secretary of our profession's primary organization, the American Association of Teachers of Slavic and East European Languages…AATSEEL…and he ruled it like a Tsar. The president of the organization, elected every year, was picked by him as a figurehead. He wanted us all to join AATSEEL and we did. His opinion was that this organization was much stronger in the ideological conflict than any of its constituent members would be individually. "The whole is even greater than the sum of its parts," he would say. He viewed AATSEEL as a kind of union. If he saw on someone's resume that they claimed to be an

AATSEEL member, he would look on his rolls to see whether their yearly dues were paid...and if not, he would telephone them and tell them that if they didn't pay up immediately he would telephone their supervisor and inform that they had misrepresented themselves on their resume. He involved all of his faculty, and we TA's were clearly considered "faculty," in the administration of the yearly AATSEEL convention, held in large cities' prominent hotels and conference centers. We personned the registration tables and did the "gopher" work of running the convention. But this was exciting for us, since he had the University of Arizona (not AATSEEL, and he paid his own way personally) pay for our travel and our hotel stays, and he always introduced us to all of our new field's 'big shots.' We noticed that they were uniformly afraid of him. He was a World War II combat veteran (severely wounded as a B-24 pilot in North Africa and hospitalized in Florida), a no-nonsense take-charge person not afraid to transcend excessive thought with quick actions. I can recall his strategy at the yearly AATSEEL business meetings where he would stand up with a blank paper in his hands and announce to all the present membership the "nominating committee's slate of officer candidates." There really was no "nominating committee" but him, but someone prearranged would "second" his nomination and the figurehead president would call for the vote. It was almost always unanimous...even Soviet style in some ways. But it worked. AATSEEL prospered immensely and became effective as a professional organization under his tenure as Executive Secretary.

Joe Malik also strongly advocated that we become members of the other professional organizations that touched our lives...the MLA and its affiliate RMMLA, the AAASS, the ACTR, LSA, SWCOLT, ACTFL, AZLA...you name it, he thought we should all join it. And not only that, but take it over...control the panels and the officer positions. We (Sandy Couch and I) would travel to these conventions to participate and take over these organizations in Joe Malik's own Volkswagen van. I remember long drives with diverse company to places like Albuquerque, Denver, El Paso (now THAT was a trip), and Las Vegas. On these drives I was able to "bond" with many a valuable colleague. I remember especially the U. of A. TA's Dan Winters, Rick Ruth and Al Cannon, as well as later department Head Margaret Gibson, who patiently tolerated our male jokes and antics on these trips.

In 1984 Joe Malik resigned the Executive Secretaryship of the national AATSEEL, designating our ASU Professor Sandy Couch to succeed him.

Sandy did not last long in the job. He was too seriously committed to democratic modes of operation, allowing a president or two to be elected who did not understand that they were mere figureheads. They rewrote the AATSEEL bylaws to make the presidency and advisory board more powerful. Also, Sandy disagreed with the subsequent boards about whether AATSEEL should pay for the officers' travel to the yearly conventions. The new officers favored the travel subsidies, but Sandy continued to pay his own way like Joe Malik had done, and wanted the other officers to do the same, arguing that such largess to the elite would decrease AATSEEL's impressive bank balance. Only two years later, Sandy resigned under board pressure, and, embittered, stopped participating in AATSEEL functions, even locally. But the national headquarters of the AATSEEL executive secretaryship soon returned to the University of Arizona under the administration of George Gutsche. Later it was run from the Tucson-area retirement abode of former Ohio State University professor (and U. of A. alum) Gerard Ervin.

The Arizona AATSEEL meetings, held semesterly, were our state colleagues' main forum for both professional and personal interaction. Most often these meetings occurred at ASU in the fall and at the University of Arizona in the spring, though meetings have also occurred at Northern Arizona University, the American Graduate School of International Management-Thunderbird Campus in Glendale, Yavapai Community College in Flagstaff, and even at the home of then AzAATSEEL President Pat Barrett in Mesa. In the 1970's the AzAATSEEL meetings featured after-session softball games between ASU and U. of A. students (the U. of A. won the last of these in 1981 with Joe Malik insisting to bat just months after a heart operation) and other less conventional competitions (e.g. the arm-wrestling contests or the table-tennis games between me and the U. of A. "champions" that I never lost). I have videotape of a post-session gathering at my former home in Phoenix showing Joe Malik's amazing feat—reciting the names of all the U.S. states and their capitals in thirty seconds or less. More recently the spring meetings in Tucson have often featured Russian plays, produced and directed by Instructor Roza Simkhovich with U of A Russian students acting in the featured roles. Often too, this occasion has been used for the induction of the University of Arizona's excellent students into their chapter of DOBRO SLOVO, the National Slavic Studies Honorary, which also has a chapter at ASU (the Epsilon Epsilon charter plaque is now in my ASU office). The Arizona State AATSEEL, as opposed to the national AATSEEL (of which I've been a member since 1969), has no dues and operates very collegially to encourage our scholarship and our recognition of student excellence. Last year I realized that I had presented more than thirty times at AzAATSEEL. I am attaching the list to this document so the reader can see the kind of topics I presented. One of Joe Malik's own memorable presentations was an astounding list of "high achieving Americans of Czech Heritage." Colleagues talked about it for years. And each of these presentations was just one, usually of five to seven others, presented by the people described in this book, and I cherish to this day almost ALL of the programs and associated handouts in my office files.

In 1987 as Joe Malik was considering retirement, I came up with the idea of endowing and maintaining a fund in the ASU Foundation entitled the "Joe Malik, Jr. Arizona Slavic Studies Award Fund." This fund was, as I announced to the AzAATSEEL on November 18, 1987 (the month after my son Hayden was born), to be used for "Honoring Our Own." The idea was to provide professional recognition for those who had advanced Slavic Studies in the State of Arizona. Later, after Malik's death, a national award of similar title was begun by the national AATSEEL administration. But our award has been given only to colleagues who have spent twenty years or more of their lives in the service of Arizona Slavic Studies. The award plaque (shaped like the State of Arizona and with the Arizona State governmental seal), which I designed at Joe Malik's suggestion, features the ancient Slavic letters of the Glagolitic alphabet (the national AATSEEL logo also includes Glagolitic letters for AATSEEL) spelling out the words "Слава-Glory" and "Честь-Honor." The inscription says: "Given by the judgment of peers for sustained outstanding contribution to the advancement of Slavic Studies in the State of Arizona." The first award committee was composed of just Joe Malik and me. Joe wanted the first award in his name to go to Dr. Boriss Roberts, who was retiring after twenty-six years of overload service. This happened in 1988, and then Dr. Roberts was added to the Board as was each subsequent awardee. The list is now:

Dr. Boriss Roberts, U. of A., 1988 (Boriss passed away in 2006)

Dr. Margaret Gibson, U. of A., 1989, (Margaret passed away in 1999)

Dr. Snaford C. Couch, ASU, 1991

Dr. Delbert D. Phillips, U. of A., 1992

Dr. Lee B. Croft, ASU, 1993 (the above group of awardees and Joe Malik insisted that I receive the award that I myself initiated)

Dr. Stephen K. Batalden, ASU, 1998

Dr. Frederick C. Giffin, ASU, 2000

When Steve Batalden won the award in April of 1998 I told him I thought that I could arrange for him to meet his award's namesake, Joe Malik, Jr. I called Joe's wife Paula and asked her about Joe, whom I knew to be suffering from Alzheimer's Syndrome. She told me that she had taken over Joe's care personally after more than one assisted living center had been forced by his erratic behavior to expel him. But she agreed to host a lunch for us with Joe at their long-time home on Calle Canis in Tucson. When Steve and I arrived, got out of the car and approached the entry, Joe opened the door and came out with Paula to meet us. He looked physically fine to me, the same as always, but he said nothing as he shook our hands. Very uncharacteristically, he was wearing a bright red T-shirt.

Lee Croft, Joe Malik, Jr, and Stephen Batalden at the Malik home, April 1998. Photo by Paula Malik.

It was a T-shirt that I had printed on a self-made silkscreen twenty-two years before and given to him. On it was a wild-eyed likeness of Leo Tolstoy that he liked surrounded by the Russian inscription: Русский Кружок Хочет Вас ("The Russian Club (Circle) Wants you!"...an early draft, circa 1976, of my later popular design using the Russian title of Tolstoy's story "God Sees the Truth, but Waits"). Paula had dressed him in this T-shirt, remembering that I had made it and that it bore my 1976 copyright claim on it in fine print. Immediately we posed as Paula took the photo given here. Steve showed Joe the award plaque, pointed to the Glagolitic letters and said: "This says "Slava i Chest'" ("Glory and Honor") in Glagolitic letters." Joe responded: "There was no "chest'" in Glagolitic." This was true...in Glagolitic-alphabet times the word now rendered as "chest'" for "honor" was pronounced differently as "chist'" and written equivalent to Cyrillic "чьсть." It was the only sensible utterance (showing the impressive knowledge buried somewhere in his disease-affected brain) to come out of Joe Malik during that entire visit. The lunch conversation was, from him, a complete and disturbing scramble, a filigree of names and phrases not even connected to the topics of our conversation. The Joe Malik I had so long known and revered was gone. The "Golden Years" of retirement that Paula had looked forward to in his company were an inaccessible dream. As we were leaving, Joe hunted frantically for his cigar box filled with harmonicas. He was a musically talented man who liked the Polka music of Frankie Yankovic and others. As he found the box of harmonicas in the living room, I wondered if his ability to express himself in music would be as profoundly deteriorated as his ability to express himself in speech. He began to play, and it was no polka. It was hard to make out, but then I recognized it. It was, very roughly, the hymn: "Abide with me, fast falls the eventide./The darkness deepens, Lord with me abide./When other helpers fail and comforts flee,/ Help of the helpless, O, abide with me." Steve and I were both shedding tears as we got in the car and left. Joe Malik died a month later, his operation-mended heart getting insufficient instruction from his brain to continue.

At the memorial ceremony at the Malik's home, I read the following:

"Joe Malik, Jr.: A Few Remarks at his Funeral Gathering, May 31, 1998

(These remarks pertain to Joe Malik's global legacy...his impact on the world)

Joe Malik, to paraphrase Anna Akhmatova, always knew "what was lying on the balance...what...REALLY what... was taking place" in his time...a time when "the hour for courage struck on all our clocks." What was taking place, in Joe Malik's time, were the global conflicts of ideas...freedom and democracy versus facism in World War II, then freedom and democracy versus communism in the long cold war with the Soviet Union. What was lying on the balance was the very survival of our American culture of freedom and democracy... These were indeed times for courage. And courage did not forsake Joe Malik in these struggles. As a young man he fought as a soldier, giving up his precious time to risk his life and his health so that our way of life would not only survive but triumph over the threat of facism. And as a mature man he was even more effective in bringing about the triumph of freedom and democracy over what Ronald Reagan termed the "Evil Empire" of the Soviet Union. For Joe Malik knew that the most effective combatants in the conflict of ideologies were the teachers. So a teacher he became, and a great one, then an organizer of teachers, and a career-long professional advocate for the teachers. He knew that every student he equipped with the knowledge of the Russian language and culture...every student he enabled to go forth and teach yet others...were worth, in their aggregation, far more in bringing about the great "change of mind" of our adversary than were all the troops and the missiles and the other implements of war. And so...(this is what his children and his grandchildren, who think of him in other ways, should know)...he was genuinely a hero in the conflict of ideas...a leading American teacher, incrementally bringing about the conversion of our global adversary by his advancing of Slavic Studies and by his advancing the myriad students whose focus he changed, whose own contributions he enabled. As we are all now more secure, as millions have been freed from fear...his legacy is large.

(These remarks pertain to Joe Malik's personal legacy...his impact on me)

As for me, Joe Malik was ever my mentor, my role model, and my champion...certainly one of the most influential figures in my life...from the days when he granted me, an undergraduate Math major, a graduate TA-ship in Russian and wrote to my draft board (and to Del Phillips' and

Arizona Daily Star B-6
Tucson, Sunday, May 31, 1998

Joe Malik dies, gave UA Russian program national prominence

By Tom Collins
The Arizona Daily Star

Joe Malik Jr., who built the UA Russian and Slavic Languages Department into a nationally recognized program, died early Thursday morning. He was 78.

Malik died of heart failure at his daughter's ranch near Benson. He had also suffered from Alzheimer's disease, family members said.

In 1960, Malik was hired away from the University of Texas to start a Russian program at the University of Arizona.

"With Sputnik and all that, it really set Russian on fire," said Pauline Malik, his wife. "Everybody wanted to learn."

Malik was the first Russian professor in Arizona; the department became independent from the UA's German Department in 1970.

He headed the department until 1985, and he retired in 1989. By then he had built bachelor's and master's programs that rivaled any in the country, said George Gutsche, the current department head.

The department currently has eight faculty members and has from 35 to 70 graduate and undergraduate majors, Gutsche said.

Pauline Malik said her husband thought learning Russian was important for students' futures.

"Joe was one to go out and find people and educate them about why this is important," she said.

Joe Malik saw education as the best route to ending communism, said Lee Croft, an Arizona State University Slavic Languages professor who studied under him from 1968-70.

"In his time we were engaged in a conflict of ideas," Croft said. "Freedom and democracy vs. fascism and, later, freedom and democracy vs. communism.

"Joe Malik was a primary combatant in that conflict... The most effective combatants in a conflict of ideas are teachers."

On Oct. 21, 1968, Malik saw firsthand the artillery of that conflict. He was in a hotel in Prague, Czechoslovakia, when Russian tanks rolled in, squelching anti-Soviet resistance. Malik's daughter was about to enter an exchange program there.

"They came down to the lobby and there was a Soviet tank blocking the door," Croft said.

Croft said Malik used his Czech language skills to get his

> He was in a hotel in Prague, Czechoslovakia, when Russian tanks rolled in, squelching anti-Soviet resistance.

daughter, the Czech student involved in the exchange, another American professor and that professor's wife out of the country.

Pauline Malik said that above all, her husband of 53 years valued students, and that was the key toward building the department.

"He was most interested in students, not so much in research, but in working with the students," Pauline Malik said. "His office was open 7 a.m. to 5 p.m."

In the end, it was not being able to remember students that frustrated the Charles, Ill., native, Pauline Malik said.

"For a person who could name over a hundred students in a class ... to get Alzheimer's and not be able to remember anyone's name was very hard," she said.

Malik was executive secretary of the American Association of Teachers of Slavic and European Languages for 17 years, and served on the board of directors of Saguaro Credit Union.

There will be no funeral service for Malik, but a memorial service is planned for today at 5 p.m. at the family home, 6933 E. Calle Canis.

Malik is survived by his wife, two daughters, Lisa and Tamara, and a son, Joe Malik III.

others) in support of my deferment from Vietnam-era military service, for further study at Cornell and in finding me the job I have today at ASU, through his constant example as the Executive-Secretary of AATSEEL, right up to his post-retirement support of my contentious promotion. He was always, as my own father, a boxer in his youth, would say, a "good man to have in your corner." I certainly thank him for that…and for the many precious memories…for those wonderful road trips in the VW Van to professional meetings which bonded many of us non-professionally for life…for his vociferous resistance to my attempts to convince him he was really a Republican…For his greeting me in ribald fashion with the question: "How's your whole…family?" Indeed his character is deeply stamped in mine…in whatever I have done and whatever I will do, his legacy is large.

--Lee B. Croft"

"Publishing Ourselves—A History of AzAATSEEL"
Professor Lee B. Croft, ASU
Arizona AATSEEL Conference at ASU,
Tempe, AZ. November 4, 2006

A List of Prof. Croft's Presentations at AzAATSEEL conferences, 1973-

Prof. Lee B. Croft, ASU (President 3X: 1975-6, 1986-8, 1992-4):

1. "Modality in Russian" collateral with AZ ACTFL, U of A Tucson, Nov. 10, 1973
2. "Covert Sound Symbolism in Russian" ASU, Tempe, March 9, 1974
3. "Palindromic Symmetry and Poetic Structure" U of A, Tucson, Nov. 2, 1974
4. "The 'Dramatic Imperative' and the Aorist: A Case of Linguistic Analogy?" ASU, Tempe, Nov. 8, 1975
5. "Attempts at a Revival of Russian in Maricopa County High Schools," U. of A, Tucson, Nov. 13, 1976
6. "American Institute for Foreign Study Tour Possibilities to the Soviet Union," U. of A., Tucson, April 30, 1977
7. "Two Poems on Grammar and Love" U of A, Tucson, Nov. 26, 1980
8. "OBERIU and Monty Python," U. of A., Tucson, Sept. 26, 1981

9. "ASU's Russian Program: Recent Developments," U. of A., Tucson, April 14, 1984
10. "Spontaneous Human Combustion in Literature: Brown, Melville, Dickens, and Gogol," ASU, Tempe, Nov. 17, 1984
11. "Soviet Television in U.S. Russian Language Instruction: The Satellite Solution," U. of A., Tucson, May 3, 1985
12. "Two to the Third Power: Miller and Jakobson," ASU, Tempe, Nov. 16, 1985

(L-R): Dr. Lee Croft, Dr. Joe Malik, Jr. (holding award in his name) and the 1992 winner of the award, Dr. Delbert Phillips. At ASU, Valerie Hathaway photo.

13. "Honoring Our Own," ASU, Tempe, Nov. 18, 1987…Founding of the Joe Malik, Jr. Arizona Slavic Studies Award and its associated fund in the ASU Foundation. Awardees to date are: Boriss Roberts (1988), Margaret Gibson (1989), Snaford Couch (1991), Delbert

Phillips (1992), Lee Croft (1993), Stephen Batalden (1998) and Frederick Giffin (2000).
14. "Trichotomy and Subliminal Eisegesis," U. of A, Tucson, April 30, 1988
15. "Ivan Petrovich Myatlev's Macarony" ASU, Tempe, Nov. 12, 1988
16. "General A. A. Vlasov and the Russian Liberation Movement: Time for a Historical Reevaluation?" ASU, Tempe, Nov. 18, 1989
17. "Two Recent Attempts to 'Flesh Out' the Biography of Pushkin," U. of A., Tucson, April 21, 1990
18. "George Anton Schaeffer: Peripatetic Polyglot," at AGSIM-Thunderbird, Glendale, AZ, April 10, 1991
19. "Nikolai Ivanovich Kibalchich: Revolutionary and Scientist?—The Need for a New Kind of Biography," NAU, Flagstaff, AZ, Oct. 26, 1991
20. "Another Interesting Person" (George Anton Schaeffer), U. of A., Tucson, April 14, 1992
21. "The Promotion Case of a Slavist at ASU: Cause for Concern?" U. of A., Tucson, May 7, 1994
22. "Nikolai Gogol and Spontaneous Human Combustion: A Story Thrice Told" ASU, Tempe, Dec. 10, 1994
23. "Knowing Who Our Students Are, Why They Study With Us, and What They Wind Up Doing," U. of A., Tucson, April 12, 1997
24. "Correspondence of Russian Prospective Brides as a Cultural Perspective" ASU, Tempe, Nov. 15, 1997
25. "BABELFISH?" U. of A., Tucson, April 25, 1998
26. "The Krasnyi Arkhiv as a Source of G. A. Schaeffer's 'Hawaiian Fluency'," ASU, Tempe, Nov. 21, 1998
27. "The 'WHY' of Aorist Replacement in Slavic," ASU, Tempe, Oct. 30, 1999
28. "Supplemental Iconicity in Marshak's Translation," ASU, Tempe, Nov. 18, 2000
29. "George Anton Schaeffer (1779-1836) and the Moscow Balloon Project against Napoleon in 1812" at President Pat Barrett's home in Mesa, AZ, Dec. 8, 2001.
30. "The Mnemonic Function of Poetic Palindromy" U. of A, Tucson, April 26, 2003
31. "A Soviet Spy Visits ASU: WHY?" ASU, Tempe, Sept. 26, 2003
32. "The 'Triple Whammy' Approach to Russian Conversational Pedagogy," at Yavapai Community College (conjoint with AZLA convention), October 9, 2004.

33. "Russians in Australia to the End of Lachlan MacQuarrie's Governorship (1810-1821)" U. of A., Tucson, April 16, 2005
--"Award of Russian Academy of Natural Sciences V. I. Vernadsky Silver 'Ten Years of RANS Medal' to Lee B. Croft" by Prof. Valentin F. Olontsev (Akademik-RANS-Perm Division) at post-AzAATSEEL reception, Croft residence, Phoenix, Nov. 19, 2005, and subsequently at ASU's Russian and East European Center, Dec. 1, 2005
34. (with Shamella Tribble) "Russians and Rapa Nui Hieroglyphics" U. of A., Tucson, April 22, 2006.

Other University of Arizona Faculty Profiles

Barker, Adele M., B.A., M.A., Ph.D., Professor of Comparative Cultural and Literary Studies and affiliated Professor of the Department of Russian and Slavic Languages. Interviewed by Aimee M. Raymer.

Born in Washington D.C., Professor Adele Barker earned her B.A. in Russian from Northwestern University in 1970. From there Adele went on to earn her Ph.D. in Comparative Literature from New York University in 1978. Having finished her studies at NYU, Dr. Barker left for the Pushkin Institute in Moscow with the American Council of Teachers of Russian (ACTR). She studied also at Moscow State University in 1979 with the IREX Language Teachers Exchange. In 1979 also, Professor Barker was hired as Assistant Professor of Russian at the University of Arizona. Between 1979 and 1985 she conceived and carried out, with the support of her department Head and college Dean, the project to bring active Soviet television programming into the University of Arizona's Russian language program and also into the new area-studies major program called "Russian and Soviet Studies (RASS)" she was instrumental in creating. With these technological, grant, and program creation achievements taking her time, it is amazing how she managed to teach as well as to write and have

Prof. Adele Barker. Photo by Aimee M. Raymer, 2007

published scholarly articles in <u>American Imago, SEEJ-Slavic and East European Journal, Slavic Review</u>, and <u>Russian Literature</u>. By 1985 she had earned tenure and promotion to the rank of Associate Professor. Her first book, <u>The Mother Syndrome in the Russian Folk imagination</u> was published by Slavica Publishers in 1986, earning her wide esteem by its positive reviews and numerous subsequent citations. In 1990 Prof. Barker left the University of Arizona to work as an Associate Professor at the University of Washington in Seattle. She was the only woman tenured faculty member there and was intended to Chair the department, but for a host of reasons she didn't like it there and so, upon the promise of a University of Arizona Vice President that she "could always come back," she decided to return to the University of Arizona, and did so in 1993. She rejoined the staff as an Associate Professor in the Graduate Program in Comparative Cultural and Literary Studies, where, until 2001, she served as Graduate Advisor, and as an affiliated faculty member of her former department of Russian and Slavic Languages. She continued to increase her professional record of scholarship, having articles, chapters, and entries published in various positively impressive places. A second book, <u>Consuming Russia: Popular Culture, Sex and Society Since Gorbachev</u> was published by Duke University Press in 1999. In 2001 she was promoted to Full Professor at the University of Arizona. During her first year in that rank she was awarded a Fulbright Senior Scholarship to study and lecture in the English Department at the University of Peredeniya, Sri Lanka. Throughout her accomplished career she has earned many awards and has been able to receive numerous grants. In 1987 she was selected as a commencement speaker at the University of Arizona—a rare honor. She was a recipient of the International Educator Award from the U. of A. and Winner of the prestigious Heldt Prize for the best book in Slavic/East European/Eurasian Women's Studies for her co-edited work (with Jahanne M. Gheith), <u>The History of Women's Writing in Russia</u>, published by Cambridge University Press in 2002. An accomplishment Dr. Barker is particulary proud of is being the Founding Director of the Program in Russian and Soviet Studies where she established the first student exchange between the University of Arizona and The Pedagogical Institute of Foreign Languages in Almaty, Kazakhstan. She also initiated an ongoing faculty exchange program with the Desert Institute in Ashkhabad, Turkmenia. Dr. Barker has received $277,000 in federal grant money for her various exchange programs and her seminars on Women, the Law, and Domestic Violence in Post-Communist Russia. About this work, she states: "I'd like for you to mention my work with the 'Rule of Law' program in Washington, D.C. My Russian counterpart was Nadezhda Azhgikhina, Head of the Russian Association of Women Journalists. We brought women activists from the provinces, Siberia, etc. to Moscow for one week to meet with a team that I brought over of counselors, Heads of rape crisis centers and shelters to share our experiences and see what of our experience might work for them. We had hundreds of pages of materials translated into Russian and got amazing coverage on Russian T.V. *This was the best thing I've ever done cause it actually helped someone, as opposed to writing another article about the wart on Gogol's nose* (italics ours, LBC/AMR)." At the state level Prof. Barker has received $18,984 for her educational exchange programs and her work on her various books. She also has received nearly $100,000 from private foundations to initiate new teaching positions for geography and sociology and to bring speakers to the University of Arizona from abroad. She is currently working on <u>The Russian Reader</u> with Professor Bruce Grant, "Searching for Mother Russia in the Films of Aleksandr Sokurov," for <u>Heroines of the Soviet and Post-Soviet Screen</u> and "War is not a Joke: Anti-Chechen Humor in Post-Soviet

Russia," a commissioned chapter for <u>Humor in Post-Soviet Russia.</u> Despite her extremely outstanding academic career, Dr. Adele Barker considers herself "a non-traditional academic involved in not always academic enterprises."

Dunkel, Alexander, B.A., M.A., Ph.D., Associate Professor of Russian: (material here from a page of the UA College of Humanities website www.coh.arizona.edu/newandnotable/dunkel/dunkel2.html.) Information pursuant to interview arrangements by Aimee M. Raymer.

Dr. Alexander Dunkel has taught at the University of Arizona since 1973. During his career, he has taken the lead in introducing a broad range of innovative courses from "Cinema and Literature" at New York University, where he completed his Ph.D., to Video-Campus presentations of "Great Cities" and "Twentieth Century Russian Humanities" at the University of Arizona. His interest in art led him initially to a Bachelor of Fine Arts in design and art history at Hunter College. Today his courses in Russian literature and culture vary from large enrollment undergraduate survey and general education offerings such as "Utopian Visions, Promise and Reality -Russian Art in the Twentieth Century," conducted in English, to graduate seminars such as "Tolstoy's <u>Anna Karenina</u>," conducted in Russian. <u>Readings in Russian Literature Through the Nineteenth Century</u>, a pioneering interpretation of the subject first published in 1981, was devised and edited by Professor Dunkel, who also contributed translations. This text was used at a number of other universities, including ASU.

Dr. Dunkel has traveled to and resided in Russia and the USSR numerous times during the past thirty-six years. He has conducted research, participated in a National Endowment for the Humanities Institute at the Hermitage and Russian Museums, been the faculty Resident Director of the IREX-Moscow State University Summer Faculty Exchange of Language Teachers, and a lecturer on University-sponsored cultural tours of the Volga and Dnieper Rivers. He has also served as an interpreter for the U.S. Department of State for various educational, cultural and scientific delegations, as well as for luminaries such as the composer Dmitri Shostakovich and the writer Chinghiz Aitmatov.

In addition to his work in Russian and Slavic Languages, Professor Dunkel is also the founding Director of the College of Humanities' Critical Languages Program. Since its inception in 1987, this remarkable program has offered thousands of students courses in twenty-four less commonly taught languages not otherwise available at the University. During the past decade he has also participated in three major National Security Education Program grants: 1) as principal investigator for a project that produced introductory CD-Rom based lessons in Korean, Mandarin Chinese, Cantonese, Turkish, Brazilian Portuguese, and Kazakh 2) as a contributor to the National Foreign Language Center's "Infrastructure Enhancement for Critical Languages: A National Strategy," which expanded and enhanced the National Association of Self-Instructional Language Program's services on the Internet, and 3) most recently as principal investigator for an award of more than $500,000 that will make MaxAuthor, a language authoring program refined at Critical Languages, available on the Internet for downloading by language teachers around the world. He is working with Professor Ofelia Zepeda of the University's Linguistics Department on a CD-ROM project for elementary Tohono O'odham, one of Southern Arizona's indigenous languages. Dr. Dunkel has also served as an officer of the leading organizations of his profession, and since 1997 has been the Executive Director of NASILP, North America's oldest and largest professional organization for the Less Commonly Taught Languages.

Fielder, Grace, B.A., M.A., Ph.D. (UCLA), Professor of Russian and Slavic Languages and Literatures.

Grace Fielder earned her Ph.D. in Slavic Linguistics from UCLA and taught at the University of Virginia from 1983 to 1992, when she moved to the University of Arizona. Since 2000 she has served on the National Policy Advisory Committee of the Slavic and East European Languages Resource Center at Duke University/University of North Carolina and she

Professor Grace Fielder, 2007 Photo by Lee B. Croft

has been Chair of the Discipline Advisory Committee for the Resource Center's Fulbright Program. She is a very experienced teacher of Russian and has, in recent years, supervised the teaching of the under-division Russian language offerings at the University of Arizona.

Prof. Fielder's areas of Research interest include not only Russian, but Bulgarian, Macedonian, and Balkan Linguistics, discourse analysis, and grammaticalization. She is the author of several articles in these areas in both major journals and international conference proceedings (e.g. Slavic and East European Journal, Balkansko Ezikoznanie, Proceedings of the International Congress of Slavists, etc.), important anthologies, and has written an influential book, The Semantics and Pragmatics of Verbal Categories (Edwin Mellen, 1993). She is a leading expert on the dynamics of languages in contact and has lectured widely on "Discourse Markers" in Bulgarian. Major lectures in just the past three years include: "Adversative Connectives in Bulgarian: Conjunctions or Discourse Markers?" at the 9th International Pragmatics Conference in 2004, "Discourse Markers as Balkanisms" as the Kenneth Naylor Memorial Lecture at Ohio State University in April of 2005, "Balkan Discourse Markers: Acting Out Identity in Popular Culture" in the University of California at Davis' Russian Program's Distinguished Slavicist Lecture Series in October of 2006, and (together with John Leafgren (below)) a participant lecture, "Discourse Markers as Flags of Identity" at the Southeast European Studies Association (of which ASU and UA graduate Elisabeth Elliott is the President) Conference, April 26-8, 2007.

Prof. Fielder has traveled widely in Southeastern Europe and has lead groups of travelers to this area as a tour leader for the prestigious National Geographic Expeditions. A touting brochure online informs us that "Grace Fielder is an expert on the history, culture, and languages of the Dalmatian Coast…Her courses on Balkan History focus on the emergence of distinct national identities following a century of ethnic and political conflict. Grace has studied the local lore, music, and cuisine of this region, and has even moonlighted as a lavender harvester on the Island of Hvar."

Garrard, John G., B.A. (Oxford U.), M.A., graduate RASS certificate and Ph.D. (Columbia U.), Professor of Russian Studies. Interviewed by Aimee M. Raymer

Prof. John Garrard is not actually a teacher of the Russian language in Arizona, though he does, of course, know Russian. It's just that the teaching of the Russian language intricately involves the teaching of the Russian culture, because the language and the culture are codeterminate and, as mathematicians say, "are intricately bound." Prof. Garrard is a specialist in the culture itself, its history, society, politics, and religion.

Prof. John G. Garrard

Therefore he gives his title as "Professor of Russian Studies," and he certainly shines brightly in that role.

Prof. Garrard came here in 1984 from the University of Virginia to replace Joe Malik, Jr. as Head of the Department of Russian and Slavic Languages at the University of Arizona. A U. of A. Dean enforced his hire on the department after their search committee had recommended someone else, and this made his position as Head difficult from the beginning. Even more complicating was the fact that he was absent most of his first year at the university as a result of his position as a Woodrow Wilson Fellow at the

Kennan Institute necessitating his research abroad. And this was a time (1984-6) coinciding with an inter-institutional competition between the University of Arizona and Arizona State University for U.S. Department of Education funding as the Southwest National Resource Center in Russian and East European Studies. The two departments were temporarily cast as rivals, preparing their cases for funding separately, ASU under its REESC Director Stephen Batalden and U. of A. under its Russian and Slavic Languages' Head John Garrard sometimes operating from a distance by proxy. Eventually the Department of Education program officer demanded that the two universities consolidate their efforts and that we apply as ONE university consortium. But there remained the key question: "Whose university, ASU or the U. of A., would be the primary conduit for the granted money, meaning that it, the primary conduit university, would benefit by the grant's "indirect" apportionment? After considerable stalling and politicking, it was decided—ASU's Office of Research Grants and Contracts (ASU's Org. & C., now acronymed (appropriately) ORCA) would administer the money for both ASU and the U. of A. This was essentially a victory in the struggle for ASU, but then, after all that, the joint ASU/UA consortium application for a USDE National Resource Center grant was denied (and neither of us have applied again in subsequent cycles). This left a bitter taste in everyone's mouth and unjustified blame was assigned to several of the involved, and even some non-involved, parties. No doubt this was unpleasant for John Garrard and, after five years, he resigned the position of departmental Head. His term as Head was, however, marked by several notable and positive developments. Important was his recognition of the value of using the Soviet television broadcasts in Russian language pedagogy and in cultural studies. So he supported the work of his department's Professor Adele Barker to gain the technology (beating the earlier-begun ASU project to it) and hired as a teaching interpreter/aide a Russian expert on Soviet television named Val Golovskoi. A "television room" was provided to faculty and students and it rapidly filled with videotaped content and commentary. Also, it was Garrard who hired the charismatic scholar Alex De Jonge to give the U. of A. program more public visibility with his mass-publication books on Stalin and the Shaping of the Soviet Union (Wm. Morrow & Co. paperback edition came out in 1987) and The Life and Times of Grigorii Rasputin (Carrol and Graf paperback edition came out in 1989). Although De Jonge subsequently left, Prof. Garrard remains at the University of Arizona teaching courses in "Russian Studies" and publishing truly world-class scholarship on a host of important issues in the Russian culture's reevaluation of its history, and its reconsideration of its religious, social, and political values.

Prof. Garrard is one of those faculty members who has warranted a broad and deep internet presence now in addition to a "library presence" in scholarship. There are other "John Garrards" cited on the web, but our U. of Arizona Prof. John G. Garrard has a great number of sites recording reviews and discussions of his published works. One of the most controversial of these works is The Bones of Berdichev: The Life and Fate of Vasily Grossman (Simon &Schuster, NY, 1996) written together with his wife, Dr. Carol Garrard. We can only suggest that the reader become familiar with this fine work and with reviews of it as well. But Prof. Garrard's work is not circumscribed by considerations of the WWII holocaust on Slavic territory by any means. Indeed I (Lee Croft) once cited his biography of Mikhail Lermontov in an encyclopedia article on Lermontov I authored. He has always been a major literary scholar in our field. In the Spring 2003 issue of Religion and Literature appeared his insightful article, "The Twelve: Blok's Apocalypse." This is an exemplar of both literary scholarship and explication of religious symbolism, based on a personal examination of Russian poet Alexander Blok's bible, on which he jotted marginalia.

On the website www.berdichev/org/prof_john_garrrard.htm is a first-person relation of Prof. Garrard's "Biography." As he tells his fascinating personal history to us, and explains to us his motivations in scholarship, we cannot but come to a very positive appreciation of the kind of human resource to which the University of Arizona is exposing its Russian-language students. We are including it here:

"As a young private in the Royal Inniskilling Fusiliers, I was posted to Northern Ireland, an experience that left me with a lifelong commitment to religious tolerance. While queuing for injections to be posted to the Suez Canal, I was instead seconded to British Intelligence as an officer-cadet and sent to Cambridge to learn Russian in a then secret operation run by the Joint Services School for Linguists. I mustered out as an Interpreter, and took up the place that had been held for me for two years at Oxford University.

How had a Cockney boy rocketed from the working class to 'Oxbridge?' The British Education Act of 1944 gave me my chance. Having survived the Blitz, the V-1 and V-2 rockets (my baby sister did not), as well as evacuations to a dozen different schools, I passed the '11-

plus' exam and was admitted to an elite grammar school. The classical education I received there (including Latin) prepared me to win a State Scholarship to Oxford. A single law meant I was the first in my family not forced to quit school at 14 and go to work.

After graduating from Oxford (Merton) in 1958 with a B.A. in Persian and Turkish Studies, I emigrated to Canada. I created a Russian studies program at Carleton University in Ottawa, then left to earn a Ph.D. and a graduate certificate in Soviet Studies at Columbia University on a generous fellowship. I have lived and worked in the United States ever since, becoming a citizen on July 4, 1977 at Monticello. Plans to become a citizen during the 1976 Bicentennial derailed when the Immigration Service misfiled my application.

For my first twenty years as a professor I concentrated on Russian literature in European perspective, directing NEH Summer Seminars for College Teachers and creating the Center for Russian and East European Studies at the University of Virginia. Then, in 1988, I was asked by a Moscow friend to write a biography of a Soviet Jewish writer, Vasily Grossman, who had been virtually 'erased' by CPSU censorship. I agreed that, as soon as my book, Inside the Soviet Writer's Union, was published, I would.

In 1991 the collapse of the Soviet Union opened up vast new areas of research, as formerly sealed archives were now accessible. I was thus able to work in archives dealing with the Holocaust in Nazi-occupied Soviet territory. The NKVD had captured many important German documents as well during the Red Army's advance to Berlin. Soviet archives were the basis of my research for The Bones of Berdichev: The Life and Fate of Vasily Grossman (1996). Berdichev was the site of one of the first mass murders of Jews during World War II. Among the 20,000 victims was Grossman's own mother.

Though I worked on Berdichev for nearly eight years, I was only able to recover about 1,000 names of victims. However, I discovered in the Belarus archives that the Germans themselves had recorded the names and biographical details of nearly 12,500 Jews forced into the Brest ghetto. I organized the digitization of these files into a searchable database, the *Brest Ghetto Passport Archive.* The website is hosted by the Jewish Genealogical Society.

After my research was featured in a Swiss documentary, Fading Traces: Postscripts from European Memory, I switched to a new focus: Russia's emergence from the carapace of the Soviet shell. Even while working on the 'Holocaust in the Occupied Soviet Union,' I had become involved in organizing medical missions of mercy for an Orthodox Church and a school in Moscow. I retain a unique memory of landing at Sheremetevo Airport and shepherding 20 enormous crates of medical supplies through customs to the waiting room. There two groups waited: one headed by an Orthodox priest and his deacons; the other consisting of young Jewish men in keppas, the first Hillel of Moscow University. Each little delegation had withdrawn to its own area. An unspoken question hung in the air over their huddled and puzzled heads: 'Can they be waiting for the same person we are?' It was a window into the divisions that are bubbling beneath the surface of the 'new' Russia.

During the years I worked on the Holocaust, I would be continually asked if I were Jewish. Now I am asked if I am Russian Orthodox. I long ago ceased to be surprised at the question. My current project, on the resurgence of the Russian Orthodox Church, has brought me full circle to the same issue I faced over 50 years ago patrolling 'Sniper Alley' in Northern Ireland: the critical need on this planet for religious tolerance."

Gutsche, George J., B.A., M.A., Ph.D. (University of Wisconsin, Madison), Professor of Russian and Department Head, 1994-2004: (interview by Aimee M. Raymer)

Professor George Gutsche, originally from Minnesota, began his journey to the University of Arizona in 1964 when he earned his B.A. in Russian from the University of Wisconsin, Madison. He then received an M.A. and PhD from the University of Wisconsin, Madison, as well. While working towards his M.A. and Ph.D., Dr. Gutsche was awarded the National Defense Education Act Fellowship in Russian Studies. In 1969,

Dr. Gutsche began his professional career when he joined the staff of the University of Illinois, Chicago. He stayed there for 3 years as an instructor. In 1973 Professor Gutsche earned assistant professorship at the University of Illinois, Chicago, where he stayed for another three years. Professor Gutsche then went on to join the University of Tennessee, Knoxville, in 1976 as an assistant professor. At this time he also served on the editorial board of <u>Slavic and East European Journal</u> until 1984. He remained in Tennessee for only one year and then returned to Illinois in 1978 where he joined Northern Illinois University as an assistant professor. A year after moving to NIU, he was awarded a Summer Research Grant from the Graduate School Fund. Directly after receiving his summer research grant he went on to become a NEH Summer Seminar Fellow in Contemporary Literary Theory. In 1981 Professor Gutsche earned Associate Professorship at NIU and remained there for seven years as an associate professor. During those seven years he was awarded various summer research grants and worked consistently with the Russian Research Lab. In 1988 he earned full professorship and remained at Northern Illinois University for another 3 years. During his professorship at NIU he became the Executive Director of AATSEEL, the American Association of Teachers of Slavic and East European Languages, in 1989 and he held this position until 1996. While a full professor at NIU he was also the Acting Chair from 1989 to 1990. In 1991 Professor Gutsche moved to the University of Arizona. From 1993 to 1994 he was the acting head of the Russian and Slavic Studies Department and from 1994 to 2004 he was the head of that same department. For two years Dr. Gutsche was on the editorial board of <u>Pushkin Studies</u>. Shortly after, he was selected for the editorial board for <u>North American Pushkin Studies</u>. Since joining the University of Arizona he has received many NFLRC grants for travel to conferences and workshops as well as many UA technology related grants. Professor Gutsche remains at the University of Arizona today where he teaches undergraduate courses on Russian culture, literature, literary criticism, and language and graduate courses on Russian Romanticism, Pushkin, Gogol, Dostoevsky, Literary Theory, Poetry, Balkan culture and Russian language. During his educational career he has published books, scholarly articles, and translations and has served professionally in nationally important educational positions. He is currently authoring a book about Pushkin and working on a project concerning the Balkans.

Sample Publications by George Gutsche:

Moral Apostasy in Russian Literature. DeKalb, Illinois: Northern Illinois University Press, 1986.

"Pushkin's Revisions of His Lyceum Poems for His First Collection of Poems, "*Slavic and East European Journal,* 20 (1976), 103-20.

"Pushkin's 'Andrei Shen'e' and Poetic Genres in the 1820s," *Canadian-American Slavic Studies,* 10 (1976), 189-204.

"Pushkin's 'Elegija' (1830)," *Russian Language Journal,* 120 (1981), 115-25.

"Pushkin and Belinskij: The Role of the Offended Provincial," in *New Perspectives on Russian Nineteenth-Century Prose* (Columbus, Ohio: Slavica, 1982), 41-60.

At the March 5, 2005 PUSHKINISTS' DINNER at Phoenix Westcourt in the Buttes' Marketplace Café arranged by "Poet Realtor" Mark Sconce. (L-R) Mark Sconce, Lee Croft, James Falen (Oxford University Press translator of Pushkin's EUGENE ONEGIN, the guest of honor) and George Gutsche. Photo by Lesley Hoyt Croft.

"Alexander Pushkin," in *Dictionary of Literary Biography: Russian Literature in the Age of Pushkin and Gogol,* ed. Christine Rydel (Detroit: Gale, 1998).

"Moral Fiction: Tolstoi's 'Death of Ivan Ilyich'." Revised version of chapter from *Moral Apostasy in Russian Literature.* In *Tolstoi's "Death of*

Ivan Ilyich": A Critical Companion, ed. Gary Jahn (Northwestern University Press, 1999), 55-101.

"Beneath the Surface: Pushkin's Mysteries and Meanings." In *Alexander Pushkin: A Celebration of Russia's Best-loved Writer,* ed. A.D.P. Briggs (London: Hazar Publishing, 1999), 115-124.

Leafgren, John, B.A., M.A., Ph.D. (University of Virginia), Associate Professor of Russian and Slavic Languages and Literatures.

Prof. John Leafgren with daughters Elizabeth and Tory.

Dr. John Leafgren came to the University of Arizona in 1994 with a Ph.D. in Slavic linguistics from the University of Virginia. A faculty member in UA's Department of Russian and Slavic Studies, Dr. Leafgren teaches undergraduate Russian language courses and graduate-level courses in Russian linguistics (Phonology and Morphology, Syntax and Semantics, History of Russian, Introduction to Russian Linguistics). He became the department's graduate advisor in 2005, and has served as Polish language examiner for UA's Critical Language Program since 1995 and as a member of the Executive Committee of the SLAT (Second Language Acquisition and Teaching) Interdisciplinary Ph.D. Program since 2003. He is a www.LingBUZZ featured linguist and is a past president of the Arizona State AATSEEL. Dr. Leafgren is the author of "Frequently Asked Questions (and Answers) on Russian" for the National Association of Self-Instructional Language Programs and translates article abstracts from the Bulgarian journal *Sŭpostavitelno ezikoznanie* ('Contrastive Linguistics') for Linguistics Abstracts Online (Blackwell Publishing).

Dr. Leafgren's research interests lie primarily in Bulgarian linguistics, focusing on syntax and information structure. More recent publications include:

Degrees of Explicitness: Information Structure and the Packaging of Bulgarian Subjects and Objects. [Pragmatics and Beyond; New Series 102]. 2002. Amsterdam: John Benjamins.

"Bulgarian Relative Clauses and Communicative Complexity," *Slavic and East European Journal* 48 (2004) 2: 275-91.

"The Dative Absolute in Middle Bulgarian Texts," *Zeitschrift für Slawistik* ('Journal for Slavistics') 47 (2002) 2: 147-61.

"Parallels between Possessors and Other Datives in Bulgarian," *Balkanistica* 14 (2001): 43-82.

Phillips, Delbert D., B.A., M.A., Ph.D. (New York University, 1977), Distinguished Teaching Professor of Russian and Director of the University of Arizona RUSSIA ABROAD program. Interview by Aimee M. Raymer.

Honored as a "Distinguished Teaching Professor" in Russian and Slavic Studies, Dr. Delbert Phillips is one of perhaps ten professors to carry this prestigious title at the University of Arizona. Born in South Dakota, he attended the University of Minnesota, where he earned his B.A. in Russian,

Dr. Delbert Phillips, Dr. Lee Croft, and Dr. Nick Vontsolos, cronies since 1969, at Dr. Croft's Vernadsky Medal award ceremony, ASU, December 2005. Photo by Lesley Hoyt Croft.

Latin, and Music. He then continued his education at the University of Minnesota, receiving an M.A. in Russian Area Studies in 1969. While earning his M.A., he gained experience as a Teaching Assistant/Associate in Russian and Slavic Languages at the University of Minnesota. Dr. Phillips then received a fellowship to work on his PhD at New York University. The same day (July 20, 1969) astronauts landed on the moon, Delbert Phillips landed a job as Instructor at the University of Arizona in the Department of Russian and Slavic Languages. From 1969-1995 he served as the Language Teaching Coordinator for the Russian Department. During that time, in 1977, Dr. Phillips completed his PhD at NYU in early 19th-century Russian Literature.

THE STUDY ABROAD PROGRAM: While rising through the professorial ranks to his present position, Dr. Phillips created a study abroad program, which would evolve into the current Arizona Russian Abroad Program (UARA... "The Best in the Universe"). Known as THE premiere Russian Study Abroad Program in the nation, it currently offers eight language-study options to the Russian Federation per year. Summer/semester/academic year programs are offered in St. Petersburg and Moscow. Since 1992 Dr. Phillips has been able to offer Work Internships to the Russian Federation as well. Like the language programs, the internships are held in Moscow during the summer, semester, and academic year. These programs aid students, who can either stay in convenient apartments or in "home stay" arrangements, in obtaining official Russian language proficiency ratings from the Russian Federation. This economical program (it offers not only the most contiguous leadership, but also the most credit for the least money of any university accredited Russian study-abroad program) has attracted students from over 110 universities and colleges throughout Canada and the USA. In the past 20 years, over 3,500 students have participated in this prestigious program. Dr. Phillips has also received commendation for outstanding support of non-traditional students from the UA, and was listed in Who's Who in America's Teachers. In 1993 Professor Phillips was awarded the Joe Malik Jr. Award Arizona Slavic Studies Award (one of only seven given to date, and only to those who have taught Russian in Arizona for twenty years or more) and was nominated for the Pushkin Prize in Moscow for the Russian translation of his book Spook of Spoof: The Structure of the Russian Supernatural Tale. From 1987 –present Dr. Delbert Phillips has served as an Oral Proficiency Examiner in Russian, Russian Departments Undergraduate Advisor, and Russian Departments Honors Advisor. While serving as Distinguished Teaching Professor, traveling abroad with his study abroad program, Delbert Phillips co-authored numerous textbooks and audiotapes. Dr. Phillips also received $87,500 in Federal Grants for study-abroad student scholarships, and various workshops. At the State level, he has received $5,000 for the UA Provost's Teaching Improvement Award. Throughout the course of this professional career, Professor Phillips has published a number of scholarly books, textbooks, and articles in scholarly journals. Dr. Delbert Phillips is currently working on the second volume of the grammar textbook entitled Let's Improve Our Russian due out in the summer of 2008.

Sample Publications of Delbert Phillips:

Читаем с первого дня. (Let's Read from Day #1), Vol. I. II. III. Co-authored 50% with N. Kostiuk, 2002. St.Petersburg: Zlatoust Publishers.

Вне закона. ('Outside the Law: Russian Text for Law Enforcement Officers'), Vol. I. II. Co-authored 50% with G. Judina, 2003. St. Petersburg: Zlatoust Publishers.

Let's Improve Our Russian: Advanced Grammar Topics for English Speaking Students. Co-authored 50% with N. Volkova, 2004. St. Petersburg: Zlatoust Publishers, First Edition. Forthcoming.

Методика преподавания русского языка и литературы в Америке. ('Methods of Teaching Russian Language and Literature in America') Editor. Vol. 1-1995, Vol. 2-1996, Moscow: Syntaksis Press.

With regard to Prof. Delbert Phillips' career at the University of Arizona, a career beset with even more travail than my own at ASU, I (Lee Croft) here include a letter I wrote in November of 1998. I feel that it is self-explanatory and reveals the true essence of what Del Phillips is about, teaching RUSSIAN IN ARIZONA at the U. of A.

"Prof. Adele Barker
Dept. of Comparative Cultural and Literary Studies
Box 6, Harvill Building
University of Arizona
Tucson, AZ 85721

Dear Adele,

I'm very glad that you are sponsoring the nomination of Delbert Phillips for a Distinguished Teaching Professorship at the University of Arizona. You know that in 1995 I wrote a letter of support for Delbert Phillips in which I contended that he should rightfully receive such institutional sanction for the multifarious activities which constitute his career there potentiating and championing the students. For reasons completely mysterious to me (e.g. my misspelling of the Vice Provost's name, the 5-page length being considered incredible 'overkill'...I don't know), Delbert Phillips is still not institutionally recognized as a "Distinguished Teaching Professor" there. To me, this lack of recognition of Delbert Phillips' extraordinary professional excellence...not just in this particular nomination, but in general (I have in mind here the discouraging facts of his promotion status)...is a dark blot of shame on an institution that I otherwise esteem.

What I wrote in 1995 to the U. of A.'s DTP Selection Committee is only all the more true today, and so I'd like to reprise that letter, to adapt it to present purposes, since it was, and still is, the *best I can do*. It began this way: 'My high regard for your institution (I am an alumnus there, MA 1970), compels me to profer my opinion to you that *there is absolutely nothing you can do to advance the academy toward its lofiest goals* than to give the dedicated keystone of your renowned Slavic languages program, *Dr. Delbert D. Phillips*, the sanction of the title '*Distinguished Teaching Professor.*' I am certain that he is the best you have, because, quite simply, he is, in my experience, the best there is. The sheer appropriateness, indeed the truth and the justice, of this recognition shines as brightly and as clearly as the Arizona sun. And the University of Arizona itself will be an even more illuminating place, and enlightening, potentiating place, when this important appointment is made. Allow me to share with you some of the vantages which led to this observation.

Now in my fifties, I realize that, like Delbert Phillips, over half my life has been spent in the Arizona universities. I was an undergraduate in Mathematics here at Arizona State, but, in 1969, having spent an extra year requalifying myself, I entered the University of Arizona to seek a Master's Degree in Russian. At 22, I had a wife and three children to support. Your new Department of Russian and Slavic Languages, under its founding Head, Dr. Joe Malik, Jr., recognized some promise in me and granted me a graduate teaching assistantship. Delbert Phillips, in his first year as a faculty member there (he was then an ABD from New York University), was my supervisor. His only requirement of us TA's was that we sit in on his classes every other week or so and observe his teaching. From the first hour that I did so, I could see not only his methods, so carefully learned and psychologically considered, and his constant humorous manner, so disarming and disinhibiting, but, beyond that, *I could feel his power, his magic, his interpersonal genius in the classroom.* It's really something you have to experience in order to understand. Late on, and even now, after all my years of observing Russian and other foreign-language teachers (e.g. I did so as part of a New York State pedagogy evaluation project under noted Prof. Robert A. Hall in the early 1970's, and have served on numerous teacher award and teacher evaluation committees here during my tenure at ASU, including the preparation of the majority of Arizona's high-school teachers of Russian), I can say that I know what great numbers of his students have given testimony to over the years...HE'S ABSOLUTELY THE BEST, IN THE CLASSROOM AND OUT OF IT, AT TEACHING THE RUSSIAN LANGUAGE AND CULTURE AND ADVANCING HIS STUDENTS THEREBY. He has no peers, the standard is his. Indeed he is by now legendary among Russian language students internationally (and the occasional object of admiring parody...parody being a kind of evidence of legend status, if you think about it).

If you scan students' subjective comments across the many years of student evaluations (as I have in the subsequent course of supporting his professional development), over and over again you will encounter phrases reflecting this categorical absoluteness: 'the best prof I've ever had,' 'awesome instructor—my best professor,' 'the best teacher I have ever had,' 'absolutely outstanding...my best ever,' 'fantastic...the best instructor I've ever had for any course,' and on and on and on. In my own days as a TA there, my fellow graduate students and I were afraid of Delbert Phillips' courses at our level because of the demanding expected workload and his high standards of performance. But we would muse considerably about Delbert Phillips's 'strange charisma' among the undergraduates. It was certainly not an appeal based upon appearance—he was physically bulky and always-indoors pale and he dressed, in those days, more formally than we were accustomed to seeing professors dress (he kept rewearing the same full-dress suit, blue, with long-sleeved white shirt, buttoned up even when it was hot, and a black tie). And he was so consumed with his work (he has always held up a staggering teaching, grading, advising, mentoring 'load') that we worried about his health ('old' fellow of 30 he must have been...now this is indeed amusing considering how he survives leading all those physically torturous tours to Russia while many of 'us' have perished and are gone). Our consensus was that he was 'such a sweet guy that he attracted flies.' This was our uncharitable way of referring to all the eccentric, strange, and even troubled students who flocked after him wherever he went. What tales of them I could tell! I have always said that Russian as a US academic subject, with its well-known stigma of difficulty, attracts 'the very bright and the very strange—and often the very bright ARE the very strange.' This was certainly true of his loyal student retinue in those days. But it was his close personal contact with his students which sustained him in the difficult times he has experienced as a faculty member there (recall how many students marched on and occupied the UA President's office when they found out his contract for 1974 was not to be renewed). Seriously…when I reflect now upon these matters from the viewpoint of experience (I have, as he has, accepted primary professional identification as a 'teacher'), I understand what it is that actually drives Delbert Phillips—it's LOVE…love of his subject, love of his profession, and love of his students. Somehow he has more of it to pass on through his developed skills and competencies than you, than I, than anyone. That's <u>really</u> what it is.

So I went away to Cornell University and earned my Ph.D. in Slavic Linguistics. I taught at Colgate University and then for a summer at Cornell University before returning as a faculty member to Arizona State University in Tempe. How welcoming were my former professors at the U. of A. to my entering the field of Slavic Studies here as a faculty colleague, and none so more than Delbert Phillips! In the many years since (I have been Coordinator of Slavic Languages in the Department of Languages and Literatures here at ASU with only sabbatical breaks since 1975, I am a two-time President of the Arizona Chapter of the American Association of Teachers of Slavic and East European Languages (AATSEEL), the main professional organization of our field of which Delbert Phillips is a long-time active member, and I, like Delbert Phillips, am one of six recipients to date of the *Joe Malik, Jr. Arizona Slavic Studies Award,* 'given by the judgment of peers for sustained outstanding contribution to the advancement of Slavic Studies in the State of Arizona'), we have enjoyed comparing personal notes on our parallel courses of professional development (and personal development as well…I know well his wife LaFon and his sons David and Mark). I have been a close and involved witness to his growth into international eminence as a publishing scholar. For example, I reviewed his book, <u>Spook or Spoof: The Structure of the Supernatural in Russian Romantic Tales</u> (University Press of America, Washington, D.C., 1982 and subsequently republished in Russian by Синтаксис Publishers in Moscow as <u>Нечистый дух или мистификация</u> and nominated in 1995 by the publisher to the Russian Academy of Sciences (RAN) for the prestigious Pushkin Prize) in <u>Rocky Mountain Review</u> (37:2, 281-2). I think that I know his published work as well as anyone else. I have cited his work in my own published work. It's all 'good stuff,' well regarded and without re-hash or other compromise with the bibliometrics of our institutional system of rewards. It's diverse in format. He may be, for example, the world's leading producer of Russian-language-drill audiotapes (and this fact is little known), with thousands of his forty-tape accompaniment set for <u>Русский язык для всех</u> (for a time the most widely used basic Russian textual materials in the world) and of his seventeen-part 'Russian Speech Etiquette' set in use virtually everywhere Russian is taught to English speakers. His reference work is excellent, as evidence his entries in your Prof. Alexander Dunkel's compilation, <u>Readings in Russian Literature Through the Nineteenth Century</u> (U. of A., Tucson, 1981 and used in courses here at ASU throughout the 1990's). His translations are brilliant...the most recent being his work on the esoteric 'Two Udegei Tales' in <u>Manoa: A Pacific Journal of International Writing</u> (6:2 (Winter 1994), 170-5...edited by you (Prof. Adele Barker)). And, above all—and most importantly as concerns my nomination here, the majority of his publications are STUDENT CENTERED...clear evidence of the integration of research and teaching into his work. Good examples of this are his precedent-setting (the first such works by American scholars to be published in post-Soviet Russia) anthologies of articles on the teaching of Russian language and literature in America, <u>Методика преподавания русского языка и литературы в Америке</u> (Синтаксис, Москва, 1995-6 in two volumes). I have three articles on pedagogical theory and mnemonotactics published in the second volume of these, as do many of Delbert Phillips' colleagues *and several of his former students* (myself and one of my own former student co-authors included). The point here is that Delbert Phillips has a long history of introducing his students in concrete and professionally valuable ways to the main avenues of published research, or involving them in his scholarship, and always, always of considering them as the main rationale for its production. As a student-centered scholar, Delbert Phillips has few equals, if any.

Surely you must know that Delbert Phillips is our nation's foremost director of study abroad programs in Russia. The Arizona Russia Abroad Program that he has painstakingly developed and tirelessly led is, no doubt about it, the nation's best. I could go on for pages just listing the advantages of educational quality, itinerary, cost, and internationally impactful innovation (I have in mind here the ruble-paid business internships for the students of it...an idea, now broadly copied (e.g. at Boston University and also here at ASU) which HE personally thought of and first implemented). I could elaborate upon his program's recent recognition by the Social Science Research Council...giving him $20,000 per year so that he could include certain classes of impactful individuals (e.g. Arizona Russian language teachers who had never been to Russia) into his program. But, what I, who have led my own share of these study-tours to Russia, would like to give you is some idea of the kind of herculean effort this takes...and how this effort, with its attendant student guidance, complements the picture I'm trying to give of Delbert Phillips as a 'Distinguished Teaching Professor.' Imagine leaving your family for thirty or forty trips abroad for prolonged periods of time into stressful environments of student problems in a politically adversarial or transitional culture...the jet lag, the constant sleeplessness, the dietary and health problems, all the regulations, the travel logistics, etc...it boggles the mind. Imagine explaining in Russian to upset Novgorodians, who endured the Nazi occupation during World War II, why an American student would trace out a huge swastika in their city-park snow. Imagine stopping an entire train on the Finnish border to organize a search for a student's passport. Imagine finding that the janitors of the 'Chaika' ('Seagull') student residence in St. Petersburg (an eight-story concrete nightmare with *no* stairs and malfunctioning elevators) have rented out your 'Director's room' to a homeless Russian family, and so you move into a closet-sized room with three of your students. Imagine rescuing a student by bluff and begging from the Lubyanka Prison in Moscow after he was caught sneaking photos of the unloading 'black marias,' or of freeing a party of others by post-midnight explanation from KGB arrest on assault charges brought by a linguistically able thief they caught in the act of stealing from one of them a U. of A. football warm-up coat. Imagine taking responsibility for a student's emergency appendectomy in a remote Russian hospital, or avoiding a program-threatening group quarantine by agreeing to shave the pubic hair of a student who complained to the wrong authorities about venereal crab lice (eradicated, don't you know, in the first post-war five-year plan and thus clearly an imported-from-America pest), or smuggling solid stool samples into a hospital in order to free students held there for observation of their pandemic giardiasis. Imagine that your graduate-student assistant 'falls out of the dorm's second-story window' and dies and you have to inform the parents and process the body for return to the U.S. without satisfactory explanation. Stories like this abound in the Russian study-abroad directors' lives (some are his, some are mine, some from others (including the U. of A.'s Prof. Roger Hagglund)). And yet No ONE from the UARA, the most student populous of programs, has died there, no one still languishes there in the Gulag or jail...instead all gratefully acknowledge this as one of the most maturing, broadening, and enlightening experiences of their lives. Is this providence? Is is a recurring miracle? NO, it's Delbert Phillips. He is their diplomat, their nurse, their sheriff and judge, their father-confessor...the captain of their ship in alien waters, over and over risking his program, his professional standing, his personal freedom, and even his life, FOR THEM.

A close friend of mine, the only person I know who even comes close to rivaling Delbert Phillips' record as a leader of Russian study-abroad programs, has described to me the experience of leading one of these tours, so harrowing and yet so enriching, as the *addition of another life to your soul*. My own more limited experience affirms that this is so. Each tour has its painful birth, its period of adaptation and education, its personal associations quickly tempered by shared adversity and mutual interest, its successes, its failures, its deathly end, and (importantly) its legacy. Yes, each tour is a life added to the soul. And Delbert Phillips has added more of them to his soul than anyone else I know—and these 'additional lives' have given to him that extraordinary wealth of the soul which he is so willing and ready to share with the now countless others who have participated in his program.

As an academic advisor and as a continuing, out-of-class and long-after-graduation mentor and friend, Delbert Phillips has few equals. He has worked tirelessly to student benefit even in their dorms and cafeterias as a U. of A. Faculty Fellow. His office door is never shut to them, nor is his household door. Nor is his home phone, though constantly beset, unlisted or unanswered. Even the motorhome he previously owned was not exempt, often serving as transportation for the many interest-and-enrollment-building excursions of the U. of A. Balalaika Band he founded and performed in throughout the state and the southwest. *Very few professors are asked for as many recommendations as he is.* In our Russian enrollment heydays of the late 1980's he was writing more than a hundred recommendation letters per year. This is because the students quickly come to view him, above all others, as their 'sponsor' into intellectual achievement—and not just the students in the Slavic Studies sphere by any means. They feel that they can approach him, talk to him openly about their aspirations. And they know that he wants them to do well in their studies and in their lives. They know that when he recommends them, he is *really* trying to get them the position they desire, and that his recommendation will be articulate, persuasive, and, of course, seriously regarded where it is received. And this is because of the way he views his position as a 'professor' there with you, his 'mission' in academia. This view is well revealed in an e-mail note he once sent me in the course of comiserating with me over some vagaries in the process of my promotion to full professor here:

'I feel strongly that (things) will be made right this year... But even if it never is made right, Lee, you have made such an important contribution to the field and the people (students and colleagues alike) with whom you work...your life has been/is making an enormous difference... *Try to think of your position as a great honor, really a sacred trust...that you are able to exert such a positive influence over so many...sometimes just gratitude helps (and heals)*... It is a privilege to know and work with you! –DEL.'

This is Delbert Phillips—always encouraging, potentiating, undeterred by mishap or by adversity, indefatigably positive and confident that what is right WILL inevitably come to pass. I, on the other hand, have on occasion been daunted and bowed into thinking that things which SHOULD come to pass too often don't. That is why I'm trying my best to give you and the DTP Selection Committee there the chance to make this right thing happen for him. A truly 'Distinguished Teaching Professor' is what he is. Giving him the official title would credit the University of Arizona immeasurably.

Colleagues, we who have labored for any time in the 'Research One' universities of Arizona don't need the lampoons of ill-informed outsiders to tell us that we have been paying people more and more to teach less and less. We are painfully aware of it. And we are setting the mechanisms of remedy into motion—expanding the definition of scholarship to integrate more completely the parameters of research, teaching, and service and, hopefully now, elevating to a position of emblematic distinction a truly deserving prominent scholar who has held constantly high the banner of teaching and student mentorship—Delbert Phillips.'

Adele, this ends my reprisal of the 1995 nomination letter. As I said, the content of it applies equally as well today. How anyone there, or anywhere, could possibly have been placed before him as a "Distinguished Teaching Professor" is a mystery to me. And I am confident that you feel the same way. Thank you for trying to bring about this important piece of justice in our profession.

Knowing that I haven't done anything this year more important than this, I am

Respectfully yours,

Lee B. Croft, Ph.D.

Professor and Coordinator of Slavic Languages and Literatures, ASU-DLL"

As you have read in his profile, Delbert Phillips was, as a result of the campaign sponsored by Prof. Adele Barker, named a University of Arizona "Distinguished Teaching Professor" in 1998. The ceremony there was indeed the highlight of my entire year. And, in 2004, Delbert was at long last promoted generally to the rank of Full Professor, based largely on similar evidence adduced by department Head George Gutsche. My feeling is that the citizens of Arizona and the administrators of its universities should be aware of the kind of efforts that are put into the potentiation of their next generation by Delbert Phillips and the other teachers of RUSSIAN IN ARIZONA.

Polowy, Teresa, B.A., M.A., Ph.D. (University of British Columbia), Associate Professor of Russian and Slavic Languages and Literature and Current **HEAD of the Department**. Interview by Aimee M. Raymer.

Professor Polowy came to the University of Arizona in 1990. She began her career there as an Assistant Professor and in 1995 she became an Associate Professor affiliated with Women's Prose Fiction and Comparative Cultural and Literary Studies. In 2005 she became the Head of the Department of Russian and Slavic Studies and remains in that position today. Before becoming a Professor, Dr. Polowy earned her B.A. in Slavonic Area Studies with a Political Science Concentration from the University of British Columbia. She received her M.A. and Ph.D from the University of British Columbia as well, both in Russian Literature. While working on her Ph.D she was a Graduate Teaching Assistant. After receiving her Ph.D in 1986, she became a Sessional Instructor at Simon Fraser University. She then left Simon Fraser University for UC Riverside in California, where she was a Lecturer. During her career, Dr. Polowy has

Professor Teresa Polowy. 2007 Photo by Lee B. Croft.

received over six thousand dollars in grants and various awards, such as the Ukrainian National Federation in Vancouver, B.C. Scholarship, Dr. M. Lazarchuk Scholarship in Ukrainian from the University of British Columbia, and the Distinguished Graduate Advising/Mentoring Award from the University of Arizona in the College of Humanities. Dr. Polowy is a member of numerous organizations, such as the AAASS, AATSEEL, RMMLA, AWSS, CAS, and ADFL. Her areas of specialization are Post-Stalin Russian Literature, Contemporary Russian Women's Prose Fiction, Gender, Literature, and Alcoholism, Russian Language Pedagogy, Ukrainian language, literature, and culture, and Russian and Ukrainian Folk Culture.

Sample Publications of Teresa Polowy:

The Novellas of Valentin Rasputin: Genre, Language and Style. Middlebury Studies in Russian Language and Literature, Vol. 1. New York: Peter Lang, 1988.

"Russian Women Writing Alcoholism: The Sixties to the Present." Genders No. 22 (Special Issue), Winter 1995: [appeared simultaneously in the book Postcommunism and the Body Politic. Ed. Ellen Berry. New York: New York University Press, 1995: 267-295.]

"Ol'ha Kobylianska." In The Biographical Dictionary of Women's Movements and Feminisms in Central, Eastern, and South Eastern Europe. eds. Francisca de Haan and Krassimira Daskalova. Budapest/NewYork: Central European University Press, 2006: 248-252.

"The Female Face of Violence: Russian Culture and Violence Against Women." In Times of Trouble: Violence in Russian Literature and Culture, edited by Tatyana Novikov and Marcus Levitt.University of Wisconsin Press, 2007.

Simkhovich, Roza, M.A. (University of Arizona), Senior Lecturer in Russian.

Roza Simkhovich became a faculty member in Russian at the University of Arizona in 1985. For the last twenty-two years she has been close to the "heart" of the Russian language program in the department, teaching heavy loads of the grading-intensive and student-interactive Russian composition and conversation courses. She is a former President of the Arizona State AATSEEL and is admired for the long string of one-act Russian plays she has chosen, produced and directed for her students' performance at the AzAATSEEL meetings and elsewhere. These plays have led her to found the University of Arizona Russian Drama Troupe, giving students of diverse levels the opportunity to use the Russian skills she has taught them in public dramatic performances that are diverse in repertoire and method. Roza was a pioneer in arranging "Service Learning" opportunities for her students, finding them positions using their Russian in Arizona businesses

Roza Simkhovich, Senior Lecturer. 2007 Photo by Lee B. Croft

and non-profit organizations. She is the founder and current Director of the yearly ARIZONA RUSSIAN BUSINESS FORUM, for businessmen and organizational leaders who deal with businesses and organizations of the former Soviet Union and the Commonwealth of Independent States. This year of 2007 will find this successful forum in its fourteenth year and in a new exciting venue in Wroclaw, Poland. In addition to this and her other courses of student mentorship, she is the faculty advisor to the Alpha Alpha chapter (the University of Arizona's chapter) of DOBRO SLOVO, the National Slavic Studies Honorary, recognizing student excellence since 1964. This chapter now has 383 members on its rolls (see later inclusion of its membership list).

EXECUTIVE SUMMARY: ASU's 2004 Review

This is from our B.A. program review in 2004. It recapitulates some of the sectional history given previously, but adds aspects of our developmental plans and other aspects worthy to include from our program reviews from 1991 and 1997.

The Russian language has been offered as a course of instruction at Arizona State University since 1946 when Department of Foreign Languages Head, Dr. George Portnoff, a Russian ethnic, initiated RUS-101 (Fall) and RUS-102 (Spring) courses as elective courses. The Russian courses were then moved to the part-time instruction of Ukrainian emigre, Mrs. Anna Wall, in 1949. Mrs. Wall became a full-time instructor with the addition of intermediate offerings (RUS-201, 202) in 1958-9 after the Soviet launch of the Sputnik satellite heightened U.S. interest in learning Russian. In 1962, Dr. Sanford C. Couch (Ph.D., University of Wisconsin) was hired and he began to add course offerings with an eye to beginning a full four-year Bachelor's Degree program in Russian. In 1963, Prof. Rolfs Ekmanis (Ph.D. Indiana University) was hired and Mrs. Wall soon retired.

Dr. Rolfs Ekmanis in his office, ca. 1975…always with books.

Profs. Couch and Ekmanis then added a Russian-native instructor, Mrs. Irina Krylova (both Anna Wall and Irina Krylova used the title "Mrs." here for reference and address), in 1965 as they offered the courses necessary to fulfill Bachelor's degree "core" requirements (the RUS-211-2 Basic Conversation, RUS-311-2 Intermediate Composition and Conversation, RUS-411-2 Advanced Composition and Conversation...together with the 4-sem.-hr series RUS-417-8 Applied Russian Phonetics and RUS-321-2 Survey of Literature (later made into a three-course sequence) and RUS-421,3,4,5 "Person" courses in (respectively) Pushkin, Dostoevsky, Tolstoy, and Chekhov (later the "genre" courses RUS-420 Russian Poetry and RUS-430 Short Story and RUS-440 History of the Russian Language and RUS-441 Russian Culture were added)--all to comprise a 30-semester-hour major above the 16-sem.-hr. RUS-101-202 basic series which went to fulfill the College of Liberal Arts general foreign languages requirements. The Bachelor's Degree offering was applied for and approved in 1965, and the first graduate, retired US Army Col. Bruce Powers, a faculty husband, was produced.

In the late 1960's the Russian language enrollment in the Department of Foreign Languages steadily climbed. The faculty members all taught <u>four or five</u> courses per semester (average semester load, 1965-75, was 13.2 hrs) in order to provide the students with enough courses to complete the Bachelor's Degree in four years time (We have calculated that we must field TWELVE course lines per semester to satisfy what is called "program progress" requirements for our majors). In the fall of 1973, when Ms. Krylova retired and Dr. Lee B. Croft (Ph.D., Cornell University), a former student, was hired, the total Russian enrollment was 85 students, with 10 listed as majors (see table "ASU Russian Enrollment/Graduations-1970-2004" by Lee B. Croft and Adam Orford on pp. 54). In 1976, Dr. Dora Burton (Ph.D. University of Washington) was hired. After that there were NO additional tenure-track hires for 27 years until Dr. Jeanette Owen (Ph.D. Bryn Mawr College...a specialist in second-language acquisition, teaching technology, linguistic pragmatics and Russian literature) was hired in 2003...this despite a most impressive growth of enrollment (e.g. our enrollment <u>tripled</u> in the 1980's...sectionally leading in rate-of-growth a very fast-growing department, itself by 1981 the largest unified department of foreign language instruction *in the world*) and of programmatic prestige (e.g. our Coop Program with the National Security Agency and the acceptance of our graduates into most of the nation's leading graduate programs). The enrollment pressure was handled by the hiring of .25-time Faculty Associates out of departmental "salary savings" funds. By 1990 we had seven such positions, filled by four very qualified (MA or more) instructors (one gained an official "instructorship" by the combination of 4 of the .25 lines). The four tenured faculty (Profs. Couch, Ekmanis, Croft, and Burton) and the four faculty associates (Don Livingston, Andrew Reese, Dirk Willeford, and Dr. Nick Vontsolos) were offering TWENTY course lines per semester to 410 students (over 50 majors)--that's almost one full percent of all the U.S. university and college students taking Russian (by 1990 MLA statistics...see article "Foreign Language Enrollments in United States Institutions of Higher Learning, Fall 2002" by Elizabeth B. Welles in the ADFL Bulletin, Vol. 35, No. 2 (Winter 2004), cf. Table 5 for 1990 Russian data). By any measure of quantity or quality, our ASU BA Program in Russian was a national leader by 1991. We were the single largest producer of U.S. government Russian linguists for the diverse intelligence, counterespionage, and surrogate broadcasting agencies. We had an active cooperative work-study program with the National Security Agency, we had the most graduates in the employ of the Pacific Architects and Engineers (facilities maintenance and security at USSR and related nations' US embassies and consulates after 1986), and we placed the first Russian-linguist-track FBI hire (Michael Conrad, 1986-7). In the 1990-1 academic year, according to the Comparative Guide to American Colleges (J.Cass and N. Birnbaum, eds., 15th ed., Harper Publishers, NY, 1991) we produced more Russian BA's (17) than any other university in the U.S. except Georgetown University (18). Our graduates (at peak 23/yr) had a virtually perfect placement record and were accepted into all the nation's leading graduate programs in the field, into the leading international business schools, and into the nation's leading professional schools.

In 1991 the Soviet Union dissolved itself and the primary motivation for U.S. students to study Russian changed. Our enrollment began to fall precipitously (as much as 50 students per semester) until we had only 116 students in the program (15 majors, 5 graduating) by fall of 2000. We lost all our faculty associates and only the tenured faculty (Couch, Ekmanis, Croft, and Burton) were left. Increased professional expectations in areas

This ASU Insight article by Steve Koppes described our ASU Russian language program and faculty as it was in the summer of 1991, six months before the dissolution of the Soviet Union. The picture shows the 1976 US Bicentennial contingent of ASU students of the AIFS summer program in front of St. Basil's Cathedral on Red Square in Moscow. They are holding up a sign saying "ASU RUSSIAN-Number One," celebrating their success in the Soviet faculty's final assessment of student Russian language improvement.

other than teaching (e.g. study-abroad administration, research publication, and grantspersonship) subtracted from the semesterly teaching load, but still the program faculty taught an average of 9.7 credit hours per semester (essentially a three-course-per-semester load consisting of one daily class and two 3-times-per-week classes)) in order to field the program-progress-requisite 12 course lines for our students. We responded to the enrollment challenge in several ways: 1) we kept our former high profile of extracurricular student interest-building activities (a club, honoraries, lectures, films, athletics, t-shirts...etc); 2) we augmented our students' learning experiences with credit-granting Russian-language internship programs at the Phoenix Jewish Family and Childrens Services' Russian Resettlement Project (Service Learning...though this program, initially administered by ASU graduate Brian J. Thomas and enrolling more than a dozen ASU Russian students during its tenure, lost its funding in 2001) and the Tolstoy Foundation Program for Russian Refugees (where the case officer was our graduate Beata Hajduk, but also now eclipsed...though we have had interns (Kameron Kerger, Smilija Jankovic) work in Serbo-Croatian with the Bosnian Refugees through Maricopa County Social Services); 3) we sought grant support from without (e.g. SSRC, ACLS and others from 1992 on) to support instruction of less-commonly-taught languages so as to become, as recommended by our program evaluations of both 1991 and 1997 less "Russocentric" in our offerings, founding the currently successful "Critical Languages Institute" (offering Macedonian, Serbo-Croatian, and Tatar...now expanded to Albanian, Armenian, and Polish as well); and 4) we developed increased study-abroad possibilities for our students, developing exchanges and *in situ* programs with paired institutions in Skopje, in Kazan, and in Moscow (and currently with others as well under CLI auspices). At this writing (March 2004) our sectional enrollment has turned back upwards. We currently have approximately 150 students taking our courses. Twenty students are listed as majors and we have been graduating an average of 8.25 students per year for the 1997-2003 period of evaluation (see "Student Profile" section or "Course Schedules and Teaching Load Analysis" section).

The Arizona state context is that there are three universities in the state: the University of Arizona in Tucson (approx. 38,000 students), Arizona

State University (we are by far the largest at approx. 60,000 students), now with three campuses in the Phoenix area (Tempe being the main one with over 46,000 students), and Northern Arizona University in Flagstaff (22,000 students). Northern Arizona University offers a Russian minor, lead by the instruction of Anne Slobodchikoff. Arizona State University and the University of Arizona both offer Bachelors Degree Programs in Russian. The University of Arizona in Tucson offers a Master's Degree in Russian. The history of these offerings is that, in 1968, Prof. Couch at ASU and Prof. Joe Malik, Jr. at the U. of A. both wanted to begin Master's Degree programs. Prof. Couch's Russian program at ASU existed within a greater Department of Foreign Languages. Prof. Malik, who had come to the U. of A. in 1960, had just managed to gain departmental autonomy for his Russian Program, separating from a former "Department of German and Russian" in which the German faculty dominated. It was apparent to both Profs. Couch and Malik that the Arizona Board of Regents would be unlikely to approve MA programs at both institutions. And, in 1968 (unlike today), the University of Arizona was clearly the state's leading graduate institution. So, Prof. Couch agreed to support Prof. Malik's application to begin the Russian MA program at the University of Arizona in Tucson. Prof. Malik agreed to give preferential support to ASU's Russian graduates...an agreement, which benefited me (Croft) personally with a graduate teaching assistantship in Russian to support my own MA studies there in 1969-70. The relationship between the U. of A and the ASU Russian programs has been mostly strong and positive all these years. There were some rivalry problems after Prof. Malik's retirement as U. of A. Head involving competing grant applications (e.g. a federal Resource Center designation, 1986-7) and such, but generally the relationship is still cordial and positive. At this writing the U. of A. Bachelors program in Russian enrolls approximately the same (or less...about 125) number of students than we have here at ASU. But they have NINE faculty (Profs John Garrard, George Gutsche (Chair through 2003), Grace Fielder, Asc. Profs. Delbert Phillips, Alexander Dunkel, Teresa Polowy (Chair, 2004-), John Leafgren, and Asst. Prof. Romy Taylor, with instructor Roza Simkhovich and 3 TA's) to our TWO (now Croft and Owen after the retirements of Couch, Burton, and Ekmanis, with three-course help from instructional-technology researcher Dr. Danko Šipka and a course each from Faculty Associates David Mashuri, Tatiana Keeling, Tatyana Dhaliwal and Tamara McKane). Their MA program has had enrollment problems and was, in 2002, designated for termination, but Head Gutsche effected an administrative "reprieve" and the program continues. In this state academic climate ("overstaffing" there, "understaffing" here), with our respective university presidents (ASU President Michael Crow and U. of A. President Peter Likens) "reenvisioning" discrete particular roles for our universities' missions, our program desires to "annex" U. of A. Professor Delbert Phillips, together with his nation's-largest study abroad program in Russia. This annexation has been proposed to appropriate administrators here at ASU (i.e. DLL Chair Deborah Losse and International Programs Director Bill Davey, CLAS Dean (and now university vice-president as well) David Young, and ASU Presidents Lattie Coor and now Michael Crow) and is agreed-to in formal letter by Prof. Phillips himself, who wants to come here. The actual administrative mechanism of this proposed annexation is still undecided (i.e. a direct line "transfer" has been ruled out and now a "target of opportunity hire" is under consideration). Indeed, I had Prof. Phillips written into the Spring 2003 schedule here at ASU, but the appointment was, and is, stalled (at a more recent date, now…April of 2007, with Dr. Phillips promotion to Full Professor and appointment as U of A. Distinguished Teaching Professor, this "annexation" has been rendered moot…LBC).

Program leadership is another story that should be included. As the ASU Department of Foreign Languages evolved into the world's largest academic Department of Languages and Literatures (now (2007) to be renamed again as the "School of International Letters and Cultures") with approx. 7000 students per semester learning over 20 languages in regular offerings from approx. 200 instructors), the "Russian" section (now, after curriculum reforms of 2003, formally renamed the "Slavic Languages and Literatures Section" and offering course prefixes BCS, MAK, SLV, and FLA in addition to RUS…with others, including PLC- for Polish, planned for the future) gained separate administration under a "Coordinator." This happened in 1974-5 when the de-facto leader, Prof. Couch, was in Russia as CIEE Director. New departmental by-laws, installed by former DFL Chair Michael Flys (Spanish) by 1978, specified the yearly election of language section Coordinators, and, since 1975, these elections have kept Prof. Lee Croft (me) as Coordinator…deciding course offerings, leading in the hires and terminations, representing the section on the merit board, and generally being the "person of record" for the section. As for rank, all were hired at Assistant Professor's rank. All earned tenure. Profs. Couch and Ekmanis were both Full Professors by 1973. Prof. Croft became Associate Professor in 1978 and Full Professor in 1994. Prof. Burton attained tenure in 1981 but remained at Assistant Professor's rank thereafter until retirement in 2003. A plan of gradual retirement by some incentive was recommended for our "very senior" (average service was 28 years by the 1997 review) faculty by the last evaluator (Dr. Dragan Milivojevic of the U. of Oklahoma was this 1997 evaluator, but our "last exterior evaluator" now is Prof. Laura Janda of the University of North Carolina who visited us in 2004), but no such measures were taken (I refused to support "forced" retirements and my colleagues declined several incentive-program offers over those years). Nevertheless, Profs. Couch and Burton retired in 2002 and 2003, and Prof. Ekmanis retired in 2004 after a semester's sabbatical. SO, by strictly actuarial pressures, the 1997-recommended retirements have now taken place. The problem is that not all the replacements needed to maintain the BA program have been approved (i.e. Prof. Owen replaced Prof. Burton at Assistant Professor's rank, but taught only six semesters until leaving in January 2007. No replacement for Prof. Owen has been approved despite several requests, and full professors Couch and Ekmanis remain unreplaced). As usual, the lack of administrative support in the provision of faculty endangers our program.

Professional specialities are also part of the picture. Professor Couch was the pedagogy specialist and the early designer of our curriculum. Professor Ekmanis was the contemporary literature specialist and our leading scholarly publisher, mostly in Baltic literature. Professor Burton was the specialist in the "classic" period of Russian literature, the nineteenth century, with focus on Pushkin and Chekhov. I am the linguist and the "jack of all trades" who taught what the others did not want to teach. All four of us have been dedicated TEACHERS and STUDENT MENTORS. All have won institutional commendations and awards for our work. All have constantly taught, for the "good of the cause," half again or double the usual faculty loads. The point is that the implication of specialty needs from the above replacement comments is that we should hire a senior specialist in the classic period of Russian literature (Phillips' speciality, of course) and a senior pedagogy specialist who could augment our offerings into the non-Russian languages. This latter senior appointment would be well filled by the regularization of Bosnian-Serbian-Croatian/Polish/Russian polyglot Dr. Danko Šipka, currently on a three-year "return-on-investment" position (Research Associate in Instructional Technology) under the CLAS Dean and attached to the interdisciplinary Russian and East European Studies Center (REESC, Prof. Stephen Batalden, Director) and functioning as Director of the REESC-attached

Critical Languages Institute. 2007 NOTE: The proposal here described to get Dr. Šipka a tenured full professorship in the Slavic Languages and Literatures Section of the DLL was at last successful in 2005 and Dr. Šipka has been largely engaged in building minors in Bosnian-Croatian-Serbian and in Polish (where Faculty Associate Danuta Kalisz is assisting). Since both Dr. Šipka and I are essentially linguists, we need complementary faculty in the areas of (Russian) literature and culture as well as our primary need—instructors of the basic and intermediate Russian language courses.

The faculty of the Slavic Languages and Literatures Section of the Department of Languages and Literatures (and also some non-Slavic faculty like Profs. Emil Volek (Spa), Aleksandra Gruzinska (Fr), Peter Horwath (Gr) and Ileana Orlich (Rom)) are ALL now affiliates of the greater university interdisciplinary MELIKIAN CENTER for RUSSIAN, EURASIAN, AND EAST EUROPEAN STUDIES (Melikian Center for REEES...formerly the RUSSIAN AND EAST EUROPEAN CENTER, and, before 2004, a "Consortium" and not a "Center"...see brochures and list of REESC Certificate holders, 1985- and/or by link from our website). In fact, Prof. Croft is one of the founders of this interdisciplinary organization, headed for many years by Prof. Stephen Batalden of History and, in 2006, financially endowed by the family of Gregory and Emma Melikian, leaders of the Southwest Armenian émigré community. The Melikian Center for REEES administers university exchanges with several institutions in the former Soviet sphere. It administers the yearly summer Critical Languages Institutes, now offering Albanian, Armenian, Macedonian, Polish, Serbo-Croatian, and Tatar, together with *in situ* practicums and study-abroad opportunities. It administers a scholarly publication series. It provides an auspices for grant applications. And it administers an interdisciplinary undergraduate certificate program in Russian and East European Studies. The Melikian Center-REEES is currently housed in a suite of offices in the new Coor Building, on the fourth floor. The Melikian Center-REEES has a library committee and it has a personnel committee that enters its input into the departmental promotion processes of its affiliates. It employs a full-time Executive Associate (David Brokaw) as well as staff members Susan Edgington and Kathleen Evans-Romaine. The Critical Languages Institute, under The Melikian Center-REEES auspices, is directed by Dr. Ariann Stern-Gottschalk.

SO...we are currently a "section" of a giant department (about to become a part of a "Faculty of German, Romanian, and Slavic" in a giant "School of International Letters and Cultures), contending for resources with diverse other sections, in the largest college (CLAS--College of Liberal Arts and Sciences) in one of the largest universities in the nation. We are members of an interdisciplinary center (The Melikian Center for REEES), cooperating to offer non-Russian language programs and study-abroad opportunities to our students and others, even internationally. In our section we teach languages and literatures other than Russian (now Bosnian-Croatian-Serbian, Macedonian, and Polish), but the Russian program involves about 150 students, taught by the lone remaining full-time sectional faculty member Croft (me), with non-Russian courses as well taught by Prof. Danko Šipka and FA's Danuta Kalisz, Don Livingston, Tatyana Dhaliwal, David Mashuri, and Rolfs Ekmanis (as post-retirement one-course FA). For the past five years, we have been producing 8.25 graduates a year. ASU defines us as a "low production" program, but we are, according to the Fall 2003 <u>AAASS Newsnet</u>, third in the nation in BA-Russian production behind Ohio State (12) and BYU (an amazing 47, inflated by returned missionaries). Our graduates have a most enviable placement record (still virtually 100% into government service, grad schools, professional schools, or private business). Our enrollment, always our paramount concern, is back on the increase and we are growing. Our greatest present challenge is getting former levels of faculty restored.

An Essay on Prof. Croft's Office Chair

(From the Department of Languages and Literatures' **Desert Clarion**, Dr. Young Oh, Editor, Fall 2002 issue, pp. 6-7)

A Teacher's Note: "The Chair" by   Lee Croft (Professor of Russian)

When I came here as a faculty member in fall 1973, I was assigned to LL-C-424...now LL-415d where Lisa George is. This was the "Russian arcade" with adjacent offices of Professors Couch and Ekmanis (through a windowed wall to the north) and later, after 1976, Professor Burton. In my new office was only a steel-case desk and a blond wooden chair which I inherited from my vacated predecessor, Russian instructor Irina Krylova. In all the subsequent years, including my move into another office (now 402d), I have amassed quite a collection of office furniture—shelves, cabinets, file cases, etc. But I still have that same original blond wooden chair which inhabited my office when I first entered it in 1973. Since I had appropriated a more comfortable, and caster-mobile, office chair in 1975 or so...I had always used the wooden chair as the primary seat reserved for office visitors of all kinds—predominantly students, of course.

In recent years I have come to a sense of appreciation of all the diverse personalities who have, at some time or other and for whatever reason, sat in this simple blond wooden chair...and I have tried on several occasions to list the most interesting of them into some kind of compendium of illuminati. I even speculate that some arcane aura of them, an aura still increasing, acts to imbue contemporary citizens seated there with certain advantages of personal essence unseen...in short, that desirable aspects of the illuminati who have sat there "rub off" on the subsequent sitters, thus increasing their own potential for achievement. Some of this superstition may be characteristically Russian. I recall with what alacrity the Russian General Nikolai Stoljarov, now commanding troops in Chechnya, jumped to seat himself on the chair once I mentioned to him that Barry Goldwater, arch-anti-Soviet former U.S. presidential candidate, had previously sat on it.

The single most illustrious personage to sit on this chair may have been Vladimir Putin himself, current President of Russia. In the spring of 1992, very shortly after the formal dissolution of the Soviet Union, Vladimir Putin was working for Leningrad Mayor Anatoly Sobchak as his deputy in charge of international affairs. A three-man delegation from this department traveled to Phoenix to negotiate a large foreign trade deal with Cavco Modular Homes of Buckeye, Arizona. In the company of a former student who brokered the deal, these three men visited my ASU office and at least one of them sat on the wooden chair. I remember talking with them and thinking how severe their appearance and dress seemed...dark coats over plain dark suits. I took their business cards (subsequently lost). And I listened to what seemed to me a bogus explanation of why they had been summoned back to Leningrad after only a day or so here without consummation of the important deal they'd come here to negotiate... later finding that the real reason (political scandal in the Sobchak administration there, and uncomfortable involvement in the deal here by a Russian émigré—a convicted felon, who claimed to know one of the delegates from his Leningrad days). I had forgotten about this episode almost entirely until 1997 when Vladimir Putin, previously a politically "hidden" personage because of his security (KGB) positions, came prominently into the public eye as a presidential candidate. I was then struck by a feeling of familiarity with his personal appearance. I was sure that I had met him, talked with him, before. My conclusion was that he had been one of the members of this aborted Leningrad trade delegation from 1992. For various reasons I have been unable...despite several avenues of effort... to ascertain if he was, in fact, here. I think he was here, that he sat on the chair in my office...but I'll have some more work to do to give any proof of it. I notice in Putin's autobiographical work "In the First Person" that he goes to some lengths to obscure some of his activities and the venues of these activities in that period (cf. the article on "Putin's St. Petersburg Addresses" by Boris Khodorovsky in *Russian Life*. Sept/Oct 2002, especially pp. 35 concerning his Sredneokhtinsky prospekt, 42, address).

But, Vladimir Putin notwithstanding, here is a listing of some of the people who have sat in my blond wooden office chair over the years.

<u>THE CHAIR...WHO SAT ON IT?</u>

Raul Castro (Arizona Governor), Bobby Douglas (Olympic wrestler and ASU wrestling coach), Aleksandr Medved (Olympic heavyweight wrestling champion), Don Robinson (ASU gymnastics coach, performer of the one-finger stand), Yurii Zikunov (Russian acrobat...only human to do a triple-twisting triple somersault, feet-to-feet), Vasilii Smyslov (Former world Chess champion and <u>*Pravda*</u> Chess column author), Czeslaw Milosz (Nobel laureate for literature and polish expatriot UC-Berkeley Professor), Vitalii Korotich (Editor of Russian magazine <u>Ogonyok</u> and widely published poet), Vladimir Mochalov (Famed Russian caricaturist and cartoonist), Barry Goldwater (Arizona Senator and U.S. presidential candidate), Nikolai S. Stoljarov (Soviet Major General), Herman Frazier (Olympic sprinter and athletic director), Byron Scott (NBA basketball star and New Jersey Nets coach), Rudy Campbell (Former Tempe mayor and member of the Arizona Board of Regents), Oleg Tumanov, the "Soviet James Bond" (Revealed Russian spy), Georgii Chulaki (Editor of Soviet <u>*Sputnik*</u> magazine), David Macfarland (President of Kutztown State University in Pennsylvania), Dimitrije Buzarovski (Internationally renowned composer), Olga Tissarevskaya (Russian "Princess of the Tatar

Line"), Baron Carl Wrangel-Rokossowsky (son of the famous anti-Soviet White army General Wrangel), Anna Nijinskaya (daughter of famed Russian ballet star, Vaclav Nijinsky), Helga Peterson (Tamara Poljanskaya, Soviet diplomatic defector and Radio Liberty Broadcaster), "Joe" Adamov (Soviet broadcaster for Radio Moscow), Miodrag Cedic (Concentration camp survivor and founder of Cultural Exchange Worldwide), Dieter Schneider (Director of the European Union Russian Stability Fund). And, of course, many of the members of this department.

All the best...

Lee Croft

STUDENTS OF RUSSIAN AT ASU

By:

Lee B. Croft

In this section I will try to depict our ASU students of the Russian language. Who are they? From where do they come to us and why? How do they study with us? And what do they wind up doing after they study with us? Included into this section are data from our B.A. program reviews of 1981, 1991, 1997, and 2004.

Why would a person who is not masochistic choose to continue to serve in a position so fraught with trials and tribulations, with craven colleagues, perennial administrative under-prioritization, and bureaucratic nonsense as those detailed in this narrative so far? The answer is: "the students." It's the chance, the opportunity, the rare privilege of interacting closely with the students. Student contact is this position's main compensation, its very justification to me. I recall Sandy Couch, after almost forty years here, telling me, "You know, Crofto (he uses the Slavic vocative desinence as a hypocoristic...LBC), I'd pay ASU to stay here and teach the students...I love it so. But they just can't pay me enough to GRADE any more. On grading I'm just burned out. That's why I often let the students just give themselves the grades THEY think appropriate." This amused me when he said it, but now I understand. I too would pay ASU just to keep teaching here and interacting with its students. Just walking the campus during the morning class breaks (after 9:30 am, 10:30 am, 11:30 am…) is exhilarating to me, a never-ending delight. It's a "Shanghai," as the Russians say, an "anthill" of young and rapidly moving people, attractive people, tan and fit and wearing little in the heat, all headed to the next class. Walking among them, you can feel their present power, their future potential, their indefatigable enthusiasm and optimism.

I have been privileged to be in personal contact with these students. In a real sense, they keep me motivated to come to work each day—they keep me young even as I enter old age. I have been invited to their graduations as a matter of course. I am one of the commencement "readers of the names" and I shake the hands of the students I know as they pass by me during their final ceremony here. In a translation contest we endowed in the name of a tragically deceased young US Department of State Junior Faculty Development Fellow from Volgograd, Russia, named Dmitrii Krioukov in 2003, the ASU *"alma mater"* by Hopkins and Dresskell was translated into a perfectly singable Russian version by contest winner Heather Millican with some fine tuning by our talented poetess FA Tatyana Dhaliwal. So I think of both the Russian words and the English words whenever I hear it at the THREE commencement ceremonies I attend every year. Here is the English original and the Russian translation by our first (2004) Dmitrii Krioukov Memorial Translation Contest winner Heather Millican:

Alma Mater of Arizona State University (Hopkins-Dresskell)

"Where the bold saguaros
Raise their arms on high,
Praying strength for brave tomorrows
From the western sky;
Where eternal mountains
Kneel at sunset's gate,
Here we hail thee, Alma Mater,
ARIZONA STATE."

And in Russian (Heather Millican with Tatyana Dhaliwal):

"Смело лапы вверх задрав,
Кактусы стоят.
И с молитвой, в будущее,
С запада глядят.

Здесь, вечные горы
Смотрят на закат.
Процветай, наш Альма Матер—
Аризонский Штат!"

Subsequent winners of our Dmitrii Krioukov Memorial Translation contest are: Ilana Levin (2005), Samuel Zachary "Zach" Tanner (2006) and Electronica "Nica" Kolasa (2007).

I have been invited to many student weddings (they meet in our classes), to the christening of their children, to their citizenship ceremonies, their bar admittance ceremonies, their ceremonies to receive military medals and diverse other public-service and academic awards. I have had many meals with my students, played in sports events with them, taken bicycle tours, river floats, hikes and mountain climbs with them. I have acted in plays and skits with them, sung in Russian singing groups with them, re-enacted with them the 1837 duel between Georges D'Anthes and Alexander Pushkin. In Soviet Russia I have taken them to numerous "first time" cultural events, rescued them from arrest, taken them to clinics and hospitals, making decisions for them about medical emergencies and surgical operations. And, sadly, I have attended some funerals. The death of a student is, to some degree, like the death of a child—terrible in that your own legacy is cut off with the death of this person into whom you've invested so much. I think still about the premature deaths, deaths that tragically took away people just realizing their great promise, of Edward Bergman (was a graduate of our program in the UA MA program), Susan M. Crawshaw (a dedicated animal lover and anti-cruelty advocate), Suzanne M. Park (ASU MPA grad and Assistant City Manager of Chandler), and Darrow Soll (ASU Russian grad, UA Law grad and prominent Phoenix attorney). Sue Crawshaw (1956-1986), brilliant and hypersensitive, had written to me a Russian poem:

Молодое дерево хвалит солнце	**A Young Tree Praises the Sun**
Солнце встаёт помогать нам расти,	The sun gets up to help us grow,
Под его светом мы можем цвести.	In its light we flourish, you know.
Если мы в ночи томимся, оно	If we languish in dark, the sun
Силу даёт нам накалом его.	Supports us with strength hard won.
И если буря начнёт на нас дуть,	And if a storm on us should blow,
Солнце всегда освещает нам путь.	The sun lights up the path to go.
Солнце защитник наш Несокрушимый,	The sun defends us on our every course,
И свет его наш источник любимый.	Its light our future's beloved source.

Translation by Lee B. Croft

She laminated the text of it onto a wooden plaque and presented it to me at a birthday dinner she prepared for me (Dora Burton was there too) at her Tempe apartment in 1985. I have taped a copy of her newspaper obituary onto the back of it. I keep the plaque in view to remind me of her and of all our psychological fragility.

I sometimes joke that my students of Russian are "the very bright and the very strange," commenting that very often "the very bright ARE the very strange." This characterization is supported by the facts of their grade-point averages (see below) and their achievement of diverse prestigious academic distinctions (they are among the university's leading contingents of national fellowship/scholarship recipients—Fulbright and NSEP awards in particular) as well as by their subsequent courses of employment and/or entrepreneurship.

Why do the students take Russian?

In trying to cajole students into taking Russian and populating our classrooms we used to make use of a booklet entitled <u>Why Study Russian?</u> first published, I believe, by AATSEEL during Joe Malik's tenure as Executive-Secretary and subsequently renewed. In the post-Soviet era, however, a new statement of "Why Study Russian" was necessary. Such a statement is to be found on the University of Arizona's Department of Russian and Slavic Studies home website. The posting there gives "thanks to Ben Rifkin, University of Wisconsin," one of our profession's leaders. Here is the text of this version of "Why Study Russian?" from http://russian.arizona.edu/whystudyrussian.htm.

"Russian is great for training students to think clearly, organize their work: The Russian language curriculum is challenging but manageable—We train our students to think things through, plan their work, so they learn language processing and study skills applicable to other classes and to professional lives after they graduate.

Russian is marketable for students' careers:

US Government Needs for Russian Language Expertise

70 Federal agencies report significant shortfall in staff with advanced language skills in Arabic, Chinese, Russian and Turkic languages. Congressional GAO reports 29% of all State Department jobs require such language expertise. Federal jobs pay 5-15% more for language expertise. 70% of all US Dept. of Commerce Foreign Service Officer positions in Russian are budgeted, but not filled due to lack of qualified applicants! The US military is eager to recruit linguists, paying up to $60,000 towards college tuition for military committed students of certain foreign languages, including Russian. Sample Federal Employers include: NASA, FBI, Coast Guard, USAID, US Energy Dept, the Broadcasting Board of Governors, NSA/CIA/DIA, Commerce Dept, Dept of Defense, Nuclear Regulatory Commission, Dept. of Agriculture, International Trade Commission, US Dept. of State.

Private Sector Employers with Language Needs

Sample Private Sector Employers for Russian with offices in Russia: Morgan Stanley, Microsoft, General Motors, Johnson and Johnson, Otis Elevator, Reebok, Hewlett Packard, Delta Airlines, Price Waterhouse, DeLoitte and Touche, Citibank, 3M, AT&T, Ford, Honeywell, Avon, Exxon/Mobil, Chevron/Conoco, Gillette. For more information see www.bisnis.doc.gov. Private sector employers pay more for employees with language expertise and when those employees are posted abroad, they typically are given greater responsibilities than their peers posted in the US; when foreign-based employees transfer back to the US, they generally transfer in with higher pay and higher level of responsibilities than US-based peers.

Sample Non-profit Employers for People with Language Expertise: US non-profits in Russia include: AA, Amnesty International, Citizens Watch,

Nonviolence International, Green Cross, International Resettlement Agencies, IREX, ACTR/ACCELS, Mother and Child, Church missions, Women's Crisis Center of St. Petersburg.

The Russian economy is booming: expect increased trade with the US and investment from US firms in the Russian economy. See www.amcham.ru. Note Russian plans, reported recently in the <u>New York Times,</u> to build an oil pipeline to Nakhodka. Russia is the largest or one of the largest producers of numerous natural resources and raw materials, including petroleum, diamonds, gold, copper, manganese, uranium, silver, graphite, and platinum. Russia is the second largest steel producer in the world, after Japan, and has an enormous timber reserve. Russia is the world's largest producer of natural gas, third largest producer of oil and fourth largest, in terms of the mining, of coal. Russia has an estimated 40% of the world's total reserves of natural gas, and Russia's proven oil reserves are second only to Saudi Arabia's and Russian is the TOP oil producer in the world. Russia is a tremendous potential market for US goods and services. Experts expect an increase in demand for American-made equipment, as well as aircraft, air traffic control equipment, among other economic sectors. American companies have been quick to realize the potential of the Russian market; some of these are listed at www.bisnis.doc.gov. In the year 2000, the Russian government held currency reserves valued at $30 Billion and the Russian trade balance was in surplus to the tune of $50 Billion; BUSINESS IS BOOMING!

Former students of Russian are now working or have worked: as engineers at NASA's Johnson Space Center (with Russian cosmonauts training for the Space Shuttle), at banks operating in international markets, as professors of Russian literature at small colleges and large universities, in the Peace Corps, in major accounting firms (in Russia and in the US), in large corporations with Russian operations, in large and small law firms in Europe and America, in the US State Department and Commerce Department, teaching English in Russian high schools, for American press organizations (such as the New Yorker, NY Times, Washington Post, NBC News, CNN) in the US and in Russia, for non-profit agencies such as the Carnegie Endowment for International Peace, the National Foreign Language Center, or the US/Russia Business Council, for ACTR/ACCELS and IREX both in the US and in Russia.

Russian is a world language, the national language of Russia, Kazakhstan, Kyrgyzstan, and it is spoken by many people throughout the former Soviet Republics in the Caucasus and Central Asia. The Russian Federation has a population of just under 150 million people, which constitute slightly more than 50% of the population of the former Soviet Union. Of those 150 million, slightly more than 120 million identify themselves as ethnic Russians. (There are many more ethnic Russians in other countries of the former Soviet Union) Russia spans eleven time zones and covers about $1/8^{th}$ of the world's land surface. It is the largest country in the world, almost twice the size of the United States. Put simply, Russia is huge. And with more emigres from Russia living in the US, you can speak Russian in any large American city with native speakers delighted to speak with you in THEIR language!

Russian is valuable for students' personal development and personal goals:

Students who study Russian in college usually participate in a small program with great attention from their instructors; they don't get lost in the crowd as much as students in bigger programs, such as Spanish.

Students who study Russian may have higher rates of admission to the graduate and professional school programs of their choice.

Students who study Russian have special access to Russian culture: Dostoevsky, Tolstoy, and Chekhov, Kandinsky and Chagall, Akhmatova, Pasternak and Pushkin, Tchaikovsky, Stravinsky and Prokofiev, Stanislavsky and Tarkovsky (not to mention Sokurov and his latest film to sweep the cinematic world, "The Russian Ark")—Russian arts have changed the world!

Students who study Russian have special access to understanding Russian history and Russia today: the turbulence of revolution, the tyranny of dictators, lack of freedom of expression and freedom of religion, the liberation of the collapse of communism, nationalization and privatization, democratization and the legacy of authoritarianism. All are important issues for understanding not only Russia, but much of the world today!

Russians are generally a very welcoming and hospitable people who place high value on their friendships, including friendships with American students on study abroad programs.

The Infrastructure of the Russian field is great: there is support for professionals teaching Russian in the US.

The Russian field is well supported professionally, with two professional organizations (ACTR (American Council of Teachers of Russian) and AATSEEL), a rich database of information about learning outcomes (maintained by ACTR), excellent summer immersion programs in the US and Russia (see www.aatseel.org for a complete listing of options), and a steadily increasing number and variety of instructional materials and curricular support available from commercial publishers (e.g. Prentice Hall, McGraw-Hill, Wiley and Sons, Kendall/Hunt, and others) and non-profit organizations (www.rusnet.org, maintained by ACTR). The Russian field is moving towards the implementation of an Advanced Placement Exam, which may lead to a resurgence in high school programs and therefore even greater demand on college enrollments. The Russian field has one major conference (AATSEEL) and two affiliated conferences (AAASS and ACTFL) every year, giving professionals opportunities to network and share with one another both in formal and informal contexts. SEELANGs, the AATSEEL Newsletter, ACTR Letter, and SEEJ (Slavic and East European Journal) all contribute to the field's support for each practicing teacher and scholar.

There are great study abroad programs in Russia for American students, run by ACTR, CIEE, Boston University and especially—our own Arizona Russian Abroad!

For more ideas: AATSEEL and ACTR have a great video clip on the web: "Why Study Russian?": www.russnet.org/why/index.html."

Letters From Former UA Russian Students

Here is a letter from James "Jay" Davis, who was a student of the Russian language at both ASU and at the University of Arizona. I remember that he came to us in Russian in his junior year at ASU (1982-3) when he was already close to graduating in Business-Accounting/Finance. He was a studious individual, a regular reader of the <u>Christian Science Monitor.</u> Once he heard me rant that in every issue of every newspaper in the land was some story of drug-caused tragedy or travesty. He brought with him a copy of the <u>Christian Science Monitor</u> to my office and challenged me to find a story in it of drug-associated tragedy...and I was able to find such a story in the issue, to his surprise. I recall also a student gathering at my house on Burgess Street in South Phoenix. I was barbecuing hamburgers for the students when a couple of them jumped me and threw me into the swimming pool. This started a round of other mischievous "dunkings," and Jay tried to push his classmate Karen Bollerman into the pool. She somehow held onto him and pulled him in too. We still have pictures of that gathering. My mother and father were there too, visiting from Montana. Dad helped me barbecue burgers for more than sixty students.

One day Jay came into my office and asked me for a recommendation to enroll in the Master's Degree program in Russian at the University of Arizona in Tucson. At that time he was taking our RUS-202 and was not really far enough along in language study to be able to do well in Master's Degree classes. I called colleagues at the University of Arizona (Profs. Joe Malik, Margaret Gibson, and Delbert Phillips) and explained the situation to them. Jay would be allowed to enroll on a kind of probationary basis. He would continue his undergraduate work in the language at the U. of A. while taking what graduate courses he could. But, despite the efforts of the faculty there, Jay just couldn't make up the language deficit fast enough to succeed in the graduate environment. He dropped out of the U. of A.'s M.A. program to go "home" to Illinois to work as a certified public accountant. I recall that Del Phillips called to express to me his regret that my student, Jay Davis, had not succeeded there.

But one day several years later Del Phillips, during his frequent travels to Russia, was riding in a Moscow taxi and talking to the driver. The driver told his passenger that he "knew another American from Arizona." This other American was a "big fish," had a dual apartment overlooking Kutuzovsky Prospekt, headed some huge international firm, and was an "important person in Moscow to know." As the conversation developed, Del urged the driver to deliver him to this other American's address. He went up to the posh apartment and rang the buzzer. To Del's surprise, his former student James Davis answered the door. He had a Russian wife and a baby son and was the Head of the Moscow office of the international accounting firm, DeLoitte and Touche. This letter to me was written at about that time:

"June 20, 1992
Professor Lee Croft
Arizona State University
Tempe, Arizona

James Davis-Moscow Office

Deloitte and Touche
10 Westport Road
PO Box 820
Wilton, CT 06897

Dear Professor,

Although you and I have not been in touch now for quite some time, I still think of you often and wish you well. I certainly had a great time with you and my classmates in the days when Russian language was a new frontier and am so appreciative of the kind, considerate, and enthusiastic way that you taught us all Russian.

I have no doubt whatsoever that it was your good attitude and good approach to the study of Russian that made me like it so well right from the start. It certainly has turned out to have had a far greater impact on my life than ever could have been expected.

I could not possibly tell you all that has transpired to me since you and I had the pleasure of a visit but I will give you a light-speed tour through my recent past.

My bachelor's degree was accounting as you may recall. Worked in Arizona and home state of Illinois until lack of interest in debits and credits forced me to search for something else. Friends pointed out possible opportunities of bi-lingual accountancy in developing post-perestroika Russia. Wham! What a big idea. Mailed 435 (yes I counted!) resumes over a period of thirteen months. No results. Sold my beautiful Buick in April 1991, bought ticket to Moscow. Pals and parents thought I was over the edge. Got a job in less than 10 days. Toured largest factories in Soviet Union (as it was still called at that time). Ordered production for Rubles, my company shipped to New York to sell for Dollars. Mostly furniture, and wool clothing. Bigger California company stole me away for more money. Worked there four months, tried to have high profile, meet as many business men as I could, got a better offer. Went to Radisson Hotel International Corporation in Oct. 1991. Stayed there till May 1992. Once again, through the grapevine word got out that there was some guy here who was an accountant, spoke Russian, and spent his free time voluntarily reading Russian accounting regulations. Either a nut or the find of the century for a business here (still not sure which). Got a better offer. On my 366th day in CIS/Russia started my fourth job with higher pay than I ever thought possible. Wow.

As if that wasn't enough I am also married to a princess and we have a fine little boy named Benjamin. I'd say it's been a productive year. Now that I'm finished bragging, let me get down to the reason of my letter to you. I am very appreciative of your help to me and think of Russian language students in a friendly manner. If I could help them, I want to do it. I will be of help to any of your students who would like to find employment here.

Give them my address and tell them to send me a letter with CV and I will give them the best advice possible. The one point I wish to make is that if they are to succeed in their job quest, they must give me something to sell. Being 18 years, green as grass, and speaking very bad Russian does not help. But if a person is advanced in Russian studies AND ALSO knows programming, advertising, marketing, accounting, engineering, law, or any other usefull skill, then perhaps we can work together to sell them to an employer here.

I can even tell them who is now giving the cheap airfare and rent them a cheap apartment in the city. Usually about $200 per month.

If you think this will be of interest to the kids, I am ready to help. The very best wishes to you and your family, and, of course, I would be delighted ten ways over to get a letter from you.

Yours,

Jim Davis"

And here is a letter from a former student of the University of Arizona's Russian program, Suzanne Thompson (now Eanes):

"Monday, April 23, 2007

Dear Dr. Croft,

I am Suzanne Thompson Eanes, a student of Del Phillips. He called me tonight and said that you are writing a book about the study of Russian in Arizona. He asked that I send you a description of what I have done since I studied Russian there at the University of Arizona. *I must say that my financial welfare and any success I have enjoyed in my career got a significant start due to the dedication of Del Phillips, Boriss Roberts, Margaret Gibson, and Roza Simkhovich. I will always owe them a debt of gratitude for opening my mind to the rich heritage of Russian language and culture* (italics mine, LBC).

Here is a rundown of my activities:

1980: Start study of Russian with Delbert Phillips

1981-1984: Go to Cincinnati to study music; received Bachelor's, summa cum laude, in June 1984 (a break from Russian),

June 1984: Return to Tucson to complete undergraduate *curriculum* of Russian (second-year during the summer; third and fourth years concurrently during the 1984-85 year). Note that I say *curriculum* here, because I didn't get a degree in Russian at this point (I would have had to take some science courses to get the BA; I just wanted the practical Russian exposure).

September-December 1985: Study for a semester at Pushkin Institute, Moscow (through ACTR),

October 1987: Hired by Pacific Architects and Engineers (PA & E) to work in the Consular section at the US Embassy, Moscow. During the next two years, traveled widely in the Soviet Union, including five trips to Armenia and a historic visit to the Soviet Far East (Vladivostok, Sakhalin, Khabarovsk, Ulan-Ude) with US Ambassador Jack Matlock. Interpreted, along with other embassy personnel, at a state dinner between Reagan/Gorbachev at Spaso House (held in honor of entry-into-force of the INF treaty).

1990: Took graduate courses at the UA; taught as a graduate student; in the fall, worked as Program Coordinator of the Russian and Soviet Studies Program (RASS),

1991: Began my long association with Hughes Technical Services Company (HTSC) as an interpreter at the Votkinsk Portal Monitoring Facility, extant since 1988 to monitor Soviet missile production, per the INF treaty,

1993-94: Returned to Tucson but remained on casual status for HTSC, interpreted for a delegation of On-Site Inspection Agency personnel who traveled to Kiev, Dnepropetrovsk, and Pavolgrad to discuss implementation of the START treaty with the Ukrainians,

1994-95: Returned to Moscow to work for Hughes (which during this period became Raytheon Technical Services Company (RTSC)) on starting up the Cooperative Threat Reduction (CTR) program: travel to bases throughout Russia to deliver equipment and train personnel to destroy weapons.

For much of the period between 1996 and late 2000: work for *the Moscow Times* newspaper in Moscow: start on the copy desk; then work as a reporter (features and news) and editor (first for lifestyle/travel sections, then for opinion page),

January 2001: Enroll in graduate program at UA; in the fall, work with George Gutsche as graduate assistant in the Russian culture course,

December 2001: Called by Raytheon to manage the site at Votkinsk; agreed to a two-year commitment to work as the site manager (to date, I am the only permanent site manager ever hired who was a Russian speaker). While working in Votkinsk, also did graduate work in Russian.

April 2004: Finished my site-manager tour, but remained on the reserve list; during the next two and half years, returned to Votkinsk for five tours as an interpreter and/or fill-in for the site manager.

On a personal note: I got married for the first time in December, and, after years of the fiddle-footed life, I am now trying to figure a way to use my Russian on this side of the water. I would love to teach Russian to the next generation—the younger the kids, the better—but finding a school with vision and money has proven difficult. I will keep trying.

Please let me know if you want any further information.

Best wishes on your book.

Sincerely,   Suzanne Thompson Eanes."

Of course, such a letter speaks best for itself. But I might point out that this is one Arizona Russian language student who has used her skills to impact us all positively on the international security front. We can only hope that she can find a place of positive employment among us here in Arizona so that future Arizonans can have such positive impact in this sphere as well.

Here is an email message from U. of A. Russian program graduate (B.A. 1977, M.A. 1980) Ron Mastaler:

"Hi Lee,...I started studying Russian at the U. of A. in 1973 and received my B.A. in 1977; during this time I had the opportunity to participate in the

CIEE Russian study abroad program in the summer of 1975 (with Sandy Couch of ASU as the Director) and in the fall of 1976, both in Leningrad at Leningrad State University. I was inducted into DOBRO SLOVO as an undergraduate. After a year in the Peace Corps, I returned to get my M.A. (from 1978 through academic year 1980) at the U. of A. During this time I taught beginning Russian language classes as a Teaching Assistant and translated "Baba Yaga" (and a few other short items) for a compilation of folk literature that Alex Dunkel was putting together.

After this I had something of a hiatus as far as Russian was concerned, though I ended up maintaining my Russian, and actually learning the grammar much better, by translating articles in "Optics and Spectroscopy" for the American Institute of Physics. I also translated a portion (about 200 pages of revisions) of a book entitled "Interior Structure of the Earth and Planets" by Vladimir Zharkov. I returned to the U.S.S.R. in 1989 with Del Phillips' Russian summer language program in Leningrad and Moscow. This got me going again and I convinced Del to get me a position as Resident Director of a semester program in Leningrad in the spring semester of 1990. While there, Del offered me a position teaching at the U. of A.; I taught from fall 1990 until spring 1992 as an instructor. I taught grammar classes in the first two years, a beginning conversation class (2nd year), and I developed a scientific translation class (4th semester). Since Del was taking a sabbatical leave in fall of 1992, department head Margaret Gibson offered me a position for a third year to teach third-year grammar, however, budget cuts effectively eliminated my position.

In 1992 I translated most (chapters 2 through 9) of a book called "The Planet Venus" by Mikhail Marov, finally published by the Yale University Press. In 1993 I took several college-student groups to Russia. In early 1994 I was the Russian dialogue coach for the movie *Terminal Velocity*. I was teaching (or trying to teach) the actors Nastasya Kinski, Charlie Sheen, James Gandolfini, Christopher McDonals and Gary Bullock to speak Russian; though I don't think Gary had any Russian lines in the final version.

Starting in September of 1994, I worked as a translator/interpreter for the On-site Inspection Agency (OSIA, later called the Defense Threat Reduction Agency, DTRA) in Votkinsk, Udmurtia, Russian Federation. Our support group provided all official intergovernmental translations in support of the INF and START (nuclear arms limitation and disarmament, LBC) treaties. We also provided official interpretation translating into Russian (the Russian interpreter translated into English) or both ways as the situation demanded. Because of my technical background, I was designated the official "technical" translator. After about a year, I became the so-called "Support Supervisor," managing the translators, medical personnel, and chefs. I worked there full-time until the end of 1997 and then returned for extended periods to "help out" every year until 2003.

Well, Lee, that's about it (at least the highlights). I hope this got to you "in time," whatever that means in this context. Good luck with this project and in general. All the best.

Ron Mastaler, Senior Research Specialist, Institute of Atmospheric Physics, Atmospheric Sciences Dept., University of Arizona, Tucson, AZ 85721.

HOW do we teach them?

The teaching of Russian in the academic environment to monolingual speakers of English is both a science and an art. My experience leads me to believe that teachers are born and not made. That is, you can't really teach a person to be a teacher. If they are a teacher, you can teach them specific methods and attitudes to make them better teachers. But a person is either a teacher or they are not by gift of nature and nurture, not by any academic qualification or training. This is my opinion.

That said, I am often faced with the task of denying positions in the teaching of Russian to people who think that the fact that they speak Russian natively qualifies them to teach it. In many ways, the native speaker is not ideally suited to teach the language, at least not the beginning stages of the language. They can't explain adequately why they say what they say and when they say it. And, of course, they come to me ignorant of the common textual resources, professional organizations, and other aspects of the "information flow" needed to fully potentiate the students.

Teaching Russian, or any foreign language, in an effective way is very hard WORK, especially at the beginning levels. In our program for years, our RUS-101 Elementary Russian (a 16-week semester's course I have taught more than thirty times) had fifty-minute class meetings five days per week for only four semester hours of credit. Every Thursday the students spent a mandatory hour in the basement audio laboratory listening to prerecorded supporting material and writing a three-part graded dictation. In addition, the students were required to spend an additional two hours of their time per week in the audio laboratory listening to tapes of the vocabulary, the "pattern sentences," and the "part IV" example sentences. In the textbook, Prof. Couch's Практический курс русского языка, they did daily written homework comprising both translation and composition of sentences. And separately they turned in daily declension and conjugation work. In addition I assigned the memorization and reenactment of several dialogues per semester. All this work had to be graded, meticulously recorded and returned to the students by the next class hour, and it always was, no matter the will-sapping toll this took from the instructor. We all did this ourselves, every day with large groups of students (I once had a 101 group of 47), without any aides or helpers of any kind. When I think of how Prof. Couch produced these materials, using a set of two Royal typewriters—one with English keyboard and one with Russian keyboard—exchanging the entire paper platen from machine to machine with every change of alphabet in the text, and counting letters in order to right-justify the lines, I wonder if people today, in the age of computerized polyalphabetic word-processing, can even imagine such an output of sheer WORK. And this was before the widespread availability of photocopiers too. All duplication was done on an outdated mimeograph that demanded accurate dual-language typing (on the dual set of Royals) on embedded ink masters that were not tolerant of mistakes. Believe me, professors of three-day-a-week lecture courses in areas where the building of a real skill is not demanded have NO idea of what this reality is.

In the classroom itself, inhibition is the teacher's enemy. NO instructional process should inhibit the students from making even nonsensical babbling noises in the course of acquiring the desired language behavior as a habit. We used all Russian commands from the start, even as we began imparting the Cyrillic alphabet letter by letter. Повторите, пожалуйста! (Repeat, please! And always chorally, as an entire group, before, in stages, breaking the response patterns down into smaller and smaller groups until, only when the correct response was assured, the individual student was called upon to make it). Ещё раз, пожалуйста! (Once again, please! Because repetition is truly the mother of learning). When an individual is called upon, it is always in a considered way…first the question is addressed to EVERYONE so that EVERYONE thinks that they might have to answer it. Only then, after a second or two, do you address the question to a specific named student. If, on the other hand, you mention the student who has to answer the question before you give the question, then everyone else in the class, as soon as they hear the addressed student's name, turns off their own mind, knowing that the question does not apply to them.

A good idea of how our language teaching methodology avoids student inhibition and encourages repetition of the correct language response in order to build confident fluency is shown by the structure of psychologically sophisticated auditory drills that the students encounter as recorded in the language laboratory. Imagine that the students, over the headphones, are given the task of responding orally to the Russian question "Что вы видите?" ("What do you see?"). A list of possible answers is given in the associated workbook: "стол, карандаш, молоко, Иван, Анна…" ("a table, a pencil, milk, Ivan, Anna…"). The students hear the Russian question and they are to respond, saying "Я вижу————," ("I see the_____,") inserting the correct noun as the direct object of the verb in order to answer. The point of the drill is to teach the students that Russian uses a particular ending on certain words to denote the fact that they are used as direct objects of the verb. In the case of the table, the pencil, and the milk, the student just repeats each word after the Russian "I see____" without any change at all. This is because they are masculine or neuter inanimate nouns and the rules of Russian morphology do not require that their endings be changed. After each response the voice on the tape says, "Хорошо! Повторите!" ("Good! Repeat!", meaning repeat the correct response again after the speaker on the tape). But with the nouns "Ivan" and "Anna"—animate masculine or feminine first declension nouns, the direct object relationship is signaled by different endings on the nouns. That is, the students are supposed to say "Я вижу Ивана" ("I see Ivan" adding an –a ending to the word to signal that it is accusative case, denoting here a direct object). But the student, not having mastered this rule, says (in error) "Я вижу Иван" following the pattern for the previous nouns. But, even so, the voice does NOT say "that is incorrect" or anything like that, because such a correction might inhibit subsequent student response. Just as before, the voice says "Good! Repeat!" BUT, when the correct sentence "Я вижу Ивана" ("I see Ivan, with the –a ending attached to the word "Ivan") is read for the student to repeat it, an echoic aura auditorially reinforces by its repetition (twenty five times a second) the word "Ивана, Ивана, Ивана, Ивана…" In this way the student is praised by the Russian word "Хорошо" ("Good") for making any response at all (in fact they hear the same word even if they are dead silent) and are not inhibited psychologically from making subsequent responses. And the correct response is reinforced by the echoic aura's repetitions, running the correct neurophysiological circuits in the students' brains many times more than the circuit traveled in the course of making the incorrect response. This is the sort of psychological sophistication that ruled our every action in the classroom and in the language laboratory. Only positive praise was meted out to the students, in groups and then individually. Correct responses were reinforced by repetition, the mother of learning. Our grammatical explanations were similarly sophisticated in the linguistic sense, and ordered in their presentation by psychologically sophisticated considerations of pedagogy. Even the words, once introduced in each lesson's introductory vocabulary list, were counted for subsequent opportunities for reinforcement. And the words themselves were taken from the first 2500 words in established word frequency studies of Russian language usage.

I remember the debates we used to have in this profession about the adoption of the "audio-lingual method." In later years we debated the "communicative competency" movement. Much of these discussions focused on the role of grammar and grammatical explanation. How much "grammar" is appropriate in our particular academic environment, given that daily environmental exposure to spoken Russian in Arizona is very slight if non-existent? What should we do to bring about optimum student performance? Here at ASU on my watch our approach was uniformly eclectic. That is, we always tried to cater our teaching to individual students' aptitudes, backgrounds, and learning styles. For some, grammatical explanation was paramount and effective. For others it was memorization of dialogues keyed to frequently occurring social situations. Essentially we tried everything ten minutes of class time at a time as one of four, five, or six separate activities in every class period designed to illustrate the ordered points at hand. As the pendulum of pedagogical fashion swung first grammatically and then antigrammatically from year to year, we continued to hammer away eclectically, trying our best to respond to individual student needs.

In our section we had four different tenured professors with four different personal styles of teaching. The students, by and large, had to learn to adapt to each of these styles in order to get through the program. As the administrator of the section, I maintained that each professor be allowed to choose textual materials and pedagogical approaches on their own, giving them credit for the breadth and depth of their experience and trusting that they all had the best interests of the students in their hearts and minds. When colleagues at large questioned why I "permitted" superannuated use of Prof. Couch's textual materials through the first two years of instruction clear into the twenty-first century, I always responded: "The text is not as important as the teacher. As long as Prof. Couch is teaching the courses, he chooses his own text." And that's the way it was with all of us. We did our own thing, and, in my opinion, the students benefitted from the diversity of approaches. When Prof. Couch retired, his textual materials were no longer readily available to us since the bookstore that was distributing them for him went out of business. So, in collaboration with Dirk Willeford, the Faculty Associate scheduled to teach the RUS-101 in that next summer session, I chose another set of materials (Dan Davidson, et. al's <u>Live From Moscow</u> series through two years of instruction) for us to use (and it has subsequently been adopted for use at the University of Arizona also). Prof. Jeanette Owen, who came to us in Fall 2003 to direct our first two years of language instruction in a unified way, was already invested professionally in these materials and chose to continue them, as indeed we do today under Dr. Don Livingston. All of these people, however, no matter the pedagogical philosophy or "stance" of the text and its authors, continue to do their own thing, catering the educational experience to the student in an eclectic way.

STUDENT PROFILE

Our Russian language students, majors and non-majors, are, by and large, academic "fast-trackers." That is, the majority are full-time students taking full loads of academic coursework every semester, trying their best to graduate with dispatch. This data is shown in the facts about a recent (1996-2003) group of our Russian majors. The twenty of them have amassed an average of 76.93 semester hours in an average tenure here of 5.72 semesters, meaning that they are averaging 13.45 sem. hrs. per semester. Current Data Warehouse information does not deter from the 1997 profile wherein our section's students are roughly 60% male and 40% female (the sample group here has 11 male majors and 9 female majors)...this a reversal, for some reason, of the 1991 ratio of 60% female and 40% male. The average age of our students is slightly up to 22.8 years (from 1997's 22.2) and the average age at graduation in the previous seven years is 23.9 years. The average grade point average of our Russian majors is currently 3.37, the highest in the department and one of the highest in the college. The overall ASU gpa is 2.41. In 2000 I was informed that the professors of my section (ostensibly Profs. Burton, Couch, Croft, and Ekmanis) were giving grades at an average of 3.21. This means that whereas we were in 1991 a "grade rewarding" section (giving the 49 majors with a 2.81 average gpa grades at a 3.05 rate), we have become a "grade penalizing" section, giving our 19 majors with an average 3.37 gpa grades at a 3.21 rate (same as 1997 when our majors had an average gpa of 3.26). Subjectively, I think that I'm getting to be a grading "softy" as I get older, giving more and more "A" grades to my students...BUT the objective facts do not bear this out. Perhaps the oft-lamented "grade inflation" is proceeding even more vigorously in other quarters.

There are programmatic implications of our student profile. One such implication is that we do NOT have a large consituency of middle-age, already-working-elsewhere-in-a-full-time-career students, for whom we should devise evening, after-work, course opportunities. The massive majority of our students are full-time 18-25-year-olds (though most work off-campus part-time) taking our courses in concurrent multiples in an attempt to graduate with dispatch. We, as a result, try in all ways to avoid time-conflicts in the schedule between required classes...so as to allow our students to "double-up" and "triple-up" their required classes. This is also true because for other reasons...see below.

<u>Student Advisement:</u> The situation of academic advisement has changed radically in our department since the 1997 program review. In 1997 and in all years before, the FACULTY was directly responsible for the academic advisement of the students. In our section, it was primarily done by me...Lee Croft. The 1997 report states that "Prof. Croft was the advisor of record (change of major form, program of study form, graduation petition) for 54 of the 63 grads" from 1991 on (and always before it too). I even cited my 1991-7 "glitch" rate (students went through commencement but had to come back to complete some unsatisfied requirement they or I "missed") in advisement of 8% (up from 5% in 1981-91). This academic advisement, frankly, was a lot of work and it had become ever more complex after our university advisement function was recorded on computers under the DARS (Degree Audit Reporting System) protocol

after 1997. The decision was finally made to place ALL departmental advisement into the hands of a professional to be hired for this express purpose. I had misgivings about this, feeling that something essential in the faculty-student bonding process would be lost and that I would have to surrender long-built-up prerogatives of being able to circumvent "the letter" of certain graduation requirements and so on. But I served on the committee to hire a knowledgeable advisement professional...and one was, in fact, hired...a foreign-languages instructor (French) with computer savvy named Beth Glessner (now Beth Glessner-Calkins). Her superb performance on the demanding job of advising ALL our departmental majors (from all the languages at first, but now, with help, personally doing all but Spanish) has convinced everyone, including me, that this is the way to go. She has made my life dramatically easier here, so competently has she relieved me of much of this academic advisement function. In 2007 Beth was appointed to head the computerized degree-audit system called DARS. She will be replaced by her assistant, Ellie Wouda-Preciado, and a new assistant is being sought.

The advisement data, however, have not changed much since 1997 (of course, the "glitch" rate has declined...only two students affected in the 1996-2003 list of 66 graduates= 3%). It is still the case that we don't get many freshmen who come aboard already decided to be Russian majors. Mostly we win our majors to us in the course of their taking our classes while they are undecided or majoring in something else (Psychology and Political Science are the major "contributors"). The key point in this decision is still the FOURTH or FIFTH semester. That means that we have the majority of our majors taking our courses, trying to graduate with dispatch, who only made the decision to seek our degree when they were already sophomores or juniors. This also strongly militates for us to allow concurrent registration in the required courses. They have, in their minds, only THREE or FOUR semesters to amass the required 30 semester hours of Russian "core" coursework and the required 15 "related" hours. This is difficult, yet they manage to do it. Our majors are graduating in an average of 9.6 semesters (below the university average of 11.8).

Outcomes Assessment: As for the quality of our product, deciding how well do we teach our students to read, write, speak, and understand the Russian language and its host culture, I have misgivings about measuring it by test. Perhaps in some ways I'm generally "anti-test" in my educational philosophy. That is why I eschewed the departmental convention of giving "placement" exams, preferring to assess by personal conference the students' backgrounds and abilities...then allowing them to start where mutually agreed, and, if they don't do well there, move them to where they do. The size of our program and our relationships with our students (most take numerous courses from us and therefore we know each other well) has allowed this "examless" system of placement to work very well. BUT I admit to a need to assess terminal outcomes and have contributed my thought to the instruments of this assessment.

In the 1998-9 year, I volunteered the students of my section to undergo testing, both written and oral (by telephone interview), by the staff of a joint Defense Language Institute/American Council of Teachers of Foreign Languages (DLI/ACTFL) task force to assess terminal outcomes of U.S. higher educational foreign language programs. This was an ambitious effort, designed to provide a standard as well as a relative assessment of current foreign languages instructional success. The idea was to test a program's graduates to see how well they knew the foreign language, grading them on the widely accepted ILR 5-point fluency scale.

The temptation was strong to put some "ringers" into the test. We had at the time some native Russians with Russian educational backgrounds in our program...even a couple with "American" names, like Tamara McKane, subsequently a Faculty Associate who *taught* our RUS-411,2 Advanced Comp/Conv. BUT I restrained myself, deciding to ask ALL our graduates from that year to participate and exempting the educated Russian natives. Four of the six graduating seniors that year agreed to be tested. As it turned out, these students represented well the various main constituencies of students in our program. Sarah Carney was educated only in our program, having taken our courses from RUS-101 on through and without the benefit of any study-abroad programs or intensive stateside programs. John Whitefleet came to us having worked with Russian in Army Intelligence, having graduated in Russian from the DLI itself four years before starting our program at RUS-311 and completing in two years. Chad Twitty and Aaron Miles had come to us having completed two-year LDS missions in Russia. Both of them began our program at RUS-311 but took longer to complete than John Whitefleet because they had no other college credit. Chad was a Russian major only, but Aaron completed degree requirements also in Physics. Aaron had also spent one additional summer in Russia as an aide to Prof. Couch in our exchange program with Moscow State Linguistic University.

The results of the DLI/ACTFL proficiency level assessment were never nationally published...unfortunately, in my opinion. As a test monitor I received a personal check for $26.00 from one of the test directors...and that was all. I had a subsequent telephone conversation with now-retired-from-George-Washington-University-and-living-in-Kauai Prof. Irene Thompson, who had been one of my students' actual telephone interviewers. She commented to me that our ASU contingent was one of the strongest she had encountered in the testing and commiserated with me about the decision not to publish the results. I do, however, have the data from the evaluation certificates that were sent to the students themselves. Sarah Carney's certificate recorded her ILR fluency level in Russian to be 1+. John Whitefleet's certificate gave him a 3. Chad Twitty and Aaron Miles both received 3+ evaluations. My feeling is that we are turning out a very high quality product here, even as we cater our instructional efforts to widely varying students--monolingual Americans, Russian heritage speakers, DLI grads and returned LDS missionaries, all in the same classes.

We feel that our classes are of benefit to these diverse constituencies NO MATTER WHERE THEY ARE on a scale of background, experience, or aptitude. This is simply because learning a language is a LIFE-LONG PURSUIT. We never stop learning our native languages. So too, the sequential language learners will continue to learn at some rate as long as they are involved intellectually in the task. Our job is to keep them intellectually involved in the task, trying to optimize their progress individually. Some need research skills, some need cultural knowledge, some need grammar and advanced literacy... We try to give it all in some measure to all of them. One of the mechanisms that enables this diversity of service is the "omnibus" course...a course listed as RUS-484 (internship), RUS-499 (individualized instruction) or special topics courses under RUS-494 (Special Topics) or RUS-498 (Projects) or RUS-590 (Graduate Reading and Conference). As faculty, these courses do not officially count in the reckoning of "load." But we often have ten or more students per semester registered in them...each learning in some individualized way (service learning, internships of various kinds, research projects, tutoring, translation...interaction with Russian adoptees, spouses, etc.). Additionally, in our upper-division literature, culture and linguistics courses we generally cater the language requirements to the students' individual abilities and backgrounds in terms of readings, presentations and required writings (exams and papers). We may, for instance, have a Russian native who, for reasons of advancing his or her English skills, desires to read and write in English even though the skill level in English represents a relative handicap. We have even had Latin-American Spanish speakers in our classes who were learning Russian as they learned English. We certainly can't afford to offer different classes to the different types of students. Instead, we help as we can in the classes we have and take the individual efforts into account in the grading...we don't grade competitively (or "on a curve") at all. We have no quotas of either "A's" or "E's."

At ASU I am the faculty advisor of the "Student Russian Language Club." The Club organizes extracurricular support and interest-building activities for the students. Every year we hold a student meeting and elect a President. This President is usually an upper-division Russian language student. And this President winds up doing almost everything for the club. This is our tradition, and it is our tradition too, now actually written into our Club By-laws that are on file at the Associated Students of ASU student club registry, that EVERYONE ELSE IN THE CLUB IS A VICE-PRESIDENT. That way, they can all claim a prestigious position on their resumes. I cannot now remember all of our club presidents. I remember some, however, and would like to name them here: Patt Leonard was outstanding and left us a completed album of our activities in 1981-2 that still inspires us, Jacob Cruzen was the first two-year President and he first got us funds by registering us with ASASU, Tracy West Klenk signed us up to clean up one quarter of Sun Devil Stadium after the Fiesta Bowl for $500 in 1986 (and only twelve of the desired thirty showed up on New Year's morning...it was an unforgettable day), Pamela Schwartz designed an outstanding T-shirt for us with Anna Akhmatova's likeness on it with a very appropriate quotation from her poem "Courage;" "Мы Сохраним Тебя, Русская Речь" ("We will preserve thee, Russian Speech"), and Meagan King, our current and only three-year President, has raised good sums of money for our student award fund by organizing the sales of donated books. The Club has involved itself over the years in a most diverse host of functions: film showings, field trips of all kinds (from Russian poetry readings to bicycle tours to Salt River floats), Russian meals and pizza parties, athletic competitions in ASU intramurals (volleyball champs in 1976, softball contenders several years, and once we had a candidate, Brian Stark, in the University Olympics), T-shirt design contests and sales (I had a series of literary T-shirts—Pushkin, Gogol, and Tolstoy—that sold well in the 1970's and 1980's), translation contests (first the Vladimir Nabokov Memorial Contest and then, in 2003, we renamed it the Dmitrii Krioukov Memorial Contest in honor of a deceased exchange faculty member from Volgograd), and we had a Club newsletter called Пустяки or "Trifles." This newsletter reached its zenith of size, quantity and quality under the editorship of Jeanne Palumbo in 1990-91. Jeanne is the daughter of Dennis Palumbo, an ASU Regents' Professor of Justice Studies (now emeritus), and so she knew her way around the university. Very smart, she made the advancing of our academic province the task of her journalistic acumen. She asked me to write her a letter for the Thanksgiving Break issue of 1990 in which I described for the readers what all our former Russian students were now doing. Here it is:

" To: Jean Palumbo, Editor

Feature Content for Пустяки....Nov. 26, 1990

One of the things in my closet of an office I'm proudest of is my file of recommendation letters...over 1700 since 1973...over 100 per year, mostly piled up to 10 per week in late Fall and early Spring. This is surely one of my most important functions...boosting people up, the very reason I'm here. As I scan through them I can survey all the diverse career paths that students of the Russian Language wind up taking. The file, together with those occasional wonderful "where am I now" letters I can't find the time to answer provide me with an amazing catalogue of their achievements and social contributions.

The federal government is doubtlessly our major employer... especially its intelligence and diplomatic arms. I have been told that our ASU Russian Language program is the single leading supplier of Russian Linguists for the National Security Agency (NSA) with which we have an undergraduate cooperative program of alternating work and study. I can name, when pressed to do so, more than 25 of our students who have gone to work for the NSA. Terri Langlie Hudson ('86), who returned here in 1989 as a recruiting specialist for NSA, told me that whereas 75% of the NSA's entry-level Russian Linguists are shown by test to require significant in-house schooling in Russian, only 10% of our ASU contingent there did not qualify for direct work assignments. Of course, this is why the NSA sends a recruiter here three times per academic year.

We also have a sizeable contingent of students working for the CIA, especially women students, so it seems, after 1978 or so. Former student

Glavin McGalloway ('82) was part of the Soviet Leadership Analysis team there which correctly predicted Gorbachev's succession to power. She stopped by recently to tout our program, saying that her knowledge of the language gained here gave her a definite advantage over those who had learned it elsewhere and that the "intelligence Community knows well the excellence" of our program.

Michael Conrad ('86 University Moeur Award winner) was the first Russian Language Linguist hire of the FBI and now works as a Special Agent out of their Los Angeles office. The various branches of Military Intelligence have also employed our students in both active-duty and attached-civilian capacities. Bennett McCutcheon ('78 History double major…now in ASU Law School) was awarded an Air Force Commendation medal for his valorous actions under Soviet machinegun fire as a member of the U.S. military Liaison Mission in East Germany in 1987. John ('83) Bacca served a term in Army Intelligence in Augsburg, Germany and has now returned to teach Czech (which he learned at the Defense Language Institute after his Russian B.A. here) at the D.L.I. in Monterey, California. John Smith ("83) is an officer in Army Intelligence, now a communications specialist at the Presidio in San Francisco. Don Addis ('84) finished active duty as a Captain in Marine Intelligence and was to begin employment as an agent for the Drug Enforcement Agency in drug-troubled Miami when his reserve unit was activated and sent to Saudi Arabia…Good Luck, Don! A similar assignment has been reported for Jon Sachar ('88) also a USMC officer…just married in July. U.S. Navy Intelligence sends a representative here semesterly to fill several already appropriated and freeze-proof civilian Russian analyst positions…they're still looking.

When former President Reagan "allowed" the Soviets to remove their "staff members" (KGB) from our soviet embassy and consulates, Pacific Architects and Engineers (PA&E) got the contract to provide the more secure U.S. replacement personnel. Many of our students have obtained these positions…more than any other university. Ed and Karen Brauchli ('84-5 who met and married in our program) did a two-year term at the Moscow Embassy as a janitor and a driver, but subsequently were hired upon contacts made in the State Department to work in Bogota, Columbia. Tim Riley ('85) got married in a Soviet Palace of Marriages and has now returned to find entrance into a graduate program in Slavic Studies.

Graduate work in the field…further study leading to advanced degrees…is another frequent course of post-baccalaureate action for our students. Thus I take great pride in the accomplishments of such former students as: Mark Preslar ('83 at U. of Wash. past the Ph.D. comps who returned to teach here in 86-7), Sallie Folden ('85 History M.A. now on dissertation work at U. of Wash.), Robert Shein ('87 History now completing M.A. at Brown Univ.), Walt Richmond ('85 now on to Ph.D. work and teaching at USC), Henry DuVall ('86 History double major now a Graduate Teaching Assistant of Russian at U. of North Carolina), Steven Griffen ('84 now teaching at SUNY-Albany), Alex Pobedinsky ('83 at Syracuse U.), Herman Schiller ('85, also a U. of A. M.A. '89), and our current Faculty Associate Andrew Reese ('87, then Harvard M.A. '90) who married a delightful Leningrad girl while on a Soviet study program and who currently lists a Leningrad address as his residence even while he teaches here at ASU.

Andrew Reese is not our only former student to marry a Soviet citizen. John Ziker ('88 subsequently a Soviet Projects Manager and Editor for Kiser Research Inc. and now a Professor of Anthropology at Boise State University) met his Moscow bride while on the ACTR Semester program in the USSR. Sean McIntyre met his wife Liudmila, who has been teaching Russian at the Thunderbird School of International Management and in the Phoenix Union High School District feeder system, while in Moscow with the CIEE program.

Several of our former students are now working in International Business. Susan Coady ('78 then Thunderbird '80) is now responsible for international marketing at Magnavox in Syracuse, New York. Hai Van Tran Lewis ('81 and married within our program) was a soviet trade representatative for a consortium of Honolulu hotels and has represented Croft Consultants in the islands. Debra Anderson Jaynes ('77) and Susan Speshock Pao ('84) have been working in the California offices of Japanese (?) trading companies. Jeff Boehm (Business, Russian Minor '85) showed the Soviets how to use reflective tape (traffic signs, etc.) for 3-M Corp. Patty Bailey ('83, U. of A. M.A. '86) was Moscow resident as the wife of the Soviet head of Dresser Industries. Dra Wiersema (Business, Russian Minor '83) worked with Caterpillar's Soviet Production team. And there are others, many of whom paired their Russian study with programs of Business. AGSIM-Thunderbird has attracted a dozen or so of our students to further study in this area (Tammy Shahar, Loren Krebs, Mirjana Baich, Anna Krajewsky, Marian Bohl...) as have M.B.A. programs (Kim O'Connor '89...).

The nation's finest Law Schools have admitted our Russian Language students without exception. Jim O'Haver ('78 History double major) was journal editor at U. of A. Law and then an editor for the National Association of Criminal Defense Lawyers. Now he is a public defender in Prescott, Arizona. Elizabeth Gottschalk (also a 1980 double major with history) specialized herself in Arabic, studying in both Cairo and Istanbul (with Fulbright aid), then did graduate study at the University of Chicago in Middle Eastern Studies (M.A., 1983) while competing in Judo and traveling around as a sky-diver. Achieving a super score on the Law School Aptitude Test, she won admittance to Harvard Law School and while there wrote a National Aviation Writers' awarded murder-mystery novel with a sky-diving plot called <u>Double Malfunction</u> (written from a male personna as E. P. Gottschalk, Daedalus Press, 1991). Now she is a full partner with the large law firm, Kirkland and Ellis, in New York City. Robert Baum ('82 University Moeur Award winner) graduated from Stanford Law in 1987 after interning with the World Court in Europe…but now is grant-writing to support a preferred career in art. Darrow Soll (1985 Russian major), an Army airborne veteran and former police officer, was admitted to the University of Arizona's innovative joint program to earn both an M.D. and a J.D. But he soon focused exclusively on the School of Law and became a white-collar crime specialist with Phoenix's law firm, Quarles & Brady, Streich Lang. There he became well-known advocating the case of child molesters whose terms of incarceration was expired that the State wanted to keep in prison, and in representing the former boxing champion Mike Tyson. Tragically, he died suddenly in his home (?) at age 39 in 2005. He has a www.legacy.com website where more than sixty people have recorded their positive memories of him. Working with him at Quarles & Brady Streich Lang is Scott Deeny (1988 Russian major). Edwin Aralica (1996 Russian major) is now an attorney with the "Innocence Project." Lou Horowitz and Adam Orford (Russian students of the late 1990's) both went to Columbia University's prestigious School of Law. Lou is specializing in International Law and Adam is now working at a large firm, Willkie, Farr & Gallagher, in New York City specializing in environmental law. 1998 Russian major Tamara McKane is now practicing as an eminent domain attorney in Mesa, but taught advanced Russian here at ASU from 2000 to 2003. Indeed Law Schools have always had a special liking for our Russian students. In all these thirty-plus years of recommending students to law school, there is only one student I have recommended who has not yet been admitted…and he, Enrique Canales, once an illegal alien from El Salvador, is still trying.

We even have Russian Language students who were admitted to medical schools, like Terry James ('69) in Utah, or Sue McCarter ('74) at Harvard who are now practicing. Patrick Carty ('90 Chem) completed Medical School at Loma Linda School of Medicine, earning the D.O. degree. He then became an emergency medical specialist in the Phoenix area and has opened a private medical partnership in Mesa. Several of our Russian students (e.g. Outstanding Student Award Winners David Ellingson (1999), and Richard Bentley (2000), and also Ned Williams (2001) and Benjamin Tingey (2003)) are currently in Dental Schools.

We have sent students into the journalism and broadcasting field with particular success (Catrien Ross, Alan Kenny, Robert Kelly, Paul Green, Nina Bondarook, and Thomas Bonifield, who is MSNBC broadcasting head in Moscow...). Several (most recently Jill Schiager '85) have served in the Peace Corps. Several have been or are now high school teachers (Shirley Strunk '78, Craig Plumlee '80, Pat Barrett '66, Sue Farbarik Fry '88...). And several are Slavic-area information management specialists (librarians and archivists), like Murlin Croucher ('68), Paula Bickett ('80), Suzanne Galvin ('77), and Mike Malone ('84). More than one have found careers in religion (Chris Burke '77, now in counseling, and David Fisher '80 went on to semenaries, Tracy West '88 worked for a religious mission to Eastern Europe for a time, and Patricia Bailey (now Cossette), a co-author of mine in the Phillips' **Методика...** anthology, ASU class of '83, once worked with the Slavic Gospel Society...). One of our students, Sherry Wheatley Sacino (ca. 1984) has had a multifarious career in Public Relations: first as representative of the *Phoenix Flames* indoor soccer team, then as a founder of the Moscow Marathon, then as the organizer of African pineapple processing, as an advisor to the <u>Sports Illustrated</u> magazine version for children and its allied television program, as the author of Sports Books' <u>Keeping the Drive Alive: Growing Up to be a Buccaneer</u> (a Tampa Bay Buccaneer, 1995) and as the arranger of the much celebrated "double time celebrations of the turning of the millenium" (i.e. in Tahiti on Dec.31/Jan.1 on one day, then, having crossed backwards over the international date line, in Fiji again the "next" day). Few people have held so high the standard of entrepreneurial spirit as she.

In the past month I have received letters or cards from our four current exchangees to the Soviet Union or East Europe (Alan Church, grad student in English who is in Skopje, Yugoslavia, Steve Patrick of Political Science who is in Krakow, Poland, Liz Elliott and Aggie Czerski on exchange programs in the USSR), from Major Kent Larson ('90 MA in History) who is studying further Russian in the US Army Russian Research Center in Garmisch-Partenkirchen, Germany, from Theresa Clinch ('87) who is headed for a child-care job attached to the Moscow Embassy, from Lance Kuester (84), an NSA employee in England who is applying to USARI in Germany after completing intensive Russian review work at Indiana University, from Alan Anderson ('86, U of A MA '88, USIA Soviet Exhibit Guide "89-90) who now works as a Soviet Project Manager in Washington, D.C. for Delphic Associates, from Lynn Camphire ('88, U. of Pittsburgh MA '90) who is also now applying to Delphic, from John Blakney ('88), now an account executive at Phoenix office of American Express where is now working also Tony Mormino ('88-89 Italian Instructor and Russian Student and traveler) while waiting on Law School applications, and from Karrie Gonnerman ('88, double major with Psych., U. of A. MA '90) who wrote: "I just wanted to let you know that I got my M.A. in August and have great job prospects for the future. I've been teaching in Payson where my parents live since Sept., but I Leave for the USSR within the next 6 weeks. The State department rated me a "3" speaker of Russian and I'll be a consular assistant at the embassy in Moscow for 1 year. I was also accepted at 1 of the gov't agencies—which I plan on starting after returning from the USSR..."

Hopefully these paragraphs render some kind of a representative sample of the many ways our Russian Language program has benefitted its students...government intelligence and diplomatic work, military intelligence, international business, graduate schools in Slavic Studies, Law Schools, Medical Schools, graduate schools of Business, teaching positions, library science and archival management, Seminaries, ...opportunities for foreign travel and intercultural contact as important aspects of career choice. This is what our program here is all about. This is what impact it makes.

The members of our Russian Section family here at ASU have plenty of reasons, represented by the many "success stories" above, to think that we are a real "pocket of excellence" in undergraduate education. Our enrollment steadily swells, our students go on to succeed in diverse ways, and our reputation for turning out well prepared students is well established nationally. It is, unfortunately, only here locally, within our own institution (ASU), that our particular type of human success is under-recognized and our progress is hampered by administrative under-prioritization in the current severe financial climate prevailing in higher education. Like others at ASU we have been asked to do more and more with less and less...and we have done so successfully. But we have come in many ways to feel like that "little calf" ("telenok") of the Solzhenitsyn work, that futilely "butts his head against the oak" ("bodaetsja s dubom"). Student aide positions are now gone, travel funds are a mere token, capital expense funds (for instructional aids, etc.) are minimal at best, and, most negatively impactful, requests for new faculty lines persistently denied. In this climate program growth is impossible and holding the present level of quality is ever more difficult.

What we need to make the people who count (the purse-string people) more aware of our excellence and our importance is more of what I, in my first years as a faculty member here, used to term "the three P's:" Propaganda, Proselytization, and Promotion…inform 'em, enroll 'em, and boost 'em up, advance them in life. Of course our Russian Language Club's video series, its sponsored lectures, its T-shirt design contest (Congratulations to winner Valerie Hathaway) and sales, and indeed this newsletter Pustjaki are all integral parts of our "three P's" effort. I certainly thank you all for your participation in these supportive activities.

BOL'SHOE SPASIBO!   Sincerely, Lee B. Croft, Russian Section Coordinator, DFL"

U. of A. Outstanding Senior Student Kenneth Cargill (and former Russian Drama Troupe actor), flanked by his mentors, Prof. Adele Barker (L.) and Prof./HEAD Teresa Polowy (R.). 2006 photo from www.russian.arizona.edu.

As part of our B.A. in Russian's first program review in 1991, I made an effort to list the subsequent fates of many of our graduates and posted the resultant synopsis on the sectional bulletin board headlined with the question "WHERE ARE THEY NOW?" Here is a re-edition (with additions of more recent information) of that 1991 poster:

"Many of our graduates have gone on to teach Russian or other related subjects in our own or other institutions of higher learning. We take a very special pride in teaching those who are now teaching others: Leslie Wright Smith (U. of Montana after U. Texas Ph.D.), Robert Shein (Brown U.), Steven Griffen (SUNY-Albany), Alex Pobedinsky (Syracuse U.), Kathleen McFie Ahern (NC-Greensboro after UNC-Chapel Hill Ph.D.), Herman Schiller (U. of Az.), Carl Seargent (Iowa State U.), Elisabeth Elliott (Northwestern U after U. Toronto Ph.D.), Henry Duvall (U. of Minnesota), Walter Richmond (Occidental College after USC Ph.D.), Maria Budisavljevic-Oparnica (ASU after USC Ph.D.), Andrew Reese (ASU after Harvard U. MA), Mark Preslar (U. of the South after U. Washington Ph.D.). Several of our former students are now working in Library/Archival management: Suzanne Galvin (U. of Illinois), Paula Bickett (Hoover Institute/Stanford U.), Murlin Croucher (U. of Indiana Library), Michael Malone (U. of Washington Library), Patricia Cameron, Kent Blalock, Michael Galope and Sue Farbarik (ASU Library). We have put many graduates of our program into the American Graduate School of International Management-Thunderbird Campus and on into international business: Mirjana Baich, Loren Krebs, Anna Krajewski, Marianne Bohl, Susan Coady, Tami Shahar, and Russ Van der Wurf. Several of our students have gone into religious mission work or the ministry: Patricia Bailey (Slavic Gospel Society), Tracy West Klenk, Chris Burke, and David Fischer. Jill Schiager served part of a Peace Corps term in Senegal, but was evacuated due to the possibility of armed strife there and employed as editor of a compendium of US NGO's (Non-governmental organizations) dealing with the Soviet Union. Peter Doran has been an editor for the Freedom House assessments of the world's democratization. Journalists and broadcasters include: Alan Kenny, Brian Fitzgerald, Catrien Ross, Nina Bondarook, Robert Kelley, Paul Green, and Thomas Bonifield of Moscow MSNBC. International businesses have taken many of our graduates and Russian students: David Brown (Lees Carpets), Jeff Boehm (3M in Russia), Elizabeth Myers (Texas Instruments), Alan Anderson (GE), Curt Collinsworth and Troy Tingey (US outdoor advertising in

Russia). U.S. Government agencies in intelligence and diplomatic security have taken many: Jerry Marshall, Denee Hoover, and Glavin McGalloway (CIA), Lance Kuester, Bill and Gail Andersen, Terri Langley, Ksenia Lutz, Rebecca Kendrick-Thomas, Michael Cartwright, Robert Holcomb, Cheri Bertoni Peters, Joyce Tilzey Keeler, Kathleen Monahan, Martin Sielaff, Suzanne Jensen, Michael and Linda Hicks, and Louisa Morris (NSA), Michael Conrad and Sally Smith (FBI), Timothy Riley, Ed and Karen Brauchli, Dino and Christine Mortensen, and Vincent Vedelago (PA& E Embassy/Consulate security and maintenance) and Jerry Bialek (Pentagon security maintenance. And, very importantly, we have a long list of heroes of our US military, veterans of service here and abroad in the Army (Ed Brennan, John Smith, John Bacca, Julie Henderson), Navy (Mark Simpson, Ed Hunter), Air Force (Bennett McCutcheon, Thomas Wheeler, Kameron Kerger), Marines (Don Addis, Jon Sachar) and the National Guard and Air National Guard (Phil Dunihue, Matthew Teetshorn). The many lawyers and several medical physicians and dentists are mentioned elsewhere, and recently our Barrett Honors College graduate, Svetlana Pomirchy (2006), was accepted into Pharmacy School. Clearly the answer to the question: "Where are they now" is "Everywhere…they're everywhere."

Here follows an attempt to list our Russian B.A. graduates from 1981 to 1991, taken, again, from the 1991 program review "Self Study Document."

1981: Susan Benzer, Joyce Tilzey Keeler, Tammy Shahar, Marta Dittert

1982: Constance Brown, Kevin Michael Malone, Mark Merrifield, Raymond Mark Preslar, Hai-Van Tran, Don R. Wright, Lisa Haskell, Paul Kachur, Craig Plumlee, Julie Unger

1983: Robert Baum, Sylvia Gill, Lance Kuester, John Bacca

1984: Edward Bergman, Michael Cohen, Christopher Evans, Kathleen McFie, Donald Addis, Rick Musselman

1985: Nancy Jo Brown, Paul Green, Edward Brennan, Siri Granfelt

1986: Steven Ashworth, Nancy Chaykin, Steven Griffen, Janet Kenning, Jeffrey Klossner, Michael Murza, Suzanne Park, Jill Schiager, Gail Turner, Elizabeth Venuti, Dennis Adam, Brigit Keppe, Andrew Porter, David Stensland, Patricia Cameron, Edwin Brauchli, Michael Conrad, Sean McIntyre, Susan Moore, John Nemecek, Walter Richmond, Timothy Riley

1987: Jennifer Hobbs, Daniel Kelley, Kimberly O'Connor, Martin Sielaff, Thomas Wheeler, Constance Bjella, Carol Kuester, Walter Richmond

1988: Jill Batistick, Teresa Clinch, Christina Couch, William Dyrek, Shannon Eisen, John Goldthwaite, Frank Zupan, Robert Bailey, Lizabeth Rohovit, Daniel Secklin

1989: James Bade, Bruce Burris, Lynn Camphire, Michael Galope, Joel Haddock, Suzanne Jensen, Louis Lofredo III, Alice Lohr, Jonathan Sachar, Carl Sergeant, Daniel Sikokis, Robert Simpson, Erich Schmidt, Darrow Soll, Theresa "Tracy" West (Klenk), David Bruner, Mitchell Sanders, Laura Hagberg, Terri Traynor, Marvin Welch, Jr.

1990: Joseph Altnether, Louisa Morris, Natalie Morris, Jacqueline Sullivan, Lee Wilson, Jr., Daniel Meahl, Pamela Modzelewski. That's 95 graduates in 9.5 years (doesn't count 1991 commencements)...10/yr. in that decade.

RUSSIAN BA GRADUATES, 1996-2003

Here is an attempt to list our graduates, year by year, from 1996 to 2003. The 1996 academic year was included because the 1997 report was based on a self-study document completed in 1996 before the Fall 1996 students had graduated (only the 3 Spring 1996 graduates were listed in the document). The task of determining who our graduates are is surprisingly difficult, as it is to determine who will actually graduate in any particular commencement. This list is largely taken from the commencement brochures, augmented by the Data Warehouse numbers, and a survey of the supervised theses from the Barrett Honors College (BHC), which enrolls two or three of our graduates every commencement. For this reason the numbers don't entirely jive with those on the attached "ASU Russian Enrollment/Graduations, 1970-2004" mentioned earlier (though they are close). I have tried to add what I know about the subsequent fate of all of them whose fate I know. In recent years, staying in touch with former students has been rendered easier than formerly by e-mail. We are, in fact, compiling an e-mail directory of them for use in forming a sectional "Alumni Board" for program support purposes. It was through e-mail that many of our alumni responded to our request for information. I might also mention here that this list does NOT include those students who "minored" in Russian for the purposes, after 1998, of attaining the BIS (Bachelor of Interdisciplinary Science...essentially two minors) degree. I have noted also the Russian graduates on this list who have also received the interdisciplinary Russian and East European Studies Certificate (REESC).

The REESC holders are marked with an asterisk before their names. Some 2007 information has been added:

1996 (8 graduates)

Babette Finley: Now works in ASU Human Resources Dept.

*Ronald Birks: Senior engineer for Honeywell, participant in Honeywell's paired factory program in Perm', Russian Federation
Glen Kelly: Works with adoption agency specializing in the adoption of Russian children, once sponsored a Russian refugee dentist and wife.
Daniel Kopp: have lost touch, don't know.
*Christine Michajliw: Did graduate work at Harvard University's Ukrainian Research Center, now employed in arranging international bicycle races
Theodore Rybka: have lost touch, don't know.
David Schlappy: US military intelligence, retrained at DLI in Czech (Korean?)
Loren Tomasi: Teaching language arts in a charter elementary school in Mesa.

1997 (10 graduates)

*Margaret Barney-O'Neil (BHC): Graduate Program in International Relations, Georgetown University.
Scott M. Prada: US Army Intelligence, now in middle east.
James T. Turney: Employed at Boeing in Mesa on a NASA-funded project
Jennifer M. Yungfleisch: U. of A. MLS, Librarian at U. of Illinois.
*Benjamin T. Allred: working in family agricultural business.
Michael K. Gold: UCLA law school, likely done, but...?
Chad O. Olson (BHC): Grad. School in Creative Writing, U. of Iowa
Pamela D. Schwartz: Married to senior local psychiatrist, mother of a current Russian language student in program
Paul S. Wollam: Has a private business in international security, Huarong-do master and bodyguard...translated Russian self-defense manual.
Margaret Perl: have lost touch, don't know...can't, in fact, recall her...suspect the listing may be another last name for Margaret Barney-O'Neil (above) (?)

1998 (10 graduates)

Jared Everton: Law School in Utah, passed AZ. bar, now practicing in Mesa.

Robert Foreman: Law School in Ca., practicing real estate law there.
Miki Kerrigan: Married a submarine sailor, now in WA...new daughter.
John Whitefleet: AGSIM-Thunderbird Grad School of International
  Management, works in international banking in Los Angeles.
*Sarah Carney: Public Relations for Horse Racing at Turf Paradise, Phoenix.
Jason Mainka (BHC): NSEP fellow in Russia, Newspaper Editor in Oregon.
Kristin Kuchenbacker: Teaches Russian as a grad student in a German Univ.
Aaron Miles: Won Graduate Fellowship for Ph.D. in Physics at U. Maryland,
  works with Russian scholars, including Roald Sagdeev. Now completed
  Ph.D. and working at Livermore Laboratories in California.
J. Richard Bentley: Dental School in Chicago.
*Sally J. Smith (BHC): NSEP fellow, now FBI Special Agent.

1999 (7 graduates)

*Kami K. Rynish (BHC): NSEP fellow, Ph.D. Candidate in Political Science
  at Emery University
Irina I. Ananyeva: Dual degree with Spanish, MA in Nuclear Non-
  proliferation Studies at Monterey Institute of International Studies,
  Security NGO analyst.
Peter B. Doran (BHC): worked for Freedom House compiling yearly
  democratic process assessments, now accepted with aid for MA in Russian
  and East European Studies at Georgetown University.
*Brent Levi Gunderson: Accepted at U of Az Law School, then took TA'ship
  in U. of AZ's Russian Dept. after one year, now teaching Russian there.
Staci R. Maiers: Public Relations Aide for a national politician (Washington
  senator (?)...can't remember from Alumni mag, sorry).
*Chad M. Twitty: Graduation from 1998 was delayed, Gonzaga Law School.
Eric Strachan (BHC): Dual degree req. with English, CLI-Tatar, then NSEP
  fellow in Kazan, now in ASU Ph.D. program in Political Science, teaches.

2000 (6 graduates)

Jeremiah J. Broughton: Musician in a rock band, composes Russian lyrics.
Mary L. Glenn: Retired with husband, was intern in MSLU program twice,
  is mother of a current Russian language student here...selling insurance.
*Kameron G. B. Kerger (BHC): won prestigious MLK Service Scholar
  Award as first woman (and first non-African-American for work with

Bosnian refugees) worked as Slavic languages greeter for British Airways at Sky Harbor Airport; then in US Air Force Intelligence in "middle east." Now back stateside, injured her ankle badly, got married in 2006.

Bryan M. Moody: Together with Russian-student wife started a private lawyer referral business in Scottsdale.

Jared A. West: won a Ph.D. fellowship in Russian Lang/Lit at U. of Washington but has returned here, is applying for a faculty associateship in Russian here.

David Ellingson: Triathlon competitor, dental school in Illinois.

<u>2001</u> (10 graduates)

*Dwight J. Brown: worked at Hayden Library in interlibrary loan, now working at Moscow embassy in Russia with PA&E.

*William D. Gunn: Television and summer stock actor, future star. Taking Ph.D. courses in Russian literature at USC after MA at BYU.

William A. Lester: was an intern on the IWER 2000 Project with Kazakh emergency response delegation, was on TV speaking Russian...now in ASU's MA Program in Environmental/Landscape Design.

Justin Wright: Educational Administrator in Mesa, married a Russian.

Mark Mabry: Takes wedding photos, has private audio-video business.

Russ Van Der Werf: dual degree with Business, went to Thunderbird Grad School of International Management, involved in Russian Business aid program there administered by two other former ASU Russian grads.

Pamela A. Goodrich: Real Estate agent in New Mexico.

Robert D. Heeder: Also a CLI participant in BCS, now US Army Intelligence.

*Pauline I. "Penny" Smith (BHC): working as a public health nurse.

*Jamie L. Keeton: Dual degree req. with History, won Ph.D. fellowship in Russian lang and lit at UCLA.

<u>2002</u> (9 graduates)

Regina Levin Ausloos: Works in event management (e.g. Barrett-Jackson auto auction) in Scottsdale.

Benjamin J. Fanello: have lost touch...don't know.

Broc Hendershott: ASU MA Program in Housing and Urban Development.

Sean M. Paulsen: Guitarist in rock band of another Russian student (James

Bongiovi), "Twelve and Under," and touring...also teaches tennis.

*Tina Consentino: Accepted into U. of A. MA program in Slavic Langs/Lits, conjoint wit MLS degree, considered for RA/TA-ship.

Andy Wright: worked as public relations aide with Phoenix Suns NBA basketball team, Russian interpreted for player Jake Tsakalides...now works in marketing for the University of Phoenix.

Kees Campbell: was accepted at U. of Az for MA/Russian, but went instead to dental school in California.

Catherine A. (Williams) Banash: Participated in our MSLU exchange, now works in ASU Computer Services Dept.

Enrique Gustavo Canales-Hernandez: Came to US as smuggled illegal from El Salvador, having quit school after 5th grade, graduated at 26 from Phx Central H.S. and, as first native hispanic, from our program in Russian. Aspires to law school, but now working at Sprint International Call Center as a Spanish interpreter. Won our "Dr. Nick Vontsolos Perseverance Award." He got a green card finally, obtained an El Salvadoran passport and plans to visit Russia, hoping to teach Spanish at Moscow State University.

<u>2003</u> (6 graduates)

*Andrew S. Cocchia: CLI-Tatar, NSEP fellow in Kazan. Financial analyst with Vanguard Investment Services, Scottsdale.

*Aaron H. Pratt: Works as travel agent in Mesa...has sent groups to Russia.

Christopher W. Ayers: Manager of Madstone Movie Theater in S. Tempe, shows Russian movies there, including THE RUSSIAN ARK.

*Danielle M. Ross (BHC): NSEP fellow in Kazan. Won graduate fellowship for the Ph.D. in Central Asian Studies at U. of Wisconsin and has (summer 2006) returned to teach the Tatar in our CLI.

Amy Campbell: Now employed at the Defense Intelligence Agency in Washington, DC.

Autumn "Renee" Spritzer: Worked in Human Resources Dept of International Truck dealer in Phoenix, and now enrolled with financial aid in the University of Arizona Law School.

That's 66 graduates in 8 years...average is <u>8.25 graduates per year.</u> <u>18</u> of them also received the rigorous REESC Certificate. I have lost track of several (5) and may not be current on others...but the great majority are positively employed in our society and are grateful they studied Russian at ASU.

Of the 61 whose status I'm aware of, 8 are teaching in Russian or "related" areas, 6 went to law school, 7 went to graduate schools of business or international study, 11 went to graduate schools in Russian Lang/Lit/Culture or related areas, 3 went to medical or dental schools, 10 became employed by US. Government agencies (Military Intelligence, DIA, FBI, State Dept.), and 16 became employed in private businesses or unrelated public sector agencies. It's not entirely easy to determine this, but I'd say that 29 of them use or have used Russian in their professional lives since graduation, and 32 have, by and large, not used Russian in their graduation-subsequent employment. That is OK with me. One of the main attributes we are trying to give our graduates is CONFIDENCE...the belief that they can, having succeeded in our program, succeed anywhere at anything...that they can make a significant positive contribution to our society. In every class I manage to tell them: "Don't worry about what a 'good job' you're going to get when you leave here, about who is going to hire you...instead, give some serious thought to what enterprise you should start, whom you should hire." The entrepreneurially trepidatious respond: "But I have no experience, no money...how will I begin?" I answer: "At this stage of life, you have nothing to lose. Now is the time to try something. Be a hammer, not a nail, in life. You have the important experience of succeeding here in this demanding program...you will succeed in whatever else you try." Many do.

The people named above and in the 1996-2003 graduates list with the "BHC" notation after their names completed requirements for their degree as members of the ASU Craig and Barbara BARRETT (endowing donors) HONORS COLLEGE. ASU's Barrett Honors College is a most impressive (and selective) academic enterprise and its graduates have an equally impressive record of undergraduate and post-graduate achievement. Each BHC student must complete 18 sem. hrs. of dedicated honors college course work, taught by BHC faculty. In addition, they must do "extra work," directed by the professors of their ordinary ASU coursework in an additional 18 sem. hrs. of coursework. AND they must complete and defend an honors thesis. This is done in two semesters: the first semester, RUS-492, is the research, and the second, RUS-493, is the writing and the defense...total 6 semester hours, graded for all the 6 hrs. after the defense. The theses are signed by all the members (usually 3) of the student's defense committee (the Chair and another are selected by the student, a third faculty member is selected by the BHC staff). In the past eight years I (Lee Croft) have chaired eight of these theses (not all were Russian majors...but 1 per year average) and have been a committee member on 5 more. At this writing (April 2007) I am supervising the Barrett Honors Thesis of Meagan King, the only three-time Russian Club President in our program's history. She is writing a thesis entitled "The Etymology and Onomasiology of the Generic terms for Sexually Transmitted Diseases in Contemporary Standard Russian" and will be submitting it soon. The other committee members are Dr. Danko Šipka and Dr. Don Livingston. The only other sectional faculty member to be a BHC thesis committee member is Prof. Ekmanis...who may have done 1 or 2, but not, to my memory, as Chair. Profs. Burton and Couch did not participate.

Our faculty has had great relative success in mentoring our students in the most prestigious national and international fellowship and scholarship competitions. In the past decade or so, this effort has been channeled through a special office set up for this purpose. It is called ONSA—the Office of National Scholarship Advisement, and it is a part of the Barrett Honors College at ASU. The Dean there, Dr. Janet Burke, and her Assistant, Suzanne Balamenti, make it their job to find outstanding students at ASU they can help obtain these prestigious fellowships and scholarships—the Rhodes Scholarship at Oxford, the Marshall Fellowship, the Truman Fellowship, The Bill and Melinda Gates Fellowship at Cambridge, the Danforth and Goldwater Fellowships, the Fulbright Scholarships, and, especially relevant for us, the David Boren Act National Security Education Program (NSEP) scholarships. These NSEP scholarships are meant to pay for a student's study abroad and language acquisition in areas critical to the national security. The candidates are identified, informed, coached, recommended, and faculty juried into submitting competitive proposals for study and for plans of how to utilize the required "compensatory government service" in ways maximally beneficial to the candidate. Many of these proposals eventuate in honors theses, master's theses, doctoral dissertations, and highly responsible courses of permanent employment in national-security-critical areas of the world. Every year, those of us who participate in this mentorship (I should cite here my colleagues Stephen Batalden of History and the Melikian Center, Danko Šipka, Ariann Stern-Gottschalk, and Ileana Orlich in particular), take great pride when ASU is listed nationally among the leaders in the numbers of its students receiving such prestigious scholarships and fellowships and when we see that our Slavic Studies "enterprise" has generated more than a proportional share of those.

In the first-floor hallway of Irish Hall within the Barrett Honors College campus are displayed the photographs of the recent ASU winners of Rhodes, Gates, Marshalls, Trumans, Goldwaters, Fulbrights, and NSEP nationally competitive fellowships and scholarships. The walls of this hallway are literally covered with 8 X 12 framed photographs of our students. When I walk that hallway, these photos recall to me memories of these talented, hard-working, sky-high aiming young people. I imagine to myself that I have worked with (i.e. had in class, recommended and/or juried) a larger share of the students reflected in these photographs than any other faculty member (with the possible exception of Steve Batalden, with whom I've shared many). Here is a list of those jotted onto a piece of paper after a recent visit to that hallway:

Bill Katsinas (Fulbright then NSEP to Lithuania, arms monitor)
Julie Nachtigal (Fulbright then NSEP to Macedonia, graduate school)
Steven Patrick (Fulbright then Grad NSEP to Hungary, graduate school)
Steven Gillen (Fulbright then Grad NSEP to Macedonia, now diplomat)
James Frusetta (Fulbright then Grad NSEP to Macedonia, now journalist)
Dmitri Tartakovsky (Fulbright then Grad NSEP to Macedonia, diplomat)
Peg Barney O'Neil (NSEP to Russia, grad school)
Jason Mainka (NSEP to Russia, now editor in Oregon)
Maren Curtis (NSEP to Macedonia, grad school)
Jennipher Danielson (NSEP to Macedonia, grad school)
David Brown (NSEP to Russia, Goldwater Scholar also, grad school)
Todd Taylor (NSEP to Kazakhstan, grad school)
Kami Rynish (NSEP to Russia, grad school)
Chris Newhart (NSEP to Russia, journalism)
Danielle Ross (NSEP to Kazan, Tatarstan, grad school)
Colin Raymond (NSEP to Mongolia, then Marshall to England, having actually turned down a Rhodes (really))
Jordan Eickman (a profoundly DEAF student who took Russian from me, actually teaching me Russian sign language, USA TODAY 1st Team Academic All-Star, Marshall Fellowship to England, grad. School)
Kerry Pace (Meyer) (NSEP to Russia).
Kameron Kerger (NSEP to Russia)
Kimberly Hill (NSEP to Russia)
Melissa Archibald (NSEP to Russia)
Erin Traeger (Fulbright to Macedonia)

Others that I've had some lesser contact with include: Patricia Mah, Pat Gilbert, Lauralyn Beaty, Allison Bryce, and Beth Altringer. Currently I am waiting to hear word of the NSEP success of several, including one of this year's sectional "outstanding student" award winners, Laurie L. Dermer, and my current honors thesis mentoree and Russian Club President Meagan King. Very few university faculty members anywhere have been as blessed as I have with outstanding students and high-potential young people.

Recent Emails from Former ASU Russian Students

In the 1990 letter to Russian Club Newsletter *Pustjaki* editor Jeanne Palumbo I mention "those occasional wonderful 'where are they now' letters I never have time to answer." Of course, we are now in the "email era" of such communication and I find answering much easier. So here is a selection of such email communications I have received in the past few years. I am entering them here as best I can in the chronological order (oldest to most recent) of the graduation dates, adding notes of identification.

First in this sample is the email message of Anthony "Tony" Parella. He was my student in the 1970's, graduating in 1977. He is one of the translators of poetry in my first book, Russian Symbolist Poetry: Verse Translations from the Silver Age (Four Continent Books, NY, 1977...a single used copy is now for sale on Amazon for $100.00). After he left ASU he was, for a couple of years, a professional golfer. Then he did graduate study in Russian at the University of Washington in Seattle. He writes:

"Dear Prof. Croft,

Occasionally I receive these bulk-rate newsletters from the alumni folks who, misguided, believe a little taste of the old college days will induce me to throw a few bucks their way, and I hate to disappoint so I don't read them. Can't say why I leafed through their latest attempt, Fall 2002, but in it I found an amusing article regarding a certain chair (see earlier in text, LBC) that I may have sat in once or twice myself.

I'm sure that after all these years you won't remember that I sat in your Russian classes in 1973 and beyond, a Russian language major even, the class of '77. I also recall fondly and vividly your penchant for the

Nabokovesquen fable; so if I tell you that I detect a slight whiff of the apocryphal in the saga of the chair you must understand that I also recollect your claim to have been acquainted with the originator of the infamous pyramid hoax and that you yourself penned a pseudo-scientific satire linking the transmission of language learning and, what was it...cytoplasm?

Upon reading "The Chair," I was reminded of a great many things about my university days, and I thought it is long past due to express my gratitude and appreciation to you for the excellent and much valued education I received from you and Professors Couch and Ekmanis. I believe the study of the language and literature of Russia has had a profound and enriching effect on my intellectual life, and while the working world has led me in what often seemed to be divergent directions, I've remained at the core a Russophile. I'll bet there's not a day goes by that a certain poem of Pushkin (once memorized at your wise insistence) doesn't go rattling through this old brain. Actually, after almost thirty years, I now find myself doing work where the language training is occasionally useful: I'm booking romance tours to Russia...and the less said about that the better.

Warmest regards from your former student, Tony Parella."

In RUS-211/212, a year-long course called Basic Conversational Russian, I have required that the students memorize and recite on a schedule a number of classic Russian poems—from Derzhavin, through Pushkin and Lermontov to Blok, Esenin, Akhmatova, and Pasternak. Memorization of material in a foreign language is difficult, I know, and I sympathize with their frequent complaints. But while the task forces the blazing of new psychoneurological trails in their brains and arms them forever with the grammatical linguistic templates that have made these works the immortal cultural masterpieces they are, they wind up with a ready-made "something to say in Russian" when asked. And, as it turns out, they can still do this many years after their university days. Egregious recent examples: 1976 Russian graduate W. Michael "Misha" Welsch shows up at an ASU Russian Club table on the mall in 2003 and comiserates with the students at the table about "that Prof. Croft, still requiring students to learn Derzhavin's long and difficult 'Monument'" (Памятник), then reciting it for them after twenty-seven years; 1977 graduate Lila Roberts reciting the same poem to me in my office in 2007 after thirty years and reciting several others of the required corpus as well; 1984 graduate, now a prominent editor and political writer for newspapers,

Paul Green, reciting to the students from Derzhavin, Pushkin, Esenin, and Pasternak and even able to sing that rollicking Russian work lament "The Sea Spreads itself out widely" (Раскинулось море широко") as well as a few bars from the patriotic anthem "Borodino." They never forget.

Bill Andersen was one of our "Coop" students, alternating work with the National Security Agency (NSA) with terms to complete his study in Russian here at ASU. He married Gail Turner, another student in our program, and both Bill and Gail went to work for the NSA in the early 1980's. They are pictured together on a poster we have in the LL-Building's hallway of the ASU Tour to Russia on Red Square in 1986. Also, they played on our Russian Club softball team, victorious over the Chinese and Italian Clubs in that season. Bill is of Scandinavian heritage and once he and Gail invited my wife Lesley and me to their apartment for "ebel skivers," a kind of Danish mini-waffle. Once, after Bill and Gail had worked in the US intelligence field for some time, another former student, Tim Riley, told me that he had encountered Gail by surprise at a formal reception for Soviet representatives in the US Trade Mission building adjacent to the US Embassy in Moscow. She told him when he recognized her and went over to her that she was "not Gail Turner" and that "he didn't know her" in that particular context. He understood and walked quickly away, not wanting to "blow her cover." Once Lesley and I tried to visit Bill and Gail at a row house they were restoring in Baltimore, but somehow we did not get together. Soon after this, we heard that they had divorced. In post-Soviet days, the NSA downsized its Russian intelligence section and Bill used his educational benefits to study computers—artificial intelligence, earning a doctorate at the University of Maryland. He even applied for and was interviewed for a professorship in this area at ASU, and when he visited us on that occasion he made a special friend of our son Hayden, who was six or seven years old, forthrightly telling Hayden that he, Bill, "was a spy."

Bill sent this email: "Hey, Lee! Bill Andersen here. Long time since we've seen each other! Anyway, I have some news that may interest you. A few years back I joined the National Guard. Now with all the call-ups and everything, my unit was activated. Since my unit was going to be guarding garbage cans or something in the U.S. for a year, I decided to jump ship to another unit (Special Operations Forces) that is headed for Afghanistan for six months. I'm going to act as Russian interpreter for them since it seems that is still a well-known language there. Also, I'm cramming Dari as fast as I can. So, it seems that I will be taking a hiatus from computer science for a while and putting to use all of those Russian skills gained at ASU 15 years ago—no small thanks to you and the rest of the faculty there. Please give everyone there my best (I still see Couch and Burton listed in the course catalogue). Hope all is well by you there. Take care and wish me some big uspekhov! Bill."

Robert "Bob" Baum was a university Moeur Award winner in 1994, essentially the class valedictorian. He transferred to us from Physics, where he had already as a high-school student amassed a record number of Advanced Placement hours. I recall that he only had one "B" grade on his academic record at ASU, and that was from Prof. Dora Burton, who felt that he just "didn't have enough personal appreciation of the humanities." He was admitted to Stanford University's School of Law, specializing in International Law. After his second year there he was selected to be an intern in the World Court, apprenticing as a clerk with an International Judge in Florence, Italy. From there, he once sent me an analysis by Leon Lipson of a speech of Josef Stalin's...his attention struck by the "palindromic patterning" of the speech's ordered sentences, a topic (palindromic symmetry) I often touch upon in my poetry lectures. When he had finished law school and gained admission to the California State Bar, Bob decided that he didn't want to practice law. Instead, he found a position as a grant-writer in the Stanford Office of research grants and contracts and began to produce works of graphic art based on Russian mythology and influenced by Russian artists and to translate Russian literature into English. His "personal appreciation of the humanities" had apparently flourished in his law-school days.

Bob Baum writes: "Hello, Professor Croft! My wife and I were in Phoenix over the weekend to see my family, and while we were in Tempe we dropped by the fourth floor on the chance any Russian professors were holding office hours (no luck). But we did notice that you had posted my previous email to y'all on your bulletin board (the message mentioning his "retooling" from law to art and translation of literature, LBC)—does this mean you read the attached poem as well? (I read it, a superb translation of Mayakovsky). All I've received as feedback is silence, which is a bad sign, since a good portion of the poem is meaningful to English speakers conversant with the early Soviet period of literature, like you for instance. I was kind of hoping for suggestions on where to shop it for publication. For a work handicapped by both length and obscurity, I didn't think it was half bad! (My memory is that I praised it by return email but had no real place where I thought it might be published to financial advantage, LBC)

How did the school year end up—another good crop of students? I met for breakfast Monday with Professor Batalden, caught up with some of REESC's recent doings, and asked him to tell you hello. Bob."

Heather Lambert and Zbyszek Frackiewicz met in my Russian classes and married. They graduated at about the same time in the mid 1980's and became teachers. Their triplets were born with extremely low birth weights (less than 2 lbs each as I recall) and their survival was in doubt for quite some time. Everyone who knew them was praying for a positive outcome. Here it is:

"Hi, Dr. Croft! How are things at ASU? I am still teaching French at Maryvale (Maryvale High School, Phoenix). We tried to get a Russian program going a couple of years ago, but they wouldn't let it go with only 8 students. But my French program is growing, and maybe someday we will get enough interest to start a Russian program.

Zbyszek is teaching 6th grade in Dysart District. He likes teaching…and wants to teach 7th or 8th grade Social Studies or Math as well. We moved to Surprise (a NW Phoenix suburb) in 2000, so he doesn't have far to drive.

The kids are doing great—they are almost 3 years old. They were in the hospital until mid-May 1999, and they haven't had any health problems since. They are growing up speaking Polish and English, and eventually we'll try teaching them Russian and French. They spend a lot of time with their grandparents, and they call them "dziadek" and "babcia" instead of grandma and grandpa. Heather Frackiewicz."

Matt Rosin was an officer in the Sigma Chi Fraternity at ASU. As a student, he had trouble "keeping focus" on academia. He had an act as a stand-up comedian and performed "gigs" around the valley, primarily in Scottsdale clubs. He took longer than the usual student to graduate, but persisted to the degree in Russian in 1988. Once, his fraternity awarded me its "Sigma Chi Professor of the Year" plaque at a banquet we attended together. When he left ASU he found a "day job" as an insurance agent while trying to establish himself as an actor and a comedian. I was touched when I discovered (only because of an attribution mistake) that he had pledged to donate $50.00 per month to our ASU foundation "Russian Language Section Benefit Account" so that subsequent students might receive financial awards for their excellence…this when, I'm sure, $50.00/mo. was a lot of money to him.

Matt writes: "Hi Prof. Croft. This is Matt Rosin, your ne'er-do-well student from yesteryear. Hope this finds you and yours well. I am back in town after several years in Reno (don't ask) and have a request/favor. May I use you as a reference? (Absolutely, LBC) I am now pursuing acting/comedy full steam in the evenings, and am applying all over for a daytime position that has good benefits. One of the guys in my comedy troupe is an ASU employee, and he suggested I apply there, which, after perusing the openings, looks like a great place. Anyway, if possible, may I use you as a reference? Thanks, Professor, for your time. Do svidaniya. Matt Rosin."

Another 1988 graduate of our Russian program was Adam Liebi. Adam was a poet, having his works ("Hose Bats Falling From Her Hair") published in the English Department student miscellany, THE ANGLE. I always told the students that all great literary careers started just like that…in some student almanac or organizational newsletter or… I remember about Adam too that he always tried to speak Russian, both in and out of class, as a way to build his power of expression in it.

Adam Liebi writes under the subject line "Zdravstvuyte!": "Hello Prof. Croft! Just dropping a note. I was a student of yours in the late 80's. Ya vyuchilsya russkomu yazyku i ya zhil tam v gorodakh raznykh. Teper; ya zhivu v shtate Kalifornii, rabotayu v oblasti public health insurance company (NOT in sales). I hope you are well. Regards, Adam C. Liebi, C.P.M., Wellpoint Sourcing & Supplier Performance."

Margaret Dower (now Margaret Dower Foley) majored in both Russian language and History, graduating in 1989. She was a very good student and a particularly empathetic person, always concerned about the other person's feelings and welfare. She writes:

"Hello Professor Croft, I wanted to let you know that all of our hard work has finally paid off! I start a job tomorrow working for the International Rescue Committee. It is a non-profit that resettles refugees throughout the U.S. I will be working out of the Sacramento office resettling refugees from the former Soviet Union. Everyone in the office is Russian and I am the lone American. I wanted to let you know that one of the reasons they chose me was because they said my Russian was outstanding. After 14 years my language skills are still strong. I wanted to thank you again for all your enthusiasm and support. I have never forgotten it. Sincerely, Margaret Dower Foley."

It's communications like this that keep me on the job. Another is from Janet Kenning. Janet was an ASU student of both English and Russian, and, like Adam Liebi above, contributed her poetry to the English

Department's student organs. I remember that she struggled some with the Russian grammar but needed no urging to memorize Russian poetry, for which she had a heightened appreciation, being a poet herself. After graduation she gained admittance to the graduate program in creative writing at the University of Iowa. She writes to me under the subject line "old student poet":

"Hey Professor Croft, poi (?) I wrote you this summer, so just wanted to pass on to you—my book manuscript was a finalist this year for the National Poetry Series. It was an honor to be a finalist—50 in the country out of 1400 entries. Maybe next year it'll win. My family is proud as I have a 2-year-old, a 3-year-old, and a 9-year-old. How anyone accomplishes anything with kids is beyond me. I'm trying to be patient. I've won a State Arts Council grant and have been a finalist for quite a few things. Anyway, I wanted to share that piece of success, as you and Prof. Burton were big influences for me. Janet Kenning."

Here is a self-explanatory email from Peggy Walker:

"Out of the distant past... Hi Dr. Croft—If you think way, way back to the late 1980's, you may remember me. I was a student in several of your Russian language courses at ASU (I actually got a B.A. in History, though), then went to George Washington University where I got an M.A. in Russian and East European Studies. I joined the State Department in 1994 and have served as a Foreign Service Officer overseas in Tijuana and Moscow (where the language skills I learned at ASU came in very handy). My next assignment is to Sarajevo, Bosnia. I start 10 months of in-house language training in Bosnian (i.e. Serbo-Croatian) this fall and will go out to Sarajevo next summer. I'm contacting you because I was interested to see on the ASU website a note about your summer program in Serbo-Croatian. Could you tell me what texts you use to teach the curriculum? I'm looking for outside material to supplement my study. I'm trying to do some work in advance of my beginning full-time language study here. When I did a brushup of my Russian before going to Moscow, I discovered that the texts the State Department used were not as useful to me as the materials that ASU used in bringing my Russian back up to speed, and have been looking at various university websites trying to find out what texts are being used to teach Serbo-Croatian. I'd appreciate any information you could give me. Many thanks, Peggy Walker."

On this, I recall my own days teaching Serbo-Croatian at Colgate University from the US Foreign Service Institute manual. Later, in my

Critical Languages Institute, our instructor, Maria Budisavljevic-Oparnica, once intended to use Thomas Magner's The Croatian and Serbian Language as a text, but the ACLS grant committee required that we change this text to another one authored by Biljana Sljivic-Simsic...this for reasons of language politics rather than grammar. I referred Peggy Walker to our Professor Danko Šipka, who teaches what we now call "Bosnian-Croatian-Serbian" (note the alphabetical order) with diverse materials, textual and online. The superior ASU Russian materials she mentions are, I presume, primarily the four editions of Prof. Couch's workbook-format Практический курс русского языка, one of the best self-instructive set of materials for Russian I've seen.

Michael "Misha" Phillips was a 1994 graduate of our program. He studied on Prof. Phillips UARA program in St. Petersburg and returned there on his own to teach English during the early years of transition from the Soviet Union to the Russian Federation. He was followed there by two other members of his student cohort, Jason Sartor (now a custom jewelry maker at a store near where I live) and Anne Marie Welsh. Misha then returned to the U.S., joined the military and was stationed for a time in Hawaii, from where we lost touch, until I received this email:

"Dr. Croft, Long time no see. Compelled to write a short biography for work, I was looking back on my time at ASU (fondly, of course), and decided to see if I could find you. God Bless Google.

Well, if it will help for your "where are they now" file, I am currently the Cooperative Threat Reduction NCOIC (non-commissioned officer in charge, for you non-military readers) in the Defense Threat Reduction Office—Moscow, here at the US Embassy (where I met your 2002 graduate Dwight Brown, who works as a Consular Aide), having just moved here after three years of fantastic travels to many parts of the FSU (former Soviet Union). In addition to traveling to Moscow and Cheboksary in those years, I also spent many months driving, flying, and taking the train all over Kazakhstan and Uzbekistan, and even managed to spend a month in Bangkok, Thailand, escorting and interpreting for a group of Uzbek virologists who were studying at a US medical facility there; specifically I was interpreting training for synthesizing DNA. I won't bore you further, but let it be known that your efforts in the classroom have shown dividends all over the world, from former chemical weapons production facilities (see attached) to the Uzbek National Security Council. And everywhere, when folks invariably ask, I tell them I learned Russian at Arizona State.

As for your students, please let them know that the opportunities in the former USSR—both public and private—are much greater than they used to be, and that they stand to reap the benefits of hard work in your undergraduate program for years. Please give my regards to Drs. Burton, Couch, and Ekmanis.   Michael Phillips."

Danielle Burleson was a 1994 graduate of our Russian program. She was one of the few students to take advantage of more than one intensive language offering in my Critical Languages Institute, studying both Macedonian and Bosnian-Croatian-Serbian. A single mother, she needed financial support to continue her study into post-graduate work and I recommended her for such support to Georgetown University's M.A. program in International Relations, where she is now a graduate student.

Danielle writes: "Prof. Croft, I just wanted to thank you again for writing so many recommendation letters for me over the years. I am in Moscow now, studying at the International University through the ACTR (American Council of Teachers of Russian). ACTR not only accepted my application, they also offered me almost full funding, which has been wonderful. The summer program is almost over, and although I am looking forward to going home (and giving my daughter a big hug and kiss), I have enjoyed being in Moscow, and have learned so much! I hope to see you when I am back in Phoenix in mid-August. If not, I hope the coming school year is a good one for you. Thank you. Danielle Burleson."

I remember Mercedes "Mercy" Wenzel (ca. 1995) as a bright student of Russian, even though she was a pre-med/lab studies major, taking Russian because she thought it might someday provide her with research access into medicine or pharamacology. She went to work as a laboratory technician after graduation and I did not see her for some time, but, when she sought admission to medical school, she asked me if I would write her a letter of recommendation. She did not feel confident in asking some of her other professors, some in the medical field, to write. She thought that some of them would not remember her and wouldn't know what to say about her. And did I think that a letter from a Professor of Russian, from whom she had had only one course, would do her any good in this regard? She seemed doubtful, but, of course, I bragged to her about the "many" (i.e. 5 or 6) previous Russian students I had recommended who had gotten into "the nation's finest medical schools" and assured her that her record of study and related nursing and laboratory work would hold her in good stead. So I wrote, and, the next spring, received the following:

"Hi all! I apologize for the mass nature of this email. However, I have been up for about 36 hours working and now making the final touches on my big move. For anyone who isn't entirely up to speed since things happened so fast, and working nights does not make it easy to stay in touch with normal people, here is where things are:

For the past year I have been working in the lab at Scottsdale Healthcare while I applied to medical school! And, like everyone who applies you expect to be turned down by schools, but I GOT IN! I will be attending Finch University in August. I am very excited and I move…well, tomorrow! I have been putting in extra hours and flying here and there for the interviews. I did find time for myself though. In February I treated myself to a trip to England. Visited some friends and just loved it. In May a friend of mine from work and I went to Germany, Italy, and Switzerland. I am so fortunate to have had this time before I start my new adventure!! Here is my new contact information. Mercy Wenzel."

Edwin Lee Aralica was a student who, though disciplined and studious in his own way, had quite limited aptitude for foreign language acquisition. He had, quite simply, to work harder than the others to succeed in it. But he graduated as a Russian major in 1996, having studied in Moscow too as a participant of Prof. Couch's exchange program with Moscow State Linguistic University. I recommended him for Law School admission and thereafter, some years thereafter, received this terse notice:

"Prof. Croft: Just wanted to pass the word to you that I passed the California State Bar Examination."

Ed has become involved in his practice of law with the "Innocence Project" which tries to find now available evidence to exonerate the incarcerated innocent. Bravo to him.

Irina Ananyeva was a Russian speaker who was at ASU majoring in Spanish…very unique indeed. Late on in her undergraduate career she decided to indulge her native culture by taking my senior seminar on Russian poetry. In this course was revealed a real talent for poetic translation, and also for employment potential using her Russian, rather than her Spanish, language abilities. In 2000 I recommended her for admission to the Monterey Institute of Foreign Study's program in Nuclear Non-Proliferation Studies. One day Lesley and I encountered her there by chance when we were visiting Lesley's friend Brenda Campbell in Monterey. When Irina graduated from this program, I recommended her to the US Defense Intelligence Agency for employment and, after lengthy security clearing, she was hired. Later, she called me by telephone to ask to use me as a continuing reference for advancement there and I readily agreed. Right after she hung up, I received a call from the Defense Intelligence Agency Human Resources Department. Here is a recent communication from her...of course I notice at the end the addition of a new last name:

"Hello, Professor Croft!! That same day I received a call from the division manager and I was offered the job! Whatever you told the HR recruiter certainly did the trick and I appreciate your help tremendously. I should be starting in about a week or two as an Arms Control Policy Analyst in the Strategy and Policy Analysis Division of SAIC. According to the job description I will be supporting U.S. Army clients, specifically DTRA (Defense Threat Reduction Agency—on-site inspectors that make sure Russia is in compliance with its treaty obligations). I will be researching and performing analyses on national security issues and arms control policies, treaties and agreements, such as START I and SORT 2002 and the joint data exchange on NMD (National Missile Defense). Ya nadeyus' chto eto put' k svetlomu budushchemu ("I hope that this is the path to a bright future" in transliteration, LBC). Thank you again for your help and I will keep in touch. Irina Eaves. PS. I am attaching my resume."

The next email is from Melissa Wallace. Melissa only took one year of Russian from me. I remember that she was in the aerospace engineering program at ASU and was taking Russian to provide her with research access and possible interpersonal communication. She was part of her college's team in a national competition to make an extraterrestial vehicle and that she traveled with the team to demonstrate it...and the team won the competition.

"Hey Professor Croft! I am not sure if you remember me (it's been over a year since I took RUS 101 and 102 from you). I wanted to say hello. I graduated from aerospace engineering in May and am now working in Houston at NASA (Johnson Space Center). However, what I think you will enjoy is that I am working as a flight controller for the International Space Station...which means I will be having to communicate with the Russians! I just did an interview with Anthony Vanchu (who says he knows you (former UT-Austin Russian prof and now Russian Language Director at the Johnson Space Center...LBC)) and got placed into a Russian course. Thanks to you, I get to start a few levels higher than the basic class. So, anyways, I know you like to hear what your Russian students are doing and how they are using their Russian, so here's my story. Take care. Melissa Wallace."

In 1998 I taught a senior seminar, RUS-441, in "Russian Culture." This class attracted a brighter-than-usual cohort of twenty-six students, including advanced members of our program, former LDS missionaries, and educated native Russians. The textual material was in both Russian and in English. For reasons of my own attraction to television contest shows like "Jeopardy" (which I was twice selected to compete on, but scuttled by cancellations of the show), I decided to have a weekly "Trivia Down" (like an elementary school "spell down") every Friday. The students would put into a hat a question…the most arcane, obscure, even implied, fact from the week's reading, lecture, and photo captions they could find (with the answer on the back of the question). Then I would ask the questions in turn. A student who could not correctly answer in five seconds was "out," and the last student left was the week's "победитель" ("Victor") earning THREE points (second-to-last out earned two, third-to-last out earned one). I kept track of the points earned throughout the sixteen-week semester and eventually awarded a Russian "Victory in WWII" "znachok" (a little metal lapel pin) to the overall winner. The competition for this overall award was absolutely fierce and the student contestants were simply amazing. But all the students, in the end, congratulated the winner, ASU Theater and Acting major William "Billy" Gunn. He was acknowledged by the best as the best. Here is a recent email from him. His younger brother Andrew Gunn is in our program now. Both Billy and Andrew are now members of our DOBRO SLOVO honorary chapter.

"Dear Professor Croft, Hello! I was doing some internet browsing and made my way to the ASU Slavic page, so I decided to send you a quick email. I don't know whether you even remember me from classes about five years ago. How is the old ASU Russian program going? And how are you doing?

I am currently at USC working on an MA/Ph.D. in Russian Literature, and I just finished an MA in Theater at BYU last year. My family is still in AZ, so I need to stop by and say hello next time I'm in town. I would love to see you. Billy Gunn."

Of course I remember him, and I was surprised to hear that he had been admitted to a Ph.D. program in Russian Literature without a recommendation from me, which I certainly would have given him. Just now we have a former student named Jamie Keeton in the Ph.D. program at UCLA. She and Billy, once classmates, are at rival southern California universities studying for doctorates in Russian literature! Nice!

Former student John Ziker is now an Assistant Professor of Anthropology at Boise State University. His recent request by email shows that he hasn't forgotten ASU as a source of Russian-competent student-scholars:

"Dear Lee, It's been a while, but I thought of you and my alma mater as I began to recruit for these (attached) positions. I have a National Science Foundation grant and funding for 2 students for our MA program in Anthropology, including a season of field research in Siberia for 2008. If you know of anyone who might be interested, I'd appreciate your forwarding this to them, or posting it. I see where your Russian and East European Studies Center there has received a large donation. That's great. John P. Ziker, Assistant Professor, Dept. of Anthropology, Boise State University."

I responded with the news of our program changes and assured John that I would post his advertisement for a student assistant. He then wrote back:

"Lee, thank you for writing back. I remember very fondly my Russian training at ASU. Your conversation classes, Prof. Couch's textbook, and starting off with Prof. Ekmanis in 101, Prof. Burton's lit class and others. I am thankful for the program. I am sorry to hear about Dora Burton passing away. Your book sounds interesting and fun. I have been working on articles mainly. Thanks for any contacts on the assistantship. Vsego Khoroshego, John."

Adam Orford took only literature survey courses from me and graduated from ASU in Italian after helping me draft a chart and graph of our program's enrollment and graduates from 1970-2000. This chart (see page 54) required some sophistication, since it was my intention visually to MINIMIZE the post-Soviet-dissolution enrollment loss. Adam came up with a logarithmic scale that flattened the apparent decline...very clever. He then went to Europe for a year, spending most of his time in Italy, from where he emailed a series of impressions that were most acute and enjoyable to read. But I always knew he would be a lawyer, and I recommended him to several top law schools. He got into Columbia and went through it in a hurry. In May 2006 I got this email from him:

"Adam Orford will graduate from Columbia Law School on May 18th with academic honors, having served as Editor-in-Chief of the Columbia Journal of Environmental Law. After studying for the New York State Bar Exam this summer, he will remain in New York City to work at the law firm of Willkie, Farr & Gallagher as an associate, pursuing a career in environmental law. Eh? Eh? Not bad, right? Three years of my life (and future plans!) reduced to THREE lines of text! But it's true."

Adam knew of my predilection for the study of THREES (e.g. see my article "People in Threes Going Up in Smoke and Other Triplicities in Russian Literature and Culture" now reprinted online at www.threes.com, where I've been listed as an author by Michael Eck. Eck and threes-fanatic Herbert O. Buckland have recognized me as the "third triophile." Even the Wikipedia *definition* of the number 3 (three) cites my work). This is why I wrote back to him:

"Dear Adam, Молодец! Браво! Поздравляю сердечно! (3X) I take great joy in reading this great news from you...and appreciate that it comes in THREE lines, and that the law firm is nominally a triad, as you might recall my treatises on Russian cultural/literary triplicity."

Soon Adam had passed the New York State Bar Exam and needed an exterior referee to attest his attorney-worthiness to the Bar. I recommended him and he was admitted. He has since sent me photos of his tiny but expensive apartment on a high floor of a Manhattan skyscraper looking out onto a several-stories-high photo of pop-figure P. Diddy hanging down an opposite building. In Manhattan also, trying to make her way, is thought-she-graduated-but-didn't senior Russian student Sofiya Analaryan. She is finishing up a RUS-499 Independent Study course with me, her last required hours to earn her degree. I keep telling her she should look Adam up, but she hasn't.

Amy Campbell is a 2003 Russian graduate who studied Tatar in the Critical Languages Institute while she was here. She wanted to do graduate work in International Relations at Georgetown University in Washington, DC, and so she planned to move there. She found out online about a volunteer internship program at the Defense Intelligence Agency in Washington, DC, and sent her resume there. The response was the kind most students dream of: they said that the unpaid internships were all filled, but they wanted to consider Amy for a full-time job. She would be able to earn a Master's Degree in Strategic Studies in their in-house school while she worked. Amy began the crucial security clearance for employment at the DIA. While this was taking place during the next six months, she went, with the agency's permission to Russia on the University of Arizona study-abroad program. When she returned the security clearance was still not complete. The DIA suggested that she enroll in the nuclear nonproliferation program at the Monterey Institute of Foreign Studies in California (where Irina Ananyeva had gone…LBC). From there she wrote to me and to Tatyana Dhaliwal:

"Hi Dr. Croft and Tatyana, I just thought I would update you with my goings on. I am still waiting for my job in DC, although I have my interim clearance.

In the meantime I am thoroughly enjoying the Monterey Institute. I love the atmosphere and the opportunities. I went to the Center for Nonproliferation Studies to apply for a research assistantship for the Fall, and it turns out that one of their summer interns is leaving early. So I am starting on Monday at CNS in their information collections area. I am hoping that I can continue with the organization in the Fall. I am told that it is a distinct possibility.

I am meeting many interesting people who are very helpful. The advisor here at the school got me in contact with a MIIS alumna who works in my agency in DC. So I have been able to talk to this individual about her experiences and she has given me some advice and insight.

I hope all is well in Tempe. Amy Campbell."

Amy did get the assistantship and complete her studies at the Monterey Institute. She did get security cleared, and when, at last, she began her work at the Defense Intelligence Agency she began at an elevated rate of pay, having further qualified herself at the agency's suggestion while she was being security cleared. Now she is both working and studying at the DIA in Washington, DC.

Autumn "Renae" Spritzer once went to high school in Conrad, Montana, fifty miles from my hometown of Cut Bank. She was a really excellent student of Russian and worked her way through ASU as a human relations secretary in a company, I-10 International Trucks, that has been a client of my wife's and my drug testing company, Croft Consultants. She found another job in a Phoenix law firm after graduating and bought a condo on her own. But then she asked me and Faculty Associate Tamara McKane (a Russian who was also an ASU Russian grad who is a practicing attorney, having graduated, also upon my recommendation, from ASU law) to recommend her to several law schools. To both of us, Renae sent this word:

"Dear Tamara and Dr. Croft, Thanks again to you for the glowing letters of recommendation you wrote on my behalf. I have been busy selling my condo and getting my affairs in order before the start of the new school year, otherwise I would have written sooner. Here is a much belated update. Your letters formed a crucial part of what turned out to be a very strong admissions file. I was offered and accepted admission to the University of Arizona at the in-state tuition rate and with a generous scholarship--$10K the first year, $8K for each of the second and the third years. Amazingly enough, I was also offered scholarships at University of Indiana-Bloomington, Baylor University, University of Utah, University of Colorado, and Yeshiva University. ASU also sent a offer of admission, but it arrived comparatively late and I committed to UA before I heard whether they were offering any scholarship money. As for the 'reach schools,' I applied to both Washington and Lee and to William and Mary (both waived the application fee, so I thought I might have had a chance), and I got wait-listed at both. Ultimately I decided I couldn't handle the stress of waiting and then possibly having to arrange a cross-country move at the last minute... (now at the UA Law School) The school year is well under way and like most of my classmates I am frazzled and fighting to stay caught up; the 'intellectual boot camp' metaphor is absolutely true... Autumn "Renae" Spritzer."

When Eric Strachan was an undergraduate at ASU he was a cross-country runner. The self-discipline of this athletic pursuit was also evident in his language work. He won one of my "outstanding beginning student" medals in the 1990s. He went on to take ALL the Russian courses in addition to the courses of his other majors (English and Political Science), but also took more than one offering of the Critical Languages Institute (Macedonian and Tatar, I think). He was admitted to the Ph.D. program in Political Science and taught there as a Graduate Teaching Assistant. I saw him once or twice in a coffee shop I patronize every morning as he lives in an apartment in my neighborhood. Like me, his formerly svelte runner's figure had grown thicker by 2006, and he seemed restless with his state of affairs. So I wasn't completely surprised when he asked me for a letter of recommendation to become a candidate for an intelligence officer's position in the U.S. Marines. He had enlisted and was headed for Marine basic training in San Diego. I had had other intellectually talented students join the Marine Corps before, and not all of them succeeded. One in particular, a post-operation female-to-male transsexual, gave Marine basic his best shot (I really HAVE heard it all), but gave it up in a week or two. He was not sorry he had tried. He had, he said, always dreamed of trying to become a U.S. Marine. I understood this well. Once I too had thought of joining the Marine Corps. I related this to Eric Strachan in my response to his request for a recommendation, along with some specification of my own summer plans. He wrote:

"Professor Croft, Thank you for your willingness to write on my behalf. I've attached a copy of my resume, which I think should provide you with the information on my language study, overseas travel, etc., that you will need to complete the letter…Hawaii and Montana sound like a couple of great places for an Arizonan to spend the summer. Do you still have family in Montana? I didn't know that you tried to join the Marines. 1965 was some time to be volunteering to join the military! May I ask what ultimately changed your mind? I remember your stories about the student housing arrangements in the Soviet Union at the time of the Vietnam War. Thank you for your help with this letter. Sincerely, Eric Strachan."

Here is my response:

"Eric,

I put into the mail today the recommendation…on the form. I noted the specification that it be on plain paper, as opposed to letterhead, if it were not to be on the form. But I made it fit on the form, checked all the 'outstanding' boxes (чистая правда) and sent it in. Good luck.

In the fall of 1965 I was boxing in a regional Golden Gloves tournament here in Phoenix, having quit the fall quarter at Montana State University in Bozeman. I was designated the Montana State Champion, even though Montana had no tournament in the Golden Gloves then and therefore had no real champion. I had merely been spotted working out by a tournament official and asked if I wanted to compete. I got through two rounds of the competition, surprising myself at the 147 light middle weight (one by default) and then was beaten by a Michigan boxer (out of our region…?) who later went to the Olympics and lost. I stayed in room 727 (top floor, end of hall on North…$15/week, I think) of the Phoenix YMCA at 350 N. 1st Avenue in the downtown. I stayed there a week or two as I recall. It was scarily hot. I needed money and went out one day as a cotton picker, but, having no experience, was told to "tromp the gleanings" in a screened trailer. The next day I couldn't walk. But I limped down the street to the U.S. Navy recruiting station on 1st Avenue nearby and talked to the Marine representative about qualifying for Officer's School. I wanted to become a pilot. He took down my name and recorded that he had enrolled me, subject to the condition that I go back to college and get five more semester hours of credit in order to qualify for Officer's Candidate School...at least that's the way I recall it. I knew that I was otherwise 1-A and subject to immediate draft. During that time also I visited a life-long girl friend (Cheryl Pritchard (now Kinder)) who was an ASU student. In trying to find her, I drove my 1957 Chevrolet up the street, where now the main pedestrian mall is, to the front of the Social Sciences Building and asked a fellow there: "Is ASU around here anywhere?" I found her in Wilson Hall, and when we left there, she suggested that I walk across to Moeur Hall and apply for admittance to ASU. I resisted this notion, but she was insistent, and so I filled out the papers and applied.

Two months later, married and working on the drilling rigs in Montana (tough in the vicious winter there), I got my draft notice ("Greetings" on the traditional yellow telegram form...I wish I still had it as a souvenir, but I lost it). I went down to Butte, Montana, in December of that year (1965) and took my preinduction physical, which I passed. I hitchhiked back to Cut Bank (325 miles) with Freddy Driscoll, another fellow from my high-school class, and we damn near froze. While I waited for my orders to report for duty, I got to thinking about how my life in the service would be better as an officer than as an enlisted man, especially since my wife was expecting our first baby. SO, I appealed my being drafted to my local, Glacier County (Montana) draft board. They called me in for an interview. I stated that I was not trying to avoid service, but only wanted to serve as an officer instead of an enlisted man...and that I had a 'deal' with the Marines to that effect. They checked this out, and the Marine recruiter here in Phoenix backed me up, telling them that I had allowed my name to be conditionally enrolled in an officer's candidate program. The draft board members asked me which university I had been admitted to. Only the day before I had received a notice from ASU saying that it would admit me. My local draft board cancelled my induction (one board member's son, also dropped out of school, went to Vietnam...as did my brother Jerry) and issued me a 2-S student deferrment. Such continued deferrments throughout the next 8 years (ASU in Math., UA in Russian, Cornell in Slavic Linguistics) kept me out of the service. Then, with a Ph.D. in a 'critical area' (extending my draft liability from age 26 to age 35) and THREE children I became subject without further deferrment to the new draft lottery. BUT I DREW A HIGH NUMBER and was not taken. This was in 1973, the year I came back to ASU as a faculty member.

As a youth, son and nephew of WWII veterans and grandson of a WWI veteran, I had always assumed that I would serve in our military. I wanted to, in fact. But it didn't happen. AND, as it turns out, I would say that I have contributed much more to our country's triumphing over its main ideological adversary (Soviet Communism and its expansionism) in the global struggle during that time as a professor of Russian here at ASU than I ever could have as a combatant in Vietnam. Every Russian-speaking student I put there caused Russian Soviets to question their political system, every diplomat and intelligence agent I trained (and that's MANY) was worth at least a missile in the perennial stand-off. Later, as a Veteran's Administration Outreach counselor of the Vietnam-era vets, I told my counselees that as a country we were right to be there in Vietnam and that our presence there, confronting the adversary in that sphere, contributed mightily to our eventual ideological victory over that adversary…that they should be proud, not troubled, by their service there. We did, in fact, win.

Stay in touch. Lee Croft."

ASU and U. of A. DOBRO SLOVO Members

It is difficult to recall the names of all our graduates, or even to find them in the university archives or digital records. And, of course, many of the students in my memory were taking Russian, but were not Russian majors and so graduated in some other subject area. SO, a good way to list a good share of the Russian language students we have had who took MORE THAN JUST ONE OR TWO CLASSES with us is to look at the rolls of DOBRO SLOVO members…the records of which are maintained by our Professor Emeritus Sandy Couch. We certainly thank him specially for providing us with such an effective spur to memory. The University of Arizona chapter, Alpha Alpha, with Roza Simkhovich as faculty advisor, has 383 members from 1964 to April of 2007. The Arizona State University chapter, Epsilon Epsilon, with Lee Croft as faculty advisor, has 403 members from 1966 to April 2007. The lists show the class of membership (1 is student, 2 is faculty, 3 is honorary), the date of the academic year inducted, and, in parenthesis, a number or numbers denoting the other chapters in which some members are also a member (e.g. I'm also in Cornell's chapter and the U. of A.'s).

Dobro Slovo Member List for Arizona State University (Epsilon Epsilon) as of 4.5.07

Name	Type	Year
ABBOT, ANDREW WILLIAM	1	06/07
ABOVYAN, PROF. MIKAEL MIKAILOVICH	3	00/01
ABRAHAMS, WILLIAM LEROY	1	74/75
ADAM, DENNIS K.	1	84/85
ADZIC, IVANA	1	02/03
ALEXANDER, CARMEN	1	94/95
ALLEN, BRANDON	1	01/02
ALLEN, BARBARA JANE	1	78/79
ALTNETHER, JOSEPH GERARD	1	89/90
ANDERSON, WILLIAM A.	1	84/85
ANDERSON, ROXANNE JOY	1	01/02
ANDERSON, ALAN JOHN	1	83/84
ARCHIBALD, MELISSA SUE	1	05/06
ARTHUR, CHARLES G.	1	74/75
ASHWORTH, STEVEN JOHN	1	85/86
ATKINS, SHERRY J.	1	67/68
AUSLOOS, REGINA L.	1	01/02
AWDZIEWICZ, MARTHA C	2	75/76
AYERS, CHRISTOPHER WAYNE	1	01/02
BACCA, JOHN RICHARD	1	82/83
BADE, JIM	1	87/88
BAEHR, ALICIA CHRISTINE	1	06/07
BAICH, MIRJANA	1	77/78
BAILEY, PATRICIA LYNN	1	78/79
BAILEY, FRANCES T.	1	67/68
BAKER, ALAN SCOTT	1	83/84
BALDINI, PIER	3	92/93
BALDWIN, DOUGLAS JOHN	3	69/90
BARNEY-O'NEIL, MARGARET G	1	95/96
BARRETT JR, PATRICK C.	1	74/75
BAUM, ROBERT C.	1	81/82
BELLIOTTI, RICK JOSEPH	1	94/95
BENZER, SUSAN LOUISE	1	80/81
BERGFOLK, GLENDON E	1	67/68
BERGMAN, EDWARD P.	1	81/82
BERNHARD, WENDY L.	1	67/69
BEYCHOK, DAVID LEONARD	1	77/78
BICKETT, PAULA	1	75/76
BIELEK, JERRY A'	1	76/77
BILLS, CATRIEN	1	73/74
BIRKS, RONALD MARTIN	1	94/95
BITNER, JEAN	1	66/67
BJELLA, CONSTANCE C.	1	84/85
BONDARCOOK, NINA	1	74/75
BONIFIELD, THOMAS R	1	89/90
BRISTOL, STANLEY	1	99/00
BROWN, DWIGHT JOSEPH	1	89/90
BROWN, MICHAEL ANTHONY	1	80/81
BROWN, CONSTANCE DIANE	1	83/84
BROWN, NANCY JO	1	75/76
BUHRIG, LINDA	1	02/03
BURGESS, NATHAN P.	1	76/77
BURKE, CHRISTOPHER E.	1	04/05
BURNETT, KATHRYN JEAN	1	88/89
BURRIS, BRUCE CAMERON	1	67/68
BURT, DIANE	1	76/77
BURTON, PROF. DORA	2	92/93
BUZAROUSKA, ELENI	3	02/03
CAMPBELL, AMY M.	1	73/74
CARLSON, DAVID JOHN	1	73/74
CARNES, DEBRA	1	77/78
CARRIERES, JOSEPH THOMAS	1	75/76
CARTWRIGHT, MICHAEL F	1	80/81
CHAROCHAK, JOHN STEVEN	1	89/90
CHURCHICH, KATHARINA	1	95/96
CLAMPITT, LORI LYNN	1	78/79
CLARK, KAREN ELIZABETH	1	77/78
COADY, SUSAN	1	99/00
COCCHIA, ANDREW SCOTT	1	82/83
COHEN, MICHAEL A	1	72/73
CONOVALOFF, TIMOTHY A.	1	84/85
CONRAD, MICHAEL J.	1	84/85
COOLEY, SCOTT J.	1	99/00
COOPER, S. THOMAS	1	89/90
COOPER, MICHAEL TERRANCE		
CORMIER, BRUCE	1	75/76
COUCH, PROF. SNAFORD C.	2	66/67
COUCH, CHRISTINA	1	83/84
COWDEN, TAMI DENISE	1	80/81
COYLE, SEAN P	1	87/88
CRAWSHAW, SUSAN M.	1	78/79
CROFT, PROF. LEE B. (48,25)	2	67/68
CROUCHER, MURLIN	1	67/68
CROWDER, LINDA CAROLYN	1	03/04
CULLON, MURRAY LEE	1	73/74
CURTIS, STPEHEN THODY	1	01/02
CURTON, PATRICK V.	1	75/76
CZERSKI, AGNIESZKA ANNA	1	87/88
DANIEL, JUDITH (5)	1	81/82
DANIELSEN, TERESA LYNN	1	75/77
DAVIS, JAMES E	1	83/84
DHALIWAL, TATYANA L	2	02/03
DI LUCIDO, MICHAEL	1	73/74
DITTERT, MARTA LOUISE	1	78/79
DITTERT, ERIC	1	75/76
DJURAEV, BOTIR	3	03/04
DOBRANSKY, MEGAN M	1	02/03
DORAN, MINFORD	1	67/68
DOWER, MARGARET MARY	1	87/88
DOYLE, DEE DEE	1	75/76
DUNIHUE, PHILIP DEAN	1	89/90
DUVAL, HENRY K	1	84/85
ECTON, JEREMY DAVID	1	89/90
ELLIOT, ELISABETH MAE	1	89/90
EVANS, CHRISTOPHER DANIEL	1	82/83
FACKLER, DEON JOELLE	1	69/90
FANELLO, BEN J	1	99/00
FETTIG, JEANETTE MARY	1	89/90
FETTIG, ANNETTE MARIE	1	89/90
FINLEY, BABETTE	1	92/93
FINN, MICHAEL	1	75/76
FISCHER, LENORE R.	1	74/75
FISHER, DAVID RAY	1	76/77
FLANAGAN, CHERYL ANN	1	89/90
FLORIAN, RICHARD ALLAN	1	89/90
FOLEY, DANNY JOSEPH	1	04/05
FRANTZ, PATTY	1	66/67
FREEMAN, MICHAEL JARRETT	1	06/07
FREITAG, CHARLES PAUL	1	77/78
FRESTEDT, MYNA DARLENE	1	76/77
GALOPE, MICHAEL RICHARD	1	87/88
GALVIN, SUSANNE T.	1	74/75
GARCIA, JOSE ALFREDO	1	06/07
GASS, VICTOR	1	74/75
GERASENKO, ARKADY	3	92/93
GERRARD JR., JACK ALLEN	1	74/75
GILL, SYLVIA RENEE	1	82/83
GILLEN, STEVEN G.	1	92/93
GLASER, MRS. EDNA	1	74/75
GLENN, BRELICE MICHAEL	1	03/04
GOLD, MICHAEL K.	1	95/96
GOLDTHWAITE, JOHN R.	1	87/88
GOODRICH, PAMELA ANN	1	99/00
GORODISSKIY, BORIS G	1	95/96
GRANFELT, SHRI	1	83/84
GREEN, MITCH BEN	1	75/76
GREEN, PAUL WEBSTER	1	83/84
GREEN, BEVERLY KAY	1	75/76
GRIFFIN, STEVEN R.	1	84/85
GRIFFIN, GRAYDON BRADLEY	1	01/02
GRIFFITH, CRAIG A.	1	74/75
GROBE, PROF. EDWIN P	3	69/70
GUNDERSON, BRENT LEVI	1	99/00
GUNN, WILLIAM D	1	99/00
GUNN, ANDREW THOMAS	1	06/07
HADDOCK, JOEL H	1	87/88
HAJDUK, BEATA URSULA	1	89/90
HALLMAN, HUGH L.	1	00/01
HANSERO, ROBERT	1	66/67
HANSFORD, KRISTINA A	1	99/00
HARANGODY, CAROL	1	83/84
HARRIS, JONATHAN JEFFREY	1	06/07
HASKELL, LISA MARGRATE	1	80/81
HATHAWAY, VALERIA J.	1	92/93
HAYWARD, JOHN WESLEY	1	95/96
HAZZARD, BEAUMONT JOHNSTONE	1	85/86
HEPFORD, ELIZABETH ANN	1	03/04
HEWLETT, LAURA CHRISTINE	1	85/86
HICKS, MICHAEL RICHARD	1	82/83
HILL, KIMBERLY MICHELLE	1	04/05
HOEPFNER, GINA MARIA	1	75/76
HOLCOMB, ROBERT SCOTT	1	76/77
HOLSTEIN, HOLLY ANN	1	05/06
HOOD, STEPHEN ROGER	1	82/83
HOROWITZ, LOUIS WILLIAM	1	94/95
HORTON, ALEX WILLIAM	1	04/05
HORWATH, PETER	3	92/93
HULS, KENNETH FREDERICK	1	88/89
HUNNICUTT, LINDA L.	1	84/85
JAMES, TERRY	1	67/68
JANEZIC, VIVIAN L.	1	75/76
JARACZESKI, JEFF J	1	84/85
JAYNES, DEBRA	1	73/74
JENSEN, SUZANNE	1	87/88
JENSEN, LORA L	1	78/79
JOHNS, RICKI L.	1	72/73
JOHNSON, JEFFREY WILLIAM	1	01/02
JOHNSON, CHRISTOPHER DAVID	1	03/04
JONES, SUSAN E.	1	89/90
KACHUR, PAUL ANTHONY	1	80/81
KANOUSE, COLBY R.	1	99/00
KASHMERICK, NADYA LOUISE	1	77/78
KELLY, ROBERT J.	1	75/76
KENNEDY, RALPH DEAN	1	04/05
KERGER, KAMERON G B.	1	99/00
KING, MARY KAY	1	77/78
KING, MEAGAN ELIZABETH	1	04/05
KLEIN, SUSAN	1	66/67
KLEIN, DAN A.	1	67/68
KOLASA, ELECTRONICA SUE	1	06/07
KORB, TIMOTHY	1	72/73
KOVACEVICH, JEREMY CHRISTOPHER	1	03/04
KOVECSI, MARY LOUISE	1	89/90
KOWALCZYK, WALTER L	1	72/73
KOWER, PETER J	1	78/79
KRAJMEROVA, MICHAELA	1	05/06
KRASNOVA, ELEONORA	3	92/93
KRYLOVA, PROF. IRYNA B.	2	69/70
KUBRIN, ALEXEY OLEGOVICH	3	00/01
KUZNETSOV, GEORGE	1	99/00
LANDAUER, KELLIE MARIE	1	04/05
LANNON, THOMAS V	1	73/74
LARSON, KENT ADAMS	1	69/90
LAYCHUK, PROF JULIAN	3	92/93
LAZARR, JULIANNE C.	1	01/02
LEAVITT, KYLE LANDON	1	01/02
LEGLER, SCOTT C.	1	04/05
LIFF, LEONARD	1	69/70
LINDBLAD, CRAIG A.	1	71/72
LINDENMAN, MAX A.	1	95/96
LINEBERRY, ANDREW	1	72/73
LINEHAN, PATRICK J.	1	72/73
LIVINGSTON, DONALD E. JR.	2	89/90
LORTI, DAVID S.	1	92/93
MABRY, MARK JR.	1	99/00
MACFIE, KATHLEEN STANTON	1	82/83
MACPHERSON, BRADLEY JAMES	1	92/93
MAIERS, STACI RACHEL-HELEN	1	95/96
MANGUM, MATTHEW WILLIAM	1	03/04
MARINOVICH, JANET	1	67/68
MARRS, GAYLE ELLEN	1	77/78
MASHURI, DAVID	2	06/07
MASON, SEAN ANTHONY	3	06/07
MATTIOLI, ROBERTA LYNN	1	78/77
MAUGANS, STACY E.	1	92/93

Name		Year
MCCUTCHEON, BENNETT B., JR.	1	75/76
MCINTYRE, SEAN DEVIN	1	85/86
MCMANIS, JENNIFER A	1	86/87
MENNING, CHADWICK L	1	92/93
MERRELL, NEIL	1	67/68
MERRIFIELD, MARK STEPHEN	1	80/81
MICKELSON, MARY KAY	1	77/78
MILES, AARON RAY	1	95/96
MILLER, DOLORES ELIZABETH	1	77/78
MILLER, CATRICIA CALYN	1	06/07
MILLICAN, HEATHER LYNN	1	02/03
MOCK, CONNIE CARILYNN	1	04/05
MODZELEWSKI, PAMELA ANNE	1	89/90
MONTOYA, DANIEL J.	1	02/03
MOODY, JULIE R.	1	99/00
MOODY, BRIAN MCKAY	1	99/00
MOORE, MAURICE BRYAN	1	03/04
MOORE, FRANKLIN DAVID, JR.	1	05/06
MOORE, JAMES E.	1	81/82
MOORE, SUSAN	1	87/88
MUSSELMAN, RICK ALAN	1	83/84
MYERS, ELIZABETH Y.	1	74/75
NACHTIGAL NEWBERG, JULIA K	1	95/96
NADER, JAMES A.	1	81/82
NEDELKO, EVA S	1	78/79
NELSON, BONITA	3	83/84
NEMECEK, JOHN M.	1	85/86
NEW, FRANCES Y	1	77/78
NICKSIC, MICHEAL J	1	75/76
NIELSON, JAMES COMSTOCK	1	05/06
NORRIS, AMY LYNN	1	85/86
NYHART, HEATHER DAWN	1	06/07
O'CONNOR, KATHLEEN T.	1	94/95
O'CONNOR, DAVID L.	1	84/85
O'CONNOR, KIMBERLY S.	1	84/85
O'HAIR, MICHELLE	1	75/76
O'HAVER, JAMES G	1	74/75
OGDEN, BETTY ANN	1	67/68
OLECKA, AGUSIA EWA	1	99/00
OLSON, KELSEY LAYNE	1	06/07
OPARNICA, MERIKAY	1	75/76
OPIE, MEITI	1	73/74
ORME, DOROTHY S	1	75/76
OWEN, JEANETTE	1	03/04
OZUNA, JOHANNA A.	1	03/04
PACA, JEANNINE KATHRYN	1	89/90
PALMA, MICHAEL D.	1	84/85
PALMER, JAIME RENEE	1	06/07
PARELLA, ANTHONY L	1	75/76
PATRIAS, KENNETH LEE	1	83/84
PAULSELL, PHYLLIS	1	72/73
PAULSON, SEAN MICHAEL	1	01/02
PEARSON, ALLEN	1	89/90
PECHTL, CORY MITCHELL	1	05/06
PETERSON, LEE MARK	1	83/84
PETERSON, MERLIN ADAM	1	01/02
PHILLIPS, MICHAEL S.	1	92/93
PIKE, BRYAN ALLEN	1	05/06
PLOVICH, PAULA M.	1	72/73
PLUMB, RON	1	73/74
POBEDINSKY, ALEXANDER	1	81/82
POLECHLA, VENITA	1	66/67
POMIRCHY, SVETLANA P	1	03/04
POWERS, COL. D. B	3	74/75
PRESLAR, RAYMOND MARK	1	80/81
PRESLER, ANDREW ELLIOTT	1	05/06
PRICE, NORMA	1	66/67
PROKOP, ROBERT S	1	73/74
RACINE, MARTIN	1	66/67
RASNICK, BARBARA	1	67/68
RAYMER, AMY MARIE	1	05/06
REYNOLDS, JOHN G	1	81/82
RICE, BARBARA S.	1	71/72
RICHARDS, JACQUELINE CHRISTINE	1	04/05
RICHARDS, BRENTON M	1	92/93
RICKETTS, DANIEL S	1	84/85
RILEY, TIMOTHY G.	1	84/85
RIOJA, FELIX K.	1	95/96
RIOS, ROSELIA LORENA	1	04/05
RITCHIE, MICHAEL KEITH	1	01/02
ROMINE, CYNTHIA M.	1	75/76
ROUDKOVSKI, GARY Y.	1	06/07
RUPPEL, ALICE	1	75/76
RYBKA, THEODORE JOHN	1	94/95
RYNISH, KAMI KATHLEEN	1	95/96
SAGNIMENI, NICHOLAS MARC	1	01/02
SAMGORODSKY, NATALY	1	02/03
SCHILLER, HERMAN DEWITT	1	82/83
SCHOOLITZ, HARRY	1	72/73
SCHULTZ, MATTHEW S.	1	92/93
SCHWAB, VIVECA	1	77/78
SCHWARZMANN, LIESEL C.	1	82/83
SCOTT, KYLE RANDOLPH	1	77/78
SECKLIN, DANIEL PHILLIP	1	85/86
SERGEANT, CARL S.	1	87/88
SHAHAR, TAMMY	1	78/79
SHAMALOV, MIKE WILLIAM	1	05/06
SHETLEY, SUSAN	1	66/67
SIMPSON, MARK STEVEN	1	83/84
SIPKA, DANKO	3	02/03
SMITH, PAULINE I.	1	99/00
SMITH, SALLY JEAN	1	95/96
SMITH, LESLIE W.	1	73/74
SMITH DE GALVEZ, EVELYN E.	1	83/84
SOBEL, BRUCE HOWARD	1	89/90
SPEDALERE, FRANK	1	75/76
SPERLING, RIANNA L.	1	94/95
SPESHOCK, SUSAN	1	81/82
SPRITZER, A. L.	1	99/00
STEINBORN, CARLA	1	66/67
STOLYAROV, DANIIL NIKOLAEVICH	1	00/01
STRONG, PATRICIA ANN	1	04/05
STRONG, TERESA	1	70/71
STRUNK, SHIRLEY J	1	74/75
SWAFFORD, SUZANNE V.	1	02/03
SWEET, KATHRYN LEE	1	04/05
SWENSON, HAROLD	1	67/68
SWIGERT, RYAN C.	1	01/02
SYLVESTER, JULIA J.	1	80/81
TANNER, BRENT JASON	1	01/02
TANNER, SAMUEL ZACHARY	1	05/06
TAPE, SEAN RICHARD	1	89/90
TAPPAN, DAVID KEVIN	1	99/00
TAPPAN, DANIEL ALLEN	1	90/91
TARENKO, NATALIE MARIE	1	80/81
TERLUK, ANNIE	1	67/68
THOMAS, BRIAN J.	1	89/90
THOMPSON, NATHAN DALE	1	02/03
TILZEY, CAROL JOYCE	1	75/76
TINGEY, TROY A.	1	01/02
TOBERMAN, MARY L.	1	92/93
TOMASI, LOREN J.	1	92/93
TONE, DIANE	1	73/74
TOWNSEND, JERRY F	1	72/73
TRAEGER, ERIN ELIZABETH	1	03/04
TRAN, HAI-VAN THI	1	80/81
TRAUSCH, JANICE KATHRYN	1	76/77
TREGO, SHERILYN G.	1	72/73
TURNER, GAIL A	1	84/85
TURNEY, JAMES THOMAS	1	95/96
TYULENOV, ALEXSEY ALEKSEEVICH	1	01/02
UNGER, JULIA L.	1	78/79
UVAYDOVA, ALBINA	1	03/04
VAN ATTA, STEPHAN DAVID	1	03/04
VAN SCOY, PROF. HERBERT A.	3	75/77
VAN WINKLE, JENNIFER LEIGH	1	04/05
VANEERDEN, JOHN WILLIAM	1	76/77
VEDELAGO, VINCENT CHARLES	1	85/86
VENUTI, ELIZABETH K.	1	84/85
VERSTRAETE, RICHARD	1	80/81
VINOGRADE, ALICE	1	75/76
WADDICAR, PAUL DOUGLAS	1	89/90
WAGNER, BENJAMIN JOSEPH	1	03/04
WAHLIN, BRETT ROGER	1	89/90
WALLACE, THERESA	1	67/68
WATERSTRADT, ELLYN JO	1	71/72
WEBB, GARY LEE	1	74/75
WEBB, TRAVIS JAMES	1	06/07
WELSCH, W. MICHAEL	1	74/75
WEST, JARED A.	1	99/00
WEST, THERESA LOUISE	1	85/86
WHITE, JULIE	1	74/75
WILCOX, LEO COLUMBUS JR.	1	02/03
WILLEFORD, DIRK M	1	75/76
WILLIAMS, PAMELA CHUNG	1	05/06
WILSON, MICHAEL GEROGE	1	95/96
WILSON, JACOB ALLEN	1	02/03
WILCOX, LEO COLUMBUS	1	03/04
WITTEL, SCOTT RUSSELL	1	01/02
WOLLERT, ANDREW JAMES	1	85/86
WOLOSCHKO, MARY	1	71/72
WORTH, KEITH A.	1	75/76
WRIGHT, BURTON POPOVICH	1	99/00
WRIGHT, JUSTIN M.	1	99/00
YUNGFLEISCH, JENNIFER MARIE	1	94/95
ZAPPE, JASON A.	1	85/86
ZUKOTYNSKI, STEPHEN H.	1	81/82
ZUPAN, FRANK NORMAN	1	87/88

403 chapter members as of 4.8.07.

Chapter mailing address:

Prof. Lee Croft
Arizona State University
Dept Foreign Language
Tempe, AZ 85287
Lee.Croft@asu.edu

Dobro Slovo Member List for U of Arizona (Alpha Alpha) as of 4.8.07

Name	Type	Year
ABBEY, ANGELA	1	94/95
ABERSATURI, LEON ANDREW	1	88/89
ABRICK, KURT	1	92/93
ACOSTA, GABRIEL	1	72/73
ACTON, ROBERT	1	70/71
ALEXANDER, JEANNINE	1	86/87
AMAN, DALE ALAN	1	86/87
ANDERSON, LYDIA DIANE	1	01/02
ANDERSON, JAMES D	1	84/85
ANDERSON, VERA	2	90/91
ANDERSON, LACINDA	1	96/97
ANDRUSYSZYN, STEPHEN PAUL	1	84/85
APPEL, CHARLES	1	84/85
APPLEBEE, LAURIE	1	80/81
ASCHERMANNOVA, HANA	1	94/95
BANKS, JOHN	1	96/97
BARTON, WILLIAM, II	1	90/91
BEDNARZ, AGNIESZKA	1	92/93
BLACKWOOD, JENNI LYNN	1	90/91
BOLIN, DAVID	1	98/99
BONGERS, ROBIN SUE	1	05/06
BORROWMAN, JOHN	1	76/67
BOSTIC, DAVID LILES	1	90/91
BRAITHWAITE, JEAN	1	84/85
BREWER, MICHAEL MEYER	1	86/87
BROWDER, ROBERT P.	3	70/71
BROWN, CLIFF	1	75/76
BROWN, MARTIN LEE	1	84/85
BROWN, URSULA	1	78/79
BURCHFIELD, LISA	1	84/85
BURNELL, DENTON	1	92/93
BUTKOVICH, STACY SUE	1	88/89
CAMPION, LAWRENCE V.	1	68/69
CARGILL, KENNETH	1	03/04
CARLSON, CYNTHIA GALE	1	90/91
CARSON, JERRI CAMILLE	1	01/02
CARTER, CARLA	1	75/76
CASH, BRYAN J.	1	96/97
CAYFORD, MARTIN YURI	1	82/83
CECCARELLI, BRIAN N	1	82/83
CEDIC, DORDE	1	75/76
CHAING, HUI-WAN	1	90/91
CHASE, KATHERINE E.	1	94/95
CHERITON, INGRID	1	78/79
CHLOPOWICZ, JANICE	1	72/73
CHRISTENSEN, CAROL	1	78/79
CHRISTENSEN, KIM DEANNE	1	90/91
CLARK, DEBRA	1	75/76
CLEMENS, MATTHEW	1	92/93
COBEAN, RYDER DAVID	1	05/06
COBURN, SUELLEN	1	65/66
COLLAER, MARY BETH	1	84/85
COLLINS, MICHAEL	1	82/83
CONFER, PATRICE	1	72/73
CONLEY, ALBERT III	1	03/04
CONNER, SUSAN	1	86/87
COOK, ALEXANDER	1	78/79
CORBIN, ELLEN	1	86/87
CORSBERG, JOHN DAVID	1	90/91
CORT, DEBORAH	1	86/87
CRAIG, MICHAEL RYAN	1	99/00
CRODDY, BRYAN WAYNE	1	84/85
CROSSWHITE, KATHERINE	1	90/91
CUFFE, DONALD	1	64/65
CULLOM, CONSTANCE	1	65/66
DAIGH, CARLA	1	84/85
DAWSON, JOHN	1	84/85
DE YOUNG, STEPHEN	1	84/85
DICKINSON, JEAN MARY	1	82/83
DIERKING, CAROL	1	72/73
DODGE, PETER XAVIER	1	88/89
DOSH, SHERYL L.	1	80/81
DUAN, LIU	1	01/02
DUNKEL, PROF. ALEXANDER	2	75/76
EARDLEY, KENNETH	1	75/76
ENGLISH, CHRISTOPHER	1	86/87
ENRIQUEZ, ELAINE	1	05/06
ERVIN, ALICE	1	65/66
ERVIN, GERARD L.	1	64/65
EWBANK, MARY L.	1	64/65
EYRICH, AMI E.	1	86/87
FAGERGREN, LAURIE ANN	1	99/00
FARMER, SUSAN	1	86/87
FELNAGLE, CATHERINE	1	98/99
FELTNER, JEANNIE	1	80/81
FIKE, JULIA R.	1	78/79
FILAPECKI, THOMAS	1	86/87
FINKELSTEIN, RAPHAEL	1	64/65
FLACK, WILLIAM CONRAD	1	90/91
FLYNN, BOB	1	82/83
FOLK, SARA H.	1	64/65
FORTIER, JANELLE MCCLARAN	1	88/89
FOY, CHERYL A.	1	82/83
FRANZ, HEATHER	1	96/97
FRITZ, PAUL	1	70/71
FUCCI, DIANA GRACE	1	90/91
GABLE, GERALDINE R.	1	64/65
GANSKI, MICHAEL J.	1	76/77
GARCIA, ANA MARIA	1	80/81
GARCIA, RICHARD	1	96/97
GARCIA, CYNTHIA	1	96/97
GARDNER, GRANT	1	68/87
GAY, MIA	3	80/81
GERSTEIN, STEVEN JAY	1	82/83
GIBSON, MARGARET	1	66/67
GIEDRAITIS, JAMES	1	76/77
GISLER, DOROTHY M.	1	78/79
GODWIN, JOSEPH SHIPMAN	1	88/89
GONNERMAN, KARRIE F.	1	88/89
GOODWIN, WALTER B.	1	94/95
GRADY, PATRICIA	1	72/73
GRAHAM, CONSTANCE	1	65/66
GRAY, TERRENCE	1	79/79
GRAYBILL, JESSICA	1	96/97
GRECO, STEVEN LEE	1	78/79
GREENE, BAIRD S.	1	84/85
GREENE, RAQUEL GINNETTE	1	90/91
GRIER, MARTHA	1	64/65
GUILD, NANCY	1	96/87
GUTSCHE, PROF. GEORGE J. (2)	2	53/64
HAGGLUND, PROF. ROGER	2	78/79
HALABY, ANTHONU	1	96/97
HAMMONDS, PHILLIP	1	90/91
HANEY, JAMES M.	1	68/69
HANNA, MARGARET	1	86/87
HANSON, JULIE	1	86/87
HARDY, VENECE	1	84/85
HARRISON, JOELLEN	1	70/71
HARRISON, JANET L.	1	82/83
HARTIGAN, JOHN K	1	90/91
HAUENSTEIN, CAROL A	1	64/65
HAYMORE, STEPHEN R.	1	96/00
HEIDEN, CHRISTINE	1	65/66
HENKLE, NANCY	3	82/83
HERBOLICH, CASH	1	84/85
HERNANDEZ, AMANDA	1	98/99
HEUSINKUELD, KAREN	1	75/76
HILSINGER, JANICE M.	1	64/65
HINKLE, CHRISTIAN M.	1	84/85
HOVEY, JAMES DONALD	1	88/89
HOYT, TANIA	1	84/85
HUK, PETER	1	92/93
HUKLE, MARIAN KAY	1	82/83
HUTCHINSON, DARION	1	75/76
IVANUK, SERGIY	1	03/04
JANSEN, DIANE C.	1	78/79
JARDINE, JACQUELINE	1	68/69
JENSON, JINDRISKA	1	72/73
JESSON, HELEN J.	1	68/69
JILLI, MARY JANE	1	80/81
JOHNSON, MICHAEL W.	1	82/83
JONES, JAMES M.	1	76/77
JOSLIN, MERRY CHRISTINA	1	82/83
JOSLIN, DAVID J.	1	05/06
JUNG, JACQUELINE	1	86/87
KACHUR, JOHN	1	86/57
KASHIMOTO, JOY AHTENA	1	82/83
KASNEY, KENNETH F.	1	78/79
KELLOG, FREDERICK	2	68/69
KELLY, COLLEEN	1	86/87
KENMAN, NAYA KAY	1	90/91
KENSKI, GLORIA	1	70/71
KENT, GEORGE	1	70/71
KERN, CHERYL J.	1	80/81
KEZELE, JOSEPH M. JR.	1	72/73
KIER, ANDREW	1	92/93
KING, JANICE D.	1	84/85
KING, ROBERT	1	86/87
KLIACHKO, PROF. SAVEL	2	64/65
KLUVER, JOHN	1	82/83
KOENIG, SUSAN ELIZABETH	1	88/89
KORDONSKY, ANNA	1	98/99
KORNREICH, BRAD	1	92/93
KOTOFSKIE, PHILLIP	1	86/87
KRASSON, MEREDITH	1	05/06
KREMP, EVA	1	70/71
KUBISTA, MARK	1	86/87
KUHNS, KATHERINE MARIE	1	88/89
LANCE, KATHRYN	1	65/66
LANDON, ROBERT	1	72/73
LANGEN, WILLIAM G.	1	64/65
LAUGHLIN, PHYLLIS	1	66/67
LAVERMAN, JULIE	1	92/93
LAZERE, JOEL H.	1	68/69
LEADENHAM, CAROL ANN	1	75/76
LEBISH, ALAN R.	1	80/81
LEE, JOHN A.	1	90/91
LEE, MARTA	1	86/87
LEHNARTZ, MICHAEL	1	99/00
LENFGREN, PROF. JOHN	2	94/95
LERNER, LORI BETH	1	88/89
LIDDLE, SUSAN	1	84/85
LINSON, LAWRENCE	1	86/87
LIVINGSTON, DONALD	1	82/83
LOMASHVILI, LEILA A.	1	01/02
LOMASZ, SARA	1	03/04
LYTLE, SHERRY E.	1	78/79
LYTLE, SUSAN	1	66/67
LYTLE, STEVEN W.	1	78/79
MACALUSO, MARK DAVID	1	84/85
MACURA, PAUL	3	84/85
MALIK, PROF JOE (45.1)	4	64/65
MARCINIK, ROGER L.	1	64/65
MARKEVICS, LAURA	1	92/93
MARSHALL, PETER	1	68/69
MARTZ, ERIN	1	86/87
MASTALER, RONALD	1	75/76
MAUL, HELEN	1	66/67
MC HENRY, WILLIAM K.	1	84/85
MCCORMICK, TIM	1	72/73
MCCULLOUGH, COLIN	1	96/97
MCHABB, RICHARD LEE	1	88/89
MCNULTY JR., JAMES	3	86/87
MEAHL, DANIEL JAMES	1	90/91
MEHRER, ANNETTE L.	1	82/83
MEYER, TONI	1	86/87
MILLER, MC LANE T.	1	82/83
MIXA, MARY SULLIVAN	1	90/91
MODICA, CONSTANCE D.	1	68/69
MOE, SHANNON	1	86/87
MORSE, KATHERINE	1	80/81
MORTIMOR, WILLIAM	1	76/77
MORTON, RICHARD	1	75/76
MURRAY, ANNA	1	88/89
NAGASHIMA, TORU	1	99/00

243

Name		Years	Name		Years	Name		Years
NELSON, DIANE GRETA	1	82/83	SIZEMORE, CINDY HOLDERMAN	1	90/91	WORLEY, CHRISTOPHER	1	90/91
NELSON, CHAD RICHARD	1	01/02	SKINNER, THOMAS T.	1	68/69	YACKLEY, JOHN R.	1	76/77
NEUBAUER, JEAN E.	1	68/69	SKVAREK, ANNE MARIE	1	01/02	YAMADA, KENZO	1	84/85
NORDAHL, RICHARD A.	1	64/65	SLAVEN, DAN	1	75/76	YAMANAKA, CHRISTOPHER	1	86/87
NOREUIL, BONNIE C.	1	68/69	SLEZAK, KATHRYN	1	86/87	YEHLING, VICKI	1	80/81
NORRIS, REBECCA	1	98/99	SLUSHER, BARBARA	1	78/79	YERGIN, APRIL ALEXANDRA	1	90/91
O'KEEFE, FRANCIS	1	75/76	SMITH, TODD ROLLINS	1	84/85	ZACK, KATHLEEN	1	76/77
O'SULLIVAN, DON	1	92/93	SMITH, MARY JO	1	80/81	ZILAVY, KATHLEEN A.	1	78/79
OKSOL, KIRI ELIZABETH	1	98/99	STENFORS, DEBRA LYNN	1	84/85			
OLSON, LINDA	1	70/71	STEPHAN, SANDRA GALE	1	78/79	383 chapter members as of 4.8.07.		
OONK, MARIANA	1	72/73	STEVENSON, JAMES	1	86/87			
OSWALD, GREGORY J	2	64/65	STEWARD, DONNA J.	1	90/91	Chapter mailing address:		
OWEN, EDWARD	1	03/04	STEWART, GRETCHEN	1	92/93			
OWEN, MICHAEL	1	70/71	STEWART-MELENDEZ, SCOTT	1	86/87	Prof. Roza Simkhovich		
PACHOLCZYK, HELEN LISA	1	88/89	STOKES, DANIEL	1	86/87	U of Arizona		
PACZOSA, THERESE	1	78/79	STORY, KIM	1	84/85	Russian Dept - Box 210067		
PARK, LAURA	1	76/77	STOYANOF, DIMITAR	1	80/81	Tuscon, AZ 85271-0067		
PARKER, RICHARD E.	1	68/69	STRANGSTALIEN, MICHAEL A.	1	80/81	Roza@dakotacom.net		
PARKER, CLAYTON S.	1	96/97	STRIMBU, LORI	1	80/81			
PAYNE, CHARLES	1	72/73	STRINGFIELD, SUZANNE	1	05/06			
PENDERGAST, JOHN MARTIN	1	01/02	STRODE, CAROLYN	1	65/66			
PERRY, JAMES W	2	64/65	STUBBS, GREGORY	1	65/66			
PERSING, SUSAN	1	75/76	SUMMERS, JOEL	1	75/76			
PETERS, JOHN	1	84/85	SWANLAND, BRUCE	1	78/79			
PFUHL, STACEY	1	78/79	SWANLAND, CHARLES M.	1	68/69			
PHILLIPS, PROF. DELBERT	2	70/71	TAYLOR, JENNIFER	1	86/87			
PINO, MICHELE	1	80/81	TAYLOR, JUDITH MARIAN	1	88/89			
PITT, DONALD	3	84/85	TAYLOR, LISA RENEE	1	88/89			
PORTER, NATHAN	1	84/85	THOMASON, ALLEN	1	66/67			
POTTER, JAMES L.	1	96/97	THOMPSON, CATHLEEN	1	70/71			
PRATER, SCOTT GREGORY	1	88/89	THOMPSON, SUZANNE	1	84/85			
PRICE, JOHN R.	1	82/83	THOMSON, ALLEN	1	66/67			
QUCK, JOHN	1	92/93	TINSLEY, PROF. ROYAL L.	2	64/65			
QUINLAN, PETER	1	75/76	TOMOFF, KIRIL DAVID	1	90/91			
QUINT, ALLA	1	05/06	TORIKAI, YAYOI	1	90/91			
REIS, RICHARD L.	1	82/83	TOWNSEND, DORIAN ALEKSANDRA	1	03/04			
REYNOLDS, ARLISSA MERRITT	1	94/95	TRANTER, REX D	1	78/79			
RIALL, KATHLEEN	1	75/75	TRAVER, WENDY	1	82/83			
RICCA, MATTHEW A.	1	05/05	TURNBERG, CAROL	1	80/81			
RIISE, SHARRON	1	84/85	TYSENN, JOAN M.	1	76/77			
RIVERA, YLIA	1	65/66	VANDEVORT, DENNIS E.	1	68/69			
ROBERTS, PROF. BORISS	3	64/65	VANEK, ANTHONY	2	64/65			
RODER, MARA	1	90/91	VASSILIEV, WALTER	1	75/76			
ROEDIG, CYNTHIA	1	90/91	VAZQUEZ, GRACIELA	1	94/95			
ROMENESKO, JAMES P.	1	03/04	VELGOS, GUY	1	80/81			
ROSE, JOSEPH C.	1	76/77	VEMULAPALLI, MOHANDAS	1	86/87			
ROY, MARIE LIVINGSTON	1	88/89	VENMAN, ELIZABETH	1	92/93			
RUDENKO, OLEKS	1	64/65	VETROVSKY, SUSAN M.	1	75/76			
RUSH, CHRISTINA	1	86/87	VIOLETTE, JO ANN	1	75/76			
RUSSELL, SHAUNA D.	1	76/77	VOHLERS, RICHARD	1	75/76			
RUTH, RICK	1	70/71	VONTSOLOS, NICHOLOS (23)	2	65/66			
SABOVIK, PAUL	1	80/81	WARDELL, DWIGHT	1	72/73			
SACK, BARBARA M	1	82/83	WATSON, ELIZABETH	1	86/87			
SALMON, PATRICK	1	75/76	WATSON, LANE TYLER	1	88/89			
SANDIDGE, HELEN	1	66/67	WEADON, PAUL	1	70/71			
SCANLON, DAVID S	1	76/79	WEAVER, KENNETH L.	1	82/83			
SCHAEFFER, ANDREA MICHELE	1	94/95	WEECH, SAMUEL	1	96/97			
SCHMIDT, ANDREW R.	1	76/77	WEINTRAUB, DANA	1	86/87			
SCHNEIDER, AMY	1	84/85	WHISHAW, LORNA H.	1	64/65			
SCHOUTEN, DARLENE	1	90/91	WHITE, CECILIA	1	88/89			
SCHUSTERMAN, ALAN	1	70/71	WHITE, THOMAS P.	1	64/65			
SCOTT, SOREN N.	1	96/97	WHYTE, JENNIFER	1	92/93			
SEABORG, CYNTHIA L.	1	80/81	WICKHAM, JOYCE P.	1	68/69			
SELDIS, PAUL	1	84/85	WIENER, WENDY	1	86/87			
SELLARI, ROBERT	1	70/71	WILLIAMS, MICHAEL	1	03/04			
SEMET, SCOTT RICHARD	1	88/89	WILLIAMS, VICKI L.	1	90/91			
SEWELL, KATHLEEN R.	1	75/77	WILLIAMSON, BARBARA C.	1	76/77			
SHARPE, CHARLES	1	70/71	WILLNER, EVAN MATTHEW	1	96/97			
SHIN, LINDA	1	86/87	WILSON, GORDON R.	1	76/77			
SHROPSHIRE, DONALD	3	82/83	WILTON, MARGO	1	70/71			
SICKOREZ, LISA	1	86/87	WINTERS, DAN	1	75/76			
SIEGEL, DVORAH	1	72/73	WOLCOTT, PETER	1	86/87			
SIKARSKIE, JEROME	1	65/66	WOOD, MARY	1	72/73			
SIKARSKIE, CONSTANCE	1	55/66	WOODS, SUSAN	1	65/66			
SIMKHOVICH, PROF. ROZA	2	88/89	WOODS, DIANNA	1	65/66			

Dobro Slovo members and certificate-holding initiates at the home of Lee and Lesley Hoyt Croft, April 18, 2007: (L-R) Danny Foley, Meagan King, Heather Nyhart, Kelsey Olson, Michael Freeman, Jaime "Olga" Palmer (front), Alicia Baehr, Andrew Abbott (red T-shirt), Andrew Gunn (back row), Jeremy Ecton, Travis Webb (back), Jose "Joe" Garcia, Lee B. Croft.

In the 1936 Ford Phaeton at the Crofts': (L-R) Alicia Baehr, Kelsey Olson, Danny Foley, and (in front) Andrew Abbott and Lee Croft (doubles ping-pong champs). April 2007 by Lesley Hoyt Croft.

What Have We Learned?

We have learned of a half-century of great effort by a handful of people... the Russian Language and Literature faculty members of the educational institutions of the State of Arizona...to potentiate and advance thousands of young Arizona residents. We have learned that these Russian-enriched young people have had a local, national, and international impact on all our lives on this world. We think that this great educational effort should find whatever support it needs to continue. If this book aids in bringing about such support from whatever quarters, then its creation will have been a worthy "capstone experience" for us all. Thank you for your attention.

Lee B. Croft, Barry Boosman, Katherine Lutz, James C. Nielsen, and Aimee M. Raymer. Arizona State University, Tempe, Arizona. May 2007.

INDEX OF NAMES

In this index are 907 names—all those many who are incremental parts of **RUSSIAN IN ARIZONA**. We are indexing all the names by last name, leaving off all titles. The index covers the text from the title page to this page, 246, including the captions of the photographs. It does NOT, however, include the lists of 746 names of the DOBRO SLOVO Honorary chapters on pages 241-244, but these can be separately accessed.

Abbott, Andrew 245
Abdow-Morgan, Miriam 39
Abell, Frances B. 11
Abernathy, Linda 30, 36
Adair, Arthur 116
Adam, Dennis 213
Adamov, Joe 181
Adams, Wallace 57
Addis, Don 206, 213
Agadjanian, Victor 72
Aitmatov, Chinghiz 143
Akhmatova, Anna 83-84, 134, 187, 204, 223
Alarcon, Justo 38
Alexander, Jeanine 80
Alexander, John 62
Alexander, Lydia 80
Alexander, Vera 80
Alexander the Great 30
Alf (dog) 20
Allred, Benjamin T. 215
Altnether, Joseph 214
Altringer, Beth 222
Analaryan, Sofiya 235
Ananyeva, Irina I. (Eaves) 216, 231-232, 236
Anderson, Alan 78, 210, 212
Andersen, William 213, 224-225
Andersen, Gail Turner 213, 224
Anderson, Waldo 23
Andreeva, Hafiza 71
Anna Karenina (Tolstoy) 142
Aralica, Edwin 208, 231
Archibald, Melissa 222
Arzumanova, Julia 72
Ashworth, Steven 213

Athena (Tatyana Dhaliwal's nom de plume) 98
Ausloos, Regina Levin 217
Avins, Carol 33
Avedisian, Katia 77, 115
Awdziewicz (Weiss), Martha 31-32, 34, 40, 71
Axford, Nadia 64
Axford, Roger 34, 64
Ayers, Christopher W. 218
Azhgikhina, Nadezhda 141

Babby, Leonard H. 25-26
Bacca, John 206, 213
Baehr, Alicia 245
Bade, James 65, 214
Baich, Mirjana 72, 207, 212
Bailey, Patricia (Cossette) 90, 207, 209, 212
Bailey, Robert 214
Balamenti, Suzanne 220
Baldini, Pier R. 12, 15, 56, 62, 64
Banash, Catherine A. (Williams) 218
Barker, Adele M. 4, 5, 47, 78, 123, 126, 139-142, 147, 161, 164-5, 211
Bar-Lev, Zev 109-111
Barney-O'Neil, Margaret 215, 221
Barrett, Barbara 219
Barrett, Craig 219
Barrett, Pat 4, 5, 60, 77, 113-117, 138, 209
Bassin, Irene 67, 83
Bassin, Stan 67
Bataille, Gretchen 63

Batalden, Sandra 5, 18-19, 72
Batalden, Stephen K. 2, 5, 18-19, 30-31, 41-44, 53, 64-66, 69, 71, 95, 112, 117, 132-133, 138, 147, 177, 226
Batistick, Jill 214
Baum, Robert 208, 213, 225-226
Beaty, Lauralyn 222
Belinskij, Vissarion 152
Bennett, Eldean 47
Bentley, J. Richard 209, 216
Benzer, Susan 213
Bergfalk, Glendon 23, 77
Bergman, Edward 183, 213
Berkoff, Dmitri 21
Berry, Ellen 167
Berry, Robb 30
Bertoni, Cheri (Peters) 213
Bialek, Jerry 213
Bickett, Paula 209, 212
Birks, Ronald 215
Birnbaum, N. 171
Bjella, Constance 213
Blackwell, Michael (Michelle) 76, 77
Blakney, John 210
Blalock, Kent 212
Blankov, Yurii 42
Blok, Alexander 148, 223
Blum, Julius 34
Bodiroga, Ronald 77
Boehm, Jeff 207, 212
Bohl, Marianne 72, 207, 212
Bollerman, Karen 188-189
Bondarook, Nina 33, 209, 212
Bonifield, Thomas 65, 209, 212
Boosman, Barry 1-2, 9, 117, 120, 246

Bor, Natalia 77
Bordwell, Robert 77
Boren, David 220
Bores, Leara 112
Bores, Leo 112
Borotynskii, Evgenii 40
Borovansky, Vladimir 72, 83
Bowers, Terri 36
Bowman, Russell 12, 14-16, 27
Brack, O. M. "Skip" 37
Brada, Josef 41-43, 56, 66, 72
Brauchli, Ed 206, 213
Brauchli, Karen 206, 213
Brecht, Richard 25
Breger, Marcus 7, 77
Breger, Martha 7, 77
Brennan, Edward 30, 213
Brewer, Michael 78-79, 123
Briggs, A.D.P. 153
Brink, Dan 47
Brink, Jeannie R. 91
Brixius, Tom 79-80
Brokaw, David 177
Broughton, Jeremiah J. 216
Browder, Robert 79
Brown, Charles Brockden 137
Brown, Constance 213
Brown, David (b) 221
Brown, David (a) 212
Brown, Dwight 217
Brown, Nancy Jo 213
Bruner, David 214
Bryce, Allison 222
Buckland, Herb O. 235
Budisavljevic-Oparnica, Maria 31, 65, 71, 212, 229
Buffington, Albert 12
Buhrig, Linda 36
Bullock, Gary 194

Burke, Christopher 209, 212
Burke, Janet 220
Burleson, Danielle 230
Burris, Bruce 214
Burton, Dora 4, 5, 32, 39-41, 44-45, 48, 54, 59, 67, 70-71, 82-84, 170-172, 174, 176, 179, 184, 200, 220, 225, 230, 234
Buzarovska, Eleni 5, 18, 30, 71, 116
Buzarovski, Dmitrije 180

Calo, Lois 77
Cameron, Patricia 212, 213
Campbell, Amy 218, 235-236
Campbell, Brenda 232
Campbell, Kees 218
Campbell, Rudy 180
Camphire, Lynn 210, 214
Canales-Hernandez, Enrique Gustavo 120, 208, 218
Cannon, Al 20, 78, 129
Capin, Justin 49, 71, 75
Carden, Patricia 25
Cargill, Kenneth 5, 211
Carlson, Ingeborg 51
Carnes, Debra, 77
Carney, Sarah 202-203, 216
Cartwright, Michael 213
Carty, Patrick 209
Carver, George 14
Cass, J. 171
Castro, Raul 180
Cattlain, Fernand 11-13
Cedic, Miodrag 65, 181
Chagall, Marc 106, 187
Chaplin, Charlie 89
Chaykin, Nancy 213

Chekhov, Anton 21, 83, 170, 176, 187
Cheppel, Alena 74, 113
Chinnov, Igor 89
Choncoff, Mary 29-31
Christian, J. Scott 65
Chulaki, Georgii 180
Church, Alan 209
Chvany, Catherine V. 61-62, 66
Clark, Ben T. 24
Clay, Eugene 31, 72
Clinch, Theresa 210, 214
Coady, Susan 72, 207, 212
Cocchia, Andrew S. 218
Cohen, Michael 213
Collinsworth, Curt 212
Combs, Sean "P. Diddy" 235
Conovaloff, Andrew John 7, 75, 110
Conrad, Michael 171, 206, 213
Consentino, Tina 218
Contreras, Bonifacio 30
Coor, Lattie 55-56, 63, 65-66, 96, 175
Cornell, Ezra 25
Corricides, Carmen 14
Couch, Christina 35, 214
Couch, Marge 35
Couch, Mark 35
Couch, Sandy 4-5, 7-9, 15-19, 21-22, 24, 26, 28, 31-32, 35-36, 39, 41, 44-45, 48-49, 51, 54, 57, 59, 63-64, 67, 70-71, 73, 77, 84-88, 109, 111-115, 125-126, 128-131, 137, 169-172, 174-176, 178, 181, 196, 199-200, 202, 220, 223, 229-231, 234

Couplan-Cashman, Louise 35
Crawshaw, Susan M. 183-184
Croft, Betty (Richter) 34, 44
Croft, Billy (William) 34, 57, 89
Croft, Christopher 34, 89
Croft, Cathy 5, 34, 57, 88-89, 94
Croft, Hayden L. 5, 9, 16, 57, 68, 89, 95, 120, 224
Croft, Jerry G. 239
Croft, Lesley Hoyt 5, 9, 16, 18-19, 29, 44, 49-51, 60, 64, 67-68, 74, 88-90, 94-95, 108, 121, 152, 155, 224, 232, 236, 245
Croft, Lee B. 1-2, 4-6, 8-10, 16, 18-19, 21-74, 76-78, 80, 84, 86-96, 111-112, 114-117, 120-122, 126-139, 141, 144, 152, 155, 157-166, 170-172, 174-184, 188-189, 193-215, 219-242, 245-246
Croft, Norma 189
Croft, William S. 68, 189
Cronkite, Walter 47
Cross, Samuel Hazzard 40
Croucher, Murlin 21, 209, 212
Crow, Michael 52, 175
Cruzen, Jacob 204
Curran, Mark 62-63
Curtis, Maren 221
Cutter, Robert Joe 12
Cvitanovic, Predrag 25-26
Cyoni, Tamayi 14
Czerski, Agnieszka Bednarz 57, 65, 72, 79, 209

Dalgleish, D. Douglas 41, 56, 71

Danielson, Jennipher 221
D'Anthes, Georges 183
Danielova, Irina 60-61
Dannenfeldt, Karl 26, 28
Daskalova, Krassimira 167
Davey, William 175
Davidson, Dan 199
Davis, Benjamin 191
Davis, James (Jay) 65, 188-191
Deeny, Scott 208
De Jonge, Alex 78, 147
De Haan, Francisca 167
Dembo 14
Demkova, Julia 73
Derizemlya, Liudmila 74, 77, 113
Dermer, Laurie 222
DeRoeck, Galina 78
Derzhavin, Gavriil 98, 223-224
Dhaliwal, David 98
Dhaliwal, Tatyana 4, 5, 68-71, 97-98, 174, 178, 182-183, 236
Dickens, Charles 137
Dillon, Mary Colleen 25
DiLucido, Michael 33
Diniciu, Carolina Varga (Morocco) 34
Dittert, Eric 33
Dittert, Marta 213
Donnelly, James 77
Doran, Peter 212, 216
D'Orssaud, Suzanne 14
Dostoevsky, Fyodor 21, 119, 151, 170
Douglas, Bobby 180
Dower, Margaret (Foley) 65, 227-228
Doyle, Dee Dee 33, 36

Driscoll, Fred 239
Dulley, Brian 24-25, 71, 73
Dunham, Vera 74
Dunihue, Phillip 65, 213
Dunkel, Alexander 4, 5, 77, 123, 126, 142-143, 161
DuPont, Robert L. 61
Durant, Martin 73
Durham, G. Homer 53
Duval, Henry 207, 212
Dyrek, William 214

Eck, Michael 235
Ecton, Jeremy 245
Edgington, Susan 177
Efimenko, Kristina 77
Eickman, Jordan 222
Eisen, Shannon 214
Ekmanis, Rolfs 4, 5, 9, 16-19-22, 28, 36-37, 41, 43-45, 48, 53-54, 56-57, 59, 64-65, 67, 70-71, 99-100, 111-112, 169-171, 174-176, 178, 200, 220, 223, 230, 234
Ekmanis, Shelley 44
Ellingson, David 209, 217
Elliott, Elisabeth 57, 79, 145 209, 212
Erasmus of Rotterdam 61
Ervin, Gerard L. 77, 113, 130
Escudero, Mary 13-14
Esenin, Sergei 223-224
Eugene Onegin (A. Pushkin) 152
Evans, Christopher 213
Evans-Romaine, Kathleen 177
Everton, Jared 216

Falen, James 5, 152
Fanello, Benjamin J. 218

Fannin, Tammy 34
Farbishel, Tatiana 76
Farbarik, Susan (Fry) 77, 209, 212
Faust 60
Feldman, Albert 2
Fettig, Annette 65, 78
Fielder, Grace 4, 5, 78, 123, 126, 143-145, 174
Filipovic, Mario 5, 69
Finley, Babette 215
Fischer, David 212
Fitzgerald, Brian 65, 212
Folden, Sally 207
Foley, Danny 245
Foos, Frederick 25
Foreman, Robert 216
Foster, David William 12, 15, 36, 62-63
Flys, Michael J. 12, 15, 31-32, 36, 38-41
Frackiewicz, Heather Lambert 77 226
Frackiewicz, Zbyszek 226
Freeman, Michael 245
Frestedt, Myna 65
Frusetta, James 221
Fyodorov, Sviatoslav 112

Galope, Michael 65, 212, 214
Galvin, Suzanne 30, 33, 36, 209, 212
Gamble, Melissa 115
Gammage, Grady 13
Gan, Adrian 25
Gandolfini, James 194
Garcia, Jose "Joe" 245
Garrard, Carol 148
Garrard, John G. 4, 5, 78, 102, 123, 125-126, 145-150, 174

Gates, Bill 220-221
Gates, Melinda 220-221
George, Lisa 178
George, Ruth 76
Gheith, Jahanne 141
Gibian, George 25
Gibson, Margaret B. 52, 65, 77, 86, 102, 125, 129, 131, 137, 189
Giffin, Frederick 5, 41-43, 51, 66, 71, 90, 132, 138
Gilbert, Patrick 222
Gill, Sylvia 213
Gillen, Steven 221
Glasse, Boris 25
Glasse, Antonia 25
Glenn, Mary L. 216
Glessner-Calkins, Beth 201
Glick, Milton 56, 63-64
Gogol, Nikolai V. 10, 31, 61, 64, 137-138, 151-152, 204
Gold, Michael 215
Goldberg, Carl 7, 49, 71
Goldthwaite, John 214
Goldwater, Barry 179-180, 220-221
Golovskoi, Valerian 78, 147
Gonnerman, Karrie, 78, 210
Gooding, Elmer 53
Goodrich, Pamela 217
Gorbachev, Mikhail 5, 17, 112, 115, 141, 206
Gottschalk, Elizabeth P. 208
Grace, Edward (Ned) 63
Granfelt, Siri 213
Grant, Bruce 141
Green, Mitch 36
Green, Paul 209, 212, 213, 224
Greil, Judi 123-124

Griffen, Steven 207, 212, 213
Grossman, Vasily 149
Grover, Glen 79-80
Gruzinska, Aleksandra 177
Gunderson, Brent Levi 216
Gunn, Andrew 233, 245
Gunn, William 77, 217, 233-234
Gunterman, Gail 67
Gutsche, George 4, 5, 9, 66, 78, 123-126, 130, 150-153, 165, 174-175, 193

Haden, C. Roland 52
Haddock, Joel 214
Hagberg, Laura 214
Hagglund, Roger 78, 111-112, 162
Hajduk, Beata 173
Hall, Robert A. 25, 158
Hammonds, Phillip 78-79
Harris, Charles S. 55-56
Hart, David 33
Hart, Pierre 74
Haskell, Lisa 213
Hatch, Aldis 14
Hathaway, Valerie 128, 137, 211
Hayden, Charles Trumball 10
Heeder, Robert D. 217
Hendershott, Broc 218
Henderson, Julie 213
Herman, George 57
Hicks, Michael 213
Hicks, Linda 213
Hildebrandt, Augusta 10
Hill, Kimberly 221
Hobbs, Jennifer 213
Hoffman, Walter S. 23
Holcombe, Robert 34, 213

Holmes, Richard 78
Homan 14
Hoover, Denee 213
Hopkins, Gerard Manley 98
Hopkins and Dresskell 182
Horowitz, Louis 208
Horwath, Peter 5, 12, 15, 24-25, 28-30, 38, 45, 51-52, 73, 177
Hoyt, Kathryn 5, 95
Hubbard, Paul 50
Hunter, Edward 213

Ivan Ilyich (L. Tolstoy) 152-153
Inumpudi, Akhila 9

Jackson, Marvin 41-43, 56, 72
Jakobson, Roman O. 40-41, 137
James, Terry 209
Janda, Laura 176
Jankovic, Smilija 173
Jaric, Avgusta L. 14, 25
Jarvis, Don 113
Jaynes, Debra Anderson 33, 77, 207
Jaynes, Rick 33
Jensen, Suzanne 213-214
Johnson, Brenda (Campbell) 232

Kachur, Paul 57, 79, 213
Kagan, Olga 90
Kalisz, Danuta 70-71, 177-178
Kashaeva, Goljihan 71
Katsinas, Bill 221
Kazanina, Tatiana 5, 49, 77, 113

Keeler, Joyce Tilzey 33, 213
Keeling, Tatiana 71, 174
Keeton, Jamie L. 217, 234
Kefeli-Clay, Agnés 31, 71
Kelley, Daniel 213
Kelley, Gerald 25
Kelley, Robert 36, 209, 212
Kellogg, Christine 34
Kellogg, Frederick 34, 79
Kelly, Glenn 215
Kendrick-Thomas, Rebecca 213
Kenman, Leon 72
Kenney, Alan 209, 212
Kenning, Janet 213, 228
Keppe, Birgit 213
Kerger, Kameron G. B 173, 213, 217, 222
Kerrigan, Miki 216
Khodorovsky, Boris 180
Khrushchev, Nikita 19
Kibalchich, Nikolai I. 89, 138
Kinder, Cheryl Pritchard 239
King, Martin Luther 217, 245
King, Meagan 204, 220, 222
Kinsinger, Jack B. 44, 47, 53
Kinsky, Nastasya 194
Kirkpatrick, Samuel 52
Kislik, Alex 76
Kiva, Alexei 18
Klein, Dan 21-22
Klein, Susan 21
Klenk, Tracy West 65, 204, 209, 212, 214
Kliachko, Savel 77
Klossner, Jeffrey 213
Koblitz, Ann Hibner 2
Kobylianska, Ol'ha 167
Kobylin, Victor 73
Koehler, Liudmila 33

Koepp, Donald 19
Kolasa, Electronica "Nica" 183
Konecni, Evica 30, 71
Kopp, Daniel 215
Koppes, Steve 172
Korb, Timothy 77
Korotich, Vitalii 180
Korovin, Lev 76
Korovina, Tatiana 76
Kostomarov, Vitalii G. 109
Kraft, Alexander 25
Krahenbuhl, Gary 52, 56, 63-66
Krajewski, Anna 72, 207, 212
Krasnova-Douglas, Eleonora 65, 71, 74, 113
Krebs, Loren 72, 207, 212
Krioukov, Dmitrii 182-183, 204
Krylova, Irina Borisovna 19, 21, 54, 71, 170, 179
Kuchenbacker, Kristin 216
Kuester, Carol 213
Kuester, Lance 210, 213
Kusevska, Marija 30, 71

Lafford, Barbara 67
Landsberg, Marge E. 65
Lang, Peter 167
Langley, Terri (Hudson) 213
Langmuir, Irving 96
Larson, Kent 209
Launer, Michael K. 66
Lazarchuk, M. 166
Leafgren, Elizabeth 153
Leafgren, John 4, 5, 78, 123-124, 126, 145, 153-154
Leafgren, Tory 153
Lee, John 78-9

Leed, Richard L. 25-26
Lenz, Helen 76, 77
Leonard, Patt 204
Lermontov, Mikhail Yu. 148, 223
Lester, William A. 217
Levin, Ilana 183
Levitt, Marcus 167
Liebi, Adam 227-228
Likens, Peter 175
Livingston, Donald E. 4, 5, 49, 53-54, 56, 65, 70-71, 73, 78-79, 101-102, 171, 178, 199, 220
Lofredo, Louis III 214
Lohr, Alice 214
Lorti, David 72
Losse, Deborah 5, 12, 15, 34-35, 40, 52, 62-63, 175
Losse, John 35
Losse, Katie 35
Losse, Owen 35
Lowe, Paulette 30
Lozano, Anthony 25
Lubbers, Lee 47
Lubensky, Sophia 113
Luey, Beth 42-43
Lunt, Horace 19-21
Lussier, Mark 96
Lutz, Katherine 1-2, 9, 106, 246
Lutz, Ksenia 213

Mabry, Mark 217
MacFarland, David 180
Mackey, Lola 22
MacQuarrie, Lachlan 139
Macura, Paul I. 77
Magner, Thomas 229
Mah, Patricia 222

Maienschein, Jane 2
Maiers, Stacy R. 216
Mainka, Jason 216, 221
Makuk, Andrew 79
Malik, Joe, Jr. 3-5, 7-9, 23-26,
44-45, 65, 77, 84, 87, 89, 102,
125-137, 146, 156, 158, 160,
174, 184, 189
Malik, Joe III 135
Malik, Lisa 135
Malik, Paula 9, 132-133, 135
Malik, Tamara 135
Malkina, Janna 73-74, 77, 115
Malloy, Molly 72
Malone, Kevin Michael 209,
212, 213
Manchester, Laurie 71
Markiw, Michael 72, 79
Markov, Georgi 43
Marov, Mikhail 194
Marshak, Samuil 138
Marshall, Jerry 213
Martinez, Quino 14
Marullo Thomas G. 25
Marx, Karl 17, 96
Mashuri, David 4, 5, 70-71,
103-104, 174, 178
Mashuri, Nargiza 103
Mastaler, Ron 78-79, 193-195
Mathews, John 99-100
Matlock, Jack 192
Maugens, Stacy 65
Mayakovsky, Vladimir 226
Mayer, Gerald 32
McCain, John 56
McCarter, Sue 209
McCutcheon, Bennett B., Jr.
33, 206, 213
McDonals, Christopher 194
McDowell, Charles 34

McFie Ahern, Kathleen 212,
213
McGalloway, Glavin 206, 213
McIntyre, Liudmila 72, 207
McIntyre, Sean 72, 207, 213
McKane, Tamara 71, 174,
202, 208, 237
McNabb, Richard 80
McNaughton, Amina 11
McNaughton, James 11
Meahl, Daniel 65, 214
Medvedev, Aleksandr 180
Melikian, Emma 44, 96, 177
Melikian, Gregory 44, 96, 177
Melville, Herman 28, 137
Menning, Chad 65
Meredith, Scott 61
Merrifield, Mark 213
Merrill, Neil 21
Metcalf, Alonzo 30
Michajliw, Christine 215
Milenkovska, Violeta 28, 71
Miles, Aaron 202-203, 216
Milivojevich, Dragan 176
Miller, George 137
Millican, Heather 182-183
Milosz, Czeslaw 180
Mitkovska, Liljana 30, 71
Mitrevski, George 31
Mochalov, Vladimir 5, 85-86,
180
Modzelewski, Pamela 214
Mohan, John 25
Monahan, Kathleen 213
Monks, Sarah 123-124
Monty Python 136
Moody, Bryan M. 217
Moore, Susan 30, 77, 213
Mormino, Anthony 210
Morris, Brent 172

Morris, Louisa 213-214
Morris, Natalie 172, 214
Mortensen, Christine 213
Mortensen, Dino 213
Mulholland, Paige 3
Murphy-Lee, Meghan 78-79, 126
Murza, Michael 213
Musselman, Rick 213
Myatlev, Ivan Petrovich 138
Myers, Elizabeth 33, 212

Nabokov, Vladimir 204
Nachtigal, Julie 30, 221
Nahas, Gabriel G. 61
Nakhimovsky, Alice Stone 25
Napoleon (Bonaparte) 67, 138
Naydan, Michael, 33
Naylor, Kenneth 145
Nelson, Roxanne 77
Nemecek, John 213
Newhart, Christopher 221
Nielsen, James C. 1-2, 9, 101, 114, 246
Nielsen, Michael 63-64
Nielsen, Tom 14
Nijinskaya, Anna 181
Nijinskii, Vaclav 181
Nilsen, Alleen Pace 58
Nilsen, Don L. F. 58
Novikov, Tatyana 167
Novosiltsev, Alla 25
Nummikoski, Marita 109
Nyhart, Heather 245

Obmanov, Viacheslav 37
O'Connor, Kim 207, 213
O'Haver, James Glenn 33, 36, 208
Olcott, Anthony 34

Olcott, Martha Brill 34
Oldani, Robert 72
Olesha, Yurii 89
Olney, Claude 57
Olney, James 57
Olontsev, Valentin F. 2, 5, 90, 95-96, 139
Olson, Chad O. 215
Olson, Kelsey L. 245
Orford, Adam 5, 54, 170, 208, 234-235
Orlich, Ileana 177, 220
Orton, Mark 25
Ostrom, Lonnie 55
Oswald, Gregory 79
Ovtchinnikova, Olga 78
Owen, Jeanette 5, 32, 71, 95-96, 103, 170, 176, 199

Pace, Kerry (Meyer) 47, 222
Palmer, Jaime "Olga" 245
Palumbo, Dennis 204
Palumbo, Jeanne 4, 204, 222
Parella, Anthony 36, 222-223
Park, Suzanne M. 183, 213
Parthe, Kathleen 25
Patrick, Steven 209, 221
Pasternak, Boris 187, 223-224
Pate, Kathy 77
Pauling, Linus 96
Paulsen, Sean M. 218
Pavlov, I. P. 82-83
Peek, George 26, 57
Perl, Margaret 215
Peterson, Eric 34
Peterson, Helga (Tamara Poljanskaya) 181
Petrosian, Sergei, 77, 113
Phillip of Macedon 30
Phillips, David 160

Phillips, Delbert D. 4, 5, 9, 23, 60, 65, 73-74, 77, 102, 110, 117, 121, 123-127, 131, 134, 137-138, 154-165, 174-175, 189, 191-192, 194, 209
Phillips, LaFon 160
Phillips, Mark 160
Phillips, Michael 65, 229-230
Pintner, Walter 25
Piper, Cary 78
Plumlee, Craig 209, 213
Pobedinsky, Alex 207, 212
Polechla, Venita 79
Polowy, Teresa 4, 5, 9, 78, 123-124, 126, 165-7, 174, 211
Pomirchy, Svetlana 213
Popovski, Mihailo 71
Porter, Andrew 213
Portnoff, Collice 15
Portnoff, George 7, 11, 13, 15, 70, 169
Powers, D. Bruce 5, 14, 19-21, 170
Powers, Doris 19
Prada, Scott M. 215
Pratt, Aaron H. 218
Prazma, Louis 23, 78, 127
Preslar, Raymond Mark 5, 49, 57, 71, 78, 85-86, 207, 212, 213
Priest, Peter 34
Proffer, Carl 20
Proffer, Ellendea 20
Prokofiev, Aleksandr 187
Pushkin, Alexander 21, 83, 138, 151-153, 170, 176, 183, 187, 204, 223-224
Putin, Vladimir 179-180

Rasmussen, David 57

Rasnick, Barbara 21, 36
Rasputin, Grigorii 147
Rasputin, Valentin 167
Rattay, Joan 7
Rauda, Maris (nom de broadcast of R. Ekmanis) 22, 99-100
Raymer, Aimee M. 1-2, 9, 124, 139-142, 145, 150, 154, 165, 246
Raymond, Colin 221
Reagan, Ronald 53, 134, 206
Reese, Andrew 49, 53-54, 65, 71, 87, 171, 207, 212
Reibman, Susan 33
Repnin-Volkonsky (Prince) 67
Richmond, Walter (Comins-) 65, 207, 212, 213
Rifkin, Benjamin 90, 184
Riley, Timothy 206, 213, 224
Roberts, Boriss 23, 77, 86, 127, 131, 137
Roberts, Lila 33, 224
Robinson, Don 180
Rodd, Laurel 52
Roffman, Bernard 33
Rogers, Don 73
Rogers, James 74
Rohovit, Lizabeth "Libby" 214
Romanesko, James 79
Romazanova, Marina 75
Rosin, Matthew 226-227
Ross, Catrien 36, 209, 212
Ross, Danielle M. 218, 221
Ruth, Rick 20, 78, 129
Rybka, Theodore 215
Rynish, Kami K. 216, 221

Sachar, Jon 206, 213-214

Sacino, Sherry Wheatley 209
Sackton, Frank J. 55-56
Samokhina, Natalia 79-80
Sanders, Mitchell 214
Sargent, Claire 56
Sartor, Jason 229
Schaeffer, George Anton 67, 138
Schaeffer, Ken 47
Schiager, Jill 209, 212, 213
Schiller, Herman 78, 207, 212
Schlacks, Charles, Jr. 41-43
Schlappy, David 215
Schmidt, Erich 214
Schneider, Dieter 181
Schwada, John W. 28
Schwartz, Pamela 204, 215
Sconce, Mark 5, 152
Scott, Byron 180
Seaborg, Cindy (Humphries) 79-80, 117
Seargent, Carl 65, 212, 214
Secklin, Daniel 77, 115, 214
Senner, Wayne M. 10, 32, 39, 65
Shahar, Tammy 72, 207, 212, 213
Shanley, Sally Clifford 64
Sharpe, Laura W. 10
Shashkevich, Olga 74
Sheen, Charlie 194
Shein, Robert 207, 212
Shen'e, Andrei 152
Sheppard, Douglas C. 12, 15, 26-28, 39
Shostakovich, Dmitrii 143
Sielaff, Martin 213
Simkhovich, Roza 4, 5, 78, 123-126, 130, 167-8, 174
Simpson, Mark 213

Simpson, Robert 214
Šipka, Danko 2, 4, 5, 9, 31, 45, 57, 67, 69-71, 103-105, 112, 174, 176-178, 220, 229
Šipka, Liljana 69
Sketch, Charles 75
Sljivic-Simsic, Biljana 229
Slobodchikoff, Anne 4, 5, 73-74, 120-122, 174
Slobodchikoff, Michael 121
Slobodchikoff, Nikolay 121
Slobodchikoff, Tanya 121
Smith, John 206, 213
Smith, Leslie Wright 212
Smith, Mary Jo 34, 79
Smith, Pauline I "Penny" 217
Smith, Sally 213, 216
Smyslov, Vasilii 180
Snipes, Linda Susan 30
Sobchak, Anatolii 179
Sokurov, Alexander 141, 187
Soll, Darrow 183, 208, 214
Solostnov, Salokhin (pseudonym of N. Vontsolos) 120
Solzhenitsyn Alexander I. 27-28, 211
Spasovski, Lupco 30, 71
Speshock, Susan (Pao) 207
Spritzer, Autumn "Renee" 218, 236-237
Stalin, Josef 7, 83
Stanislavsky, Konstantin 187
Stark, Brian 204
Starsky, Morris 57
Stensland, David 213
Stern-Gottschalk, Ariann 31, 71, 79, 178, 220
Stevens, Mary 64
Stoljarov, Nikolai S. 179-180

Story, Joyce 5, 49, 71, 75, 106-111, 117
Story, Thomas 104
Strachan, Eric 216, 237-238
Stravinsky, Igor 187
Stringfield, Suzanne 79-80
Struckmeyer, Jamie 30
Strunk, Shirley 34, 77, 209
Suny, Ronald Grigor 17
Sullivan, Jacqueline 214
Swift, Jonathon 61

Tambs, Lew 53
Tanner, Samuel Zachary "Zach" 183
Tappan, Dan 65
Tarkovsky, Andrei 187
Tartakovsky, Dmitri 221
Taylor, Romy 78, 123-124, 126, 174
Taylor, Todd 221
Tchaikovsky, Pyotr I. 187
Teetshorn, Matthew 213
Thomas, Brian J. 65, 173
Thomas, Dylan 98
Thompson, Irene 203
Thompson, Suzanne (Eanes) 78, 191-193
Tingey, Benjamin 209
Tingey, Troy 212
Tissarevskaya, Olga 181
Tito, Josip Broz 28
Tjalsma, William 25
Tolstoy, Leo N. 21, 58, 119, 133, 142, 152-153, 170, 204
Tomasi, Loren 215
Torrey, Kevin 75
Traeger, Erin 74, 113
Traicoff, Don 30
Traicoff, Gloria 30

Tran, Hai-Van 207, 23
Traynor, Terri 214
Tribble, Shamella 139
Tu, Eugenia 38
Tuman, Walter Vladimir 65-66, 72
Tumanov, Oleg (Soviet spy) 47, 138, 180
Turek, Michael, 77
Turney, James T. 215
Twitty, Chad 203-203, 216
Tyson, Mike 208

Unger, Julie 213

Valdivieso, Jorge 72
Valdivieso, Theresa 62-63
Vassiliev, Walter 78
Van der Werf, Russell 72, 212, 217
Van Scoy, Herbert 12, 22-23, 26
Vanchu, Anthony 233
Vedelago, Vincent 213
Velgos, Guy 79-80
Venuti, Elizabeth 213
Vernadsky, V. I. 45, 89, 96, 139, 155
Vinograde, Alice 33
Vinograde, Ann 33
Virgillo, Carmello 14, 53
Vlasov, Andrei Andreevich 138
Volek, Emil 7, 66, 177
Von der Heydt, Alfred 14
Vontsolos, Alexei 120
Vontsolos, Alexi 120
Vontsolos, Cathy 120
Vontsolos, George 120
Vontsolos, Lourdes 120

Vontsolos, Lucas 120
Vontsolos, Melina 120
Vontsolos, Michael 120
Vontsolos, Nicholas 4, 5, 23, 49, 53-54, 60, 65, 71, 77, 113, 117-120, 127, 155, 171, 218
Vontsolos, Nicole 120

Wakamiya, Lisa 78,126
Walker, Gary 65
Walker, Peggy 65, 228-229
Wall, Anna 14-15, 70, 114-115, 169-170
Wallace, Melissa 232-233
Walters, Marian 35
Weadon, Paul 23, 78, 127
Weidemeier, William 56, 71
Weigend, Guido 36-39, 44-45, 56
Weiner, Douglas 79
Weintraub, Victor 110
Welch, Marvin Jr. 214
Welles, Elizabeth B. 171
Welsch, W. Michael 35-36, 57, 78, 223-224
Welsh, Anne Marie 229
Welsh, William 43, 56
Wenzel, Mercedes "Mercy" 230-231
Wexler, Charles 57
Wheeler, Thomas 213
White, Charles 75
Whitefleet, John 202-203, 216
Wiersma, Dra 207
Williams, Ned 209
Willeford, Dirk 4, 5, 49-50, 54, 57, 71, 74, 78, 111-113, 171, 199
Wilmeth, James 32, 34

Wilson, Irma 11, 13-4
Wilson, Lee Jr. 214
Wilson, Woodrow 146
Winkler, Charles 25
Winters, Dan 20, 36, 78, 129
Wollam, Owen 35
Wollam, Paul S. 215
Wong, Lib 40
Woolf, Charles 31
Wooten, William 57
Wouda-Preciado, Ellie 201
Wrangel-Rokossowsky, Carl 181
Wright, Andy 218
Wright, Don R. 213
Wright, Justin 217
Wyckoff, Marla 74

Yankovic, Frankie 133
Yaroslav the Wise 42
Yeltsin, Boris 112
Young, David 175
Young, Steven 33
Yungfleisch, Jennifer M. 215

Zavada, Michael 30
Zepeda, Ofelia 143
Zharkov, Vladimir 194
Zhivkov, Todor 42
Ziegler, Ezra 74, 113
Ziegler, Henry 35
Zigelis, Andrew 25
Ziker, John 207, 234
Zikunov, Yurii 180
Zorc, R. David 25
Zovko, C. I. 7
Zukotynsky, Eva 34
Zuppan, Frank 214
Zygas, K. Paulius 25, 72